IN PRAISE OF PROFANITY

IN PRAISE OF PROFANITY

Michael Adams

OXFORD
UNIVERSITY PRESS

OXFORD
UNIVERSITY PRESS

Oxford University Press is a department of the University of Oxford.
It furthers the University's objective of excellence in research, scholarship,
and education by publishing worldwide. Oxford is a registered trade mark of
Oxford University Press in the UK and certain other countries.

Published in the United States of America by Oxford University Press
198 Madison Avenue, New York, NY 10016, United States of America.

Library of Congress Cataloging-in-Publication Data
Names: Adams, Michael, 1961- author.
Title: In praise of profanity / Michael Adams.
Description: Oxford ; New York : Oxford University Press, 2016. | Includes
bibliographical references and index.
Identifiers: LCCN 2015047784| ISBN 9780199337583 (hardback) |
ISBN 9780199337590 (ebook (updf)) | ISBN 9780199337606 (ebook (epub))
Subjects: LCSH: English language—Obscene words. | English language—Slang. |
Swearing. | BISAC: LANGUAGE ARTS & DISCIPLINES / Linguistics / General. |
LANGUAGE ARTS & DISCIPLINES / Vocabulary.
Classification: LCC PE3724.O3 A326 2016 | DDC 427—dc23 LC record
available at http://lccn.loc.gov/2015047784

1 3 5 7 9 8 6 4 2
Printed by Sheridan, USA

CONTENTS

PREFACE

Timothy Jay, America's leading scholar of profanity, noticed the absence of research on the topic in his excellent book, *Why We Curse* (2000):

> Why have scholars excluded cursing from studies of language? For over one hundred years, psychologists and linguists have developed theories of language that have excluded swearing. Certainly every scholar is aware that cursing exists and that it frequently occurs in colloquial speech. The problem is not lack of awareness; it is the nature of the topic itself. . . . Cursing is a powerful taboo in this culture and has been too taboo for linguistic scholarship . . . [but] the absence of cursing produces a theory of language that excludes the emotional and offensive aspects of speech.

Jay exaggerates the omission of profanity from linguistics, overlooking work, for instance, by James McCawley—a superlinguist, with cape and everything—and Allen Walker Read—a superhistorian of English, complete with beret—though one of Read's works on profanity and taboo appears in Jay's bibliography. Jay lists work by Arnold Zwicky, Geoffrey Pullam, and various colleagues there, too, so he would have to agree, I think, that profanity has occurred to some linguists as a suitable topic of inquiry. All of the linguists mentioned were or are renegades, however, and Jay is undoubtedly right about the mainstream of linguistic theory.

So, Jay set out to change the field of play and effectively did so in *Why We Curse* and an earlier book, *Cursing in America* (1992). As so often happens, nothing much has changed despite his heroic efforts. Geoffrey Hughes, a fine language historian, wrote *Swearing: A Social History of Foul Language, Oaths, and Profanity in English* (1991) more or less at the same time as Jay's *Cursing in America*. Articles on specific topics have appeared ever since, it's true, and recently we have gained a lot from Steven Pinker's chapter on profanity in *The Stuff of Thought* (2007), because Steven Pinker. At about that same time, Tony McEnery published *Swearing in English: Bad Language, Purity and Power from 1586 to the Present* (2006), a really cool book from a linguistic standpoint, as it combines historical sociolinguistics, problems of language planning and regulation, and cultural theory and draws on corpora to investigate how much swearing there is and has been and who the guilty parties are, by gender, class, etc. More recently, Melissa Mohr has contributed a witty, nicely proportioned, erudite, but immensely readable history of swearing, titled *Holy Shit* (2013). Given the mountains of stuff written about other linguistic subjects, Jay's view that we study profanity too little is still accurate.

In Praise of Profanity does not propose that we all proceed through life swearing as we go. Why bother? Many of us already do. Only once, towards the end of the book, do I suggest that anyone should swear more. Instead of advocating for profanity, I outline and illustrate its many benefits—personal, social, and aesthetic. Profanity has its dark side, but no one seems to spend much time thinking about the good it does, and so I've set myself the quixotic task of doing so. This book is not a history of swearing, because, after Hughes and Mohr, we don't really need another. We don't need a new map of the world of profanity because the terrain hasn't changed much since Jay's books were published, with this exception, that the profanity taboo has weakened almost—not completely—out of existence. All the more reason, if people can swear freely, to write about it freely. And while there's plenty of opportunity still to expand the linguistic discussion of profanity, again, Pinker and McEnery have made a great start.

This book is something different from all the others, but it wouldn't have come to mind in its current form without them. In each book mentioned here and some others cited in due course, the author makes some smart observation about profanity in a sentence or two and then moves on to another topic. I have taken those threads and woven them into a distinct but complementary narrative, and the tapestry that hangs before you here is shaped by some of my well-established, ongoing interests. In *Slayer Slang: A Buffy the Vampire Slayer Lexicon* (2003), *Slang: The People's Poetry* (2009), and *From Elvish to Klingon: Exploring Invented Languages* (2011), I focused on language at the social fringes, language that reflects dissatisfaction with English and other languages as they're given, such that speakers, with great linguistic creativity—an innate poetic competence—invent new forms of language to serve their social, political, and aesthetic needs—slang, jargon, Klingon, Esperanto, and the rest. These projects, as well as their products, in answering those needs, reflect an array of attitudes about language, in my work most often but not exclusively about English. So, this is a book about language we're not supposed to use, its unexpectedly beneficial and creative uses, and attitudes about it, not just manifestos against it, but the attitudes embedded in our use of profanity from frustrated exclamation to poetic diction. *In Praise of Profanity* extends and elaborates serious scholarship on profanity while at the same time extending and elaborating language issues that have preoccupied me for decades.

Now, all of that sounds serious and academic, and it should, because it is, and because profanity is a serious subject requiring serious inquiry. Jay argues rightly that we need more of it—the inquiry, if not the profanity itself. But in this book I hope also to illustrate profanity's very humane aspects, how expressive language participates in the human comedy and the human tragedy, and most often the human tragicomedy. Keep in mind the image of a young woman on a busy street in the middle of a pelting rain, juggling umbrella and bags and computer, jostled by people who don't seem to give a damn about anyone besides themselves, and all of her stuff falls into a puddle. She says, "Fuck! Fuck, fuck, fuck, fuck, fuck," as she tries to rescue herself from the vicissitudes of urban life. From a distance, from where you're standing up the street, could anything be more tragic? Could anything be funnier? Could anything raise your sympathy more surely than that exclamation followed by the stream of quiet, private *fucks*? That's one way of looking at the paradox of profanity, and the book looks at profanity paradoxically throughout. Profanity presents us with many more problems—interesting, human problems—than either its detractors or its habitual users realize or admit. One of profanity's many values is to draw our attention to those problems. But in all of this, there's much to celebrate about profanity, and this book is devoted—counterintuitively—to balancing criticism with praise.

Everyone with a keen interest and sense of humor is invited to this celebration. There's linguistics here, and literary criticism, media studies, philosophy, anthropology, cultural criticism—none of these is privileged as a disciplinary perspective, and I move freely between the classics and television, political economy and phonetics, poetics and latrine graffiti. Profanity doesn't belong to any one discipline; it's best explored from a wide variety of disciplinary angles. In doing this, I hope to include more people in a serious examination of the language—a slice of the language, anyway—that we all share. In the interest of inclusion, I've written this book, as I have several others, for educated readers rather than academics, not because I have anything against academics—some of my best friends are professors— but because specialists can glean from the book what's interesting on their terms. Why write only for their benefit? This book, I hope, is accessible and interesting to distinct but intersecting audiences. I try to keep jargon to a minimum and have placed references and most of what might appear as footnotes in the References sections at the ends of chapters.

Because I'm off in different directions from them, though partly stimulated by them, I won't cite the books I've mentioned in this preface as often as they deserve to be cited. I acknowledge them here as deeply influential. I must also acknowledge a number of other influences. Some are quite general, not tied to anything specifically about profanity. Among these I include the late Richard W. Bailey, as well as my dear friend and collaborator, Anne Curzan. Richard adjusted many of my ideas about language over time and urged me to take intellectual and professional paths I might otherwise not even have noticed, my eyes too often fixed straight ahead— Richard always knew an alley shortcut, or that you could get there, wherever that was, by ferry. Sometimes, some years on, he is still my guide.

Anne's voice is always in my head, approving or disapproving what I think and write, and I'm sure every sentence I think that makes it to the printed page is better for her real or spectral intervention—when I make a mistake here, you can be sure I should have listened better to the miniature Anne on my shoulder. Ron Butters, Connie Eble, Ed Finegan, David Skinner, and Michael Montgomery have all edited my work to its benefit and to my benefit as a writer, and I hear their voices, too, as I revise and revise again. Wendi Nichols has in one point significantly influenced my style—I wonder if she'll recognize how. Few people enjoy such an editorial chorus, and I'm happy to have their unisons and harmonies of advice.

I also benefit greatly from my fellow wordanistas, especially Ben Zimmer and Jesse Sheidlower, who are always miles ahead of me, especially about words and popular culture. Some sections of this book would never have occurred to me if they hadn't said, as they did in the same conversation at a meeting of the American Dialect Society some years back, "You should really watch *The Wire.*" The father of all American wordanistas, the late Allen Walker Read, looms larger in this book than I expected when I started writing it, and I'm grateful for his exhilarating example. *Green's Dictionary of Slang* is always on my desk, as is the *Oxford English Dictionary*, which isn't mentioned in the references below each chapter yet informs all of them—I don't want to take it for granted, but I do take consulting it as given.

Some friends deserve thanks for particular, occasional gifts, for introducing me to musicians, poets, or books, for instance, even though they couldn't have guessed at the time that they were helping me on this project—some of the introductions were made before I became principally a scholar of the English language. Thanks, then, to Nicholas P. White, the late Russell Fraser, James A. Winn, Paisley Rekdal, Jim Speese, Ed Callary, and Howard and Margaret Arbuckle. Special thanks to John Considine and Jonathon Green and several others for an early morning I'll always remember, even if they don't, and, above all, to Hugh "Andy" Anderson and his generous hospitality—he won't expect this book from the Vicar, but I'm full of surprises. At Oxford University Press, I would like to thank Hallie Stebbins, an extraordinary editor distinguished above all by her extraordinary patience.

Mostly, I thank Jennifer, my wife, and our children, Ollie and Amelia, for putting up with my obsessions, and Jennifer for reading the chapters as I thought they were ready, so that she could tell me that, no, they weren't ready yet. Fewer words here better say my love and gratitude—I wrote a lot when I was lonely and unhappy and I still write a lot now that I'm blessed with the best family and more joy than I ever imagined for me. From my experiment in living thus far, I conclude that blessed and joyful is better. I hope happiness helped me to write a better book, but that, dear reader, is for you to decide.

IN PRAISE OF PROFANITY

Chapter 1

Profanity: The Great Debate(s)

Profanity is everyday language, but it makes news, nonetheless. In the ABC situation comedy *Modern Family*, in the episode "Little Bo Bleep," which aired on January 18, 2012, two-year-old Lily Tucker-Pritchett (played by Amber Anderson-Emmons) dropped the F-bomb—a lot. Lily doesn't know what *fuck* means, but she knows people pay attention to her when she says it. So in a broad sense she does know what the word means, maybe better than her audience; she doesn't assume the supposedly worst possible meaning because she isn't old enough to have learned the obvious meanings of *fuck*, let alone how and why profanity is "bad," though she knows other people think it's "bad," so they gasp or tut, and she stoops and conquers the center of attention.

Most people just laugh. Indeed, one of Lily's fathers, Cameron Tucker, can't help but laugh even though he worries he's setting a bad example and failing (a little) at fatherhood. He feels this partly because his partner and Lily's other father, Mitchell Pritchett, disapproves of Lily's behavior and Cameron's behavior, too. Cameron's reaction is complex: it's a mixture of discomfort, approval of his daughter's precocity, and pleasure at hearing profanity—speaking profanity can release tension, but so can hearing someone else speaking it. At the end of the episode, Lily, the flower girl at a family friend's wedding, drops her last F-bomb (last of the episode, anyway) in a church: the congregation pauses and then laughs in a very life-affirming way. Maybe a child should say *fuck* at every wedding. Hundreds of years from now, this carnivalesque collision of innocence and experience might be taken for granted, as essential to the ritual. Ritual so often begins in the absurd.

Of course, Lily's profanity did not go unnoticed, and some organizations, having learned about the episode before it aired, argued prior restraint, or at least sought ABC's prior self-restraint—they wanted the episode pulled. The critics were the obvious ones, the Parents Television Council and McKay Hatch's No Cussing Club—more on the crusading Mr. Hatch below. Some people condemn profanity out of hand. Thankfully, to the delight of millions of viewers, ABC aired "Little Bo Bleep" in all its effing glory. Note that the F-word is never actually used in the episode and that Miss Anderson-Emmons never utters it, though what she does utter under the bleeps is unclear. In other words, the profanity isn't in the script but in the minds of those who hear it where it isn't.

My son Oliver, when he was a two-year-old like Lily, also inadvertently discovered profanity, or euphemisms for it. In the episode of *Our Lives* titled "Alphabet Song," which aired several times daily, Ollie (who plays himself) sang "A, B C, D, effin' G," or at least that's how it sounded to anyone who was listening. We struggled not to smile. Those outside the family circle gasped or tutted. No one picketed outside our house, and, as far as I was concerned, Ollie could sing the song any damned way he liked. But surely Ollie's *effin'* isn't as culpable as Lily's F-bomb—or is it? Or is neither culpable? Or are both of them both culpable and not? Of course, we're not pushing further, deliberate profanity on Ollie—he'll come to it on his own, soon enough. But it's not so easy to explain why we're protecting him from it, or why it bothers us that a little girl would swear—we have explanations, yes, but this book shows how they are often superficial, reductive, and inconsistent, all things I've pledged not to be, even as I try to do the right thing by my kids.

Profanity is a problem, no matter whether you use it or abhor it. It's a problem because we make it one, because we disagree, not only about its moral, social, expressive, and aesthetic value, but even about what exactly we mean when we use the term *profanity*, and about whether use of profanity exposes an underbelly of low moral character, or fits compatibly with sound moral character, or even lifts speakers in some situations to moral significance. These debates deserve some airing before we dare to praise profanity. A long, hard look at profanity discovers much that is counterintuitive and paradoxical, not at all what we expect, given our usually automatic responses, guided as they are by a conventional wisdom more conventional than wise.

IN THE BEGINNING

If you can get away with profanity on a family show like *Modern Family*, clearly you can get away with it anywhere. It suffuses twenty-first-century American culture. Because American religious culture has attempted over centuries to stamp out profanity like so much hellfire cracking through the turf of New Jerusalem, our era feels especially free—errantly free according to moralists, and linguistically libertarian according to others, those who defend the right to be profane, even in public life. In our enlightened times, parties on either side of the profanity debate recognize that profanity is itself the appropriate, ultimate focus of our attention, yet profanity is also usually taken as a symptom of more systemic cultural disease—the decline of decency, the decline of religious authority, the decline of standards, and the like—or of an increasingly free and open society, one in which individuals—individuals engaged in social networks—rather than institutions determine what counts as socially appropriate behavior. Both views are partly truth and partly mythology attached to positions in what we have come to call the culture wars. Profanity is a subject of those wars, but only one among many.

Advocates of profanity like to play with it, and they do so, of course, for sheer fun, but also to demonstrate that nothing happens when they do. Profanity isn't really taboo, though we often say it is, and no one seriously attributes low birth rate or crop failure to the god's displeasure at our using the forbidden, magic words. The Judeo-Christian-Islamic God—by self-report a jealous one—might punish us for taking His name in vain, but we have sin, I think, because we had our chance to observe taboo in the Garden of Eden and it proved an epic fail. Thus, God in His mercy graciously set before us a simpler task, and then—on various terms, depending on one's faith tradition—promised to redeem us, anyway. Once burned, twice shy.

Appropriately in our place, at our time, one measure of profanity's significance is the extent to which we consume it. We consume it a lot, exuberantly. For instance, Adam Mansbach and Ricardo Cortés's *Go the Fuck to Sleep* (2011)—according to David Byrne, of all people, a "children's book for grown-ups"—was such a runaway bestseller that it generated a franchise: *You Have to F****** Eat* (2014) and *Benjamin Franklin: Huge Pain in My…* (2015) so far, as well as euphemized versions of the effing books actually for kids, *Seriously, Just Go to Sleep* (2012) and *Seriously, You Have to Eat* (2015). Its back cover casts *Go the Fuck to Sleep* as "profane, affectionate, and radically honest," you know, as in

> The flowers doze low in the meadows
> And high on the mountains so steep.

My life is a failure, I'm a shitty-ass parent.
Stop fucking with me, please, and sleep.

It's not easy being a parent, and the book is one long, loving expletive in response. Mind you, the book has its shortcomings—it's no
Goodnight Moon—and just because it's a picture book doesn't mean
it's profound. If you don't oversimplify life, you probably can't oversimplify the value of profanity for living successfully in the real world,
but that's what *Go the Fuck to Sleep* does—it's not profanity's fault.

Mansbach and Cortés's series suggests unsubtly that profanity is
fun and funny—"pants-wettingly funny," the back cover text asserts.
But it gets better: if David Byrne approves of picture book profanity,
then profanity is also hip, the language of people exclusively and
somewhat subversively in the know. This in-the-knowingness comes
out in the pastimes of hip people, who might, for instance, while
shopping in urban boutiques have picked up a deck of *Cuss Cards*—
the European Edition (2006). Ostensibly a regular deck of cards,
the usual designations are tucked into the top left and bottom right
corners, but there's no picture of a queen or a diagram of nine spades
in the middle of a card. Each cuss card lists seven international ways
to say something supposedly profane, though the makers of the
cards quickly realized there wasn't enough easily translatable profanity for 52 cards, so *ugly* and *jerk* end up in the deck *faute de mieux*.

For no particularly good reason, the nine of diamonds is the
chicken-shit card—German *hosenscheisser*, French *poule mouillée*, Dutch
schijterd, Italian *femminuccia*, Spanish *gallina de mierda*, and Swedish
ynkrygg—and the king of diamonds is the *cunt* card—German *fotze*,
French *chatte*, Dutch *kut*, Italian *fica*, Spanish *coño*, and Swedish *fitta*.
It's one of those early mornings when you ask, "What'll we do
now?" and someone says, "Let's play cards," and you say, "Seriously?
That's so boring," but then you say, "Wait—this could be fun," and

out come the *Cuss Cards*. And while the rest of you are waiting for the slow player—there's always a slow player, especially after a night out—you can try out European profanity. Or maybe the cards are good for foreplay. You're horny—German *geil*, French *chaud*, Dutch *geil*, Italian, *arrapato*, Spanish *cachondo*, and Swedish *kåt*—and drunk—German *voll*, French *bourré*, Dutch *bezopen*, Italian *ubriaco*, Spanish *borracho*, and Swedish *full*—so you call a fuck buddy—German *fickfreund*, French *un coup*, Dutch *neuk mattje*, Italian *compagna di scopate*, Spanish *polvo*, and Swedish *knullkompis*—in order, you know, to—German *ficken*, French *niquer*, Dutch *neuken*, Italian *scopare*, Spanish *follar*, and Swedish *knulla*. Who says playing cards are things of the past? Who says profanity isn't educational? Who says it has no role in modern life? It's only sad if you're at home alone, just flipping through the cards, imagining a better night than the one you're having.

The cards are very well designed to reflect the rollicking fun of profanity, too. A brightly colored national flag accompanies each word or phrase, the background for which is pastel, and the obverse has a map of Europe with non-Anglophone capitals marked by fun iconic images: a blond, breasty Swedish woman, her aureoles oddly modestly covered with stars, for Stockholm; a marijuana leaf for, you guessed it, Amsterdam; one of those lidded pottery beer steins next to Berlin; Michelangelo's *David* for Rome; a bull and matador for Madrid; and the phallic Eiffel Tower for Paris. From the center bottom of the frame into the middle of the card is a blue hand with erect middle finger. You also find that hand on the playing side of the jokers, capped with the fool's traditional hat.

The rising tide of profanity in the first decade of this century raised a lot of ships flying the Jolly Roger. Sarah Royal and Jillian Panarese, two of the decade's language pirates, live in infamy for devising a flip-card game called *Creative Cursing: A Mix 'n' Match*

Profanity Generator (2009). There aren't that many profanities to play with, so the authors of this entertainment propose, let's see how many combinations we can come up with. The answer, if you've 128 cards in two contiguous, spiral-bound flappable piles for mixing and matching, is…um…carry the million…a lot. At random, you'll get items like *fuck dangler*, *sissy packer*, and *anus folds*, which really don't make much sense, so are bound to stimulate a certain type of conversation. But a systematic run through *meat* + X yields plausible items like *meat bagger*, *meat flaps*, *meat licker*, *meat munch*, *meat rammer*, and *meat sucker*, just to name a few—*meat waffle* is clearly a word in search of a referent. You might think a game like this has white wine spilled all over it, but I can imagine it as backseat fun during All-American road trips—college road trips, not family road trips. Its sequel, *Creative Cussin' (The Redneck Edition)* (2010), a kind of verbal whittling, could while away time in the bed of a 4 × 4.

But profanity isn't all fun and games. There's plenty of reason to take it seriously, and not merely in order to proscribe it. Jesse Sheidlower has published three editions of his historical dictionary of *fuck* and its derivatives, *The F-Word* (1995, 1999, and 2009), and yet other lexicographers—Jonathon Green comes to mind, in various works, but ultimately in his three-volume *Green's Dictionary of Slang* (2010)—show how much profanity there is and how interestingly it's used, but *The F-Word* is as good a place as any to start. For instance, you know that people use the word *fuck*, and you know that some use *cunt*, too, but did you know that there was a compound, *cunt-fuck*, both noun and verb? That seems like a lot of profanity for one word, but it makes sense when you pause at the entry for *ass-fuck* and are then reminded that there's more than one perpetratable act in question—we need language for the things people do.

The F-Word includes a word for "simulate sexual intercourse without penetration"—*dry-fuck*—and one for when lesbians "lie prone face to face and rub and stimulate each other"—*flat fuck*, which is first recorded in the anonymous *My Secret Life*, written around 1890. In any event, the entries in *The F-Word* are lexical windows onto the world, and if you're like me, you want to know what's going on out there. Also, if you're like me, you believe that learning is fun, frankly more fun than flipping cuss words into laughable combinations. *The F-Word* is just one more proof that scholarship and fun belong together like macaroni and cheese. This book, of course, is another. And to return to my original theme, profanity is interesting enough and important enough that we'll pay good money to find out what we don't know about it.

At 270 pages, *The F-Word* contains 270 more pages of profanity than its antagonists can accept, but not nearly as many pages as could be written. After all, the 270 pages account for profanity developed directly—and in euphemisms sometimes indirectly—from one überprofane word. It includes *shitfuck*, but not *shit* in its own right, let alone derivatives like *dipshit*, nor does it include *ass* or forms derived from it, like *asshat*. Green has recently pointed out that his database of slang contains an immense number of sexual and scatological items, most of which those dead-set against profanity would consider profane, including 1,740 words for 'sexual intercourse,' 1,351 for 'penis,' 1,180 for 'vagina,' 634 for 'anus' or 'buttocks,' and 540 for 'defecate'/'defecation' and 'urinate'/'urination.' There is no cell of nefarious ne'er-do-wells holed up in some bunker somewhere cooking up profanity and poisoning an unsuspecting public with acts of lexicographical terrorism. There wouldn't be so much profanity were it unequivocally vulgar; there wouldn't be so much were it not expressively useful.

Mostly, the rest of this book proves that "we," many of us, approve of profanity on at least some occasions, for one reason or another. *Approve* is a tricky word to use here, because someone who uses profanity might not in fact wholly approve of his or her own behavior—such a person might be ashamed for religious reasons or embarrassed for social ones. As we'll see, some who approve profanity do so anonymously on toilet walls, so that's probably a mixed approval, unless those who write graffiti also speak profanity loud and proud in the public square. If we voted on a profanity resolution, a majority of us might vote against profanity but also might not stop using it. Use itself casts votes of approval, no matter one's announced moral principles or dispassionate evaluation of social value or speaker motives. The best we can say is that, when it comes to profanity, we're of at least two minds.

BABEL RESTORED

As much as many enjoy profanity and might defend it, if pressed, there are many who resist it, who see it as necessarily angry or aggressive, biblically taboo, or spiritually corrosive. Because Americans too often—in my opinion—mix up their patriotism and religion—I hold out the possibility that an atheist can be virtuous and an exemplary citizen—some detractors see profanity as incompatible with red, white, and blue morals and values. Many argue against profanity from religious belief, and while I honor the belief, I must also point out that quite a few honestly religious people justify heinous behavior, both personal and political, on the basis of one or another biblical text or conventional thinking—religion can be liberating and it can be suffocating, and a moral person thinks very hard before suffocating others, even metaphorically.

But our upright atheist can be against profanity, too, and in that case the argument will take a different shape. It's not a question of taboo or top-down divine management, but rather a question of how we address one another. Profanity, from this perspective, is bad manners, and manners aren't superficial rules about which fork to use for what course at a fancy dinner or how to position a stamp on an envelope—an example that surely questions the current relevance of some sorts of manners—but an outward and visible sign of the inward and spiritual grace of politeness, the rules by which we treat others respectfully or not. In other words, reflexively, manners are moral and morality depends on manners, and if profanity interferes with respect for others—either feeling or expressing respect— then one might argue there's good reason to avoid it.

Religiously derived thinking about profanity can be sloppy and it can also be very hypocritical—another theme we'll address throughout the book—because swearers mostly object to others' swearing, and often criticism of the speech is thinly veiled criticism of the speaker. Nevertheless, one can address profanity as a problem thoughtfully, from a Christian perspective, for instance. Christopher C. Gee, who is president and CEO of HumbleGlory ministries, wrote an interesting essay on profanity titled *Swear Not at All: An Overview of the Constructs and Consequences of Foul Language* (2005), and it's to the Reverend Gee's credit that it really reflects the complexity of the issues that attend profanity's use. Unsurprisingly, his position is grounded in the Christian Bible. He reminds us of Matthew 5:22: "But I say unto you, That whosoever is angry with his brother without a cause shall be in danger of the judgment: and whosoever shall say to his brother, Raca, shall be in danger of the council: but whosoever shall say, Thou fool, shall be in danger of hell fire." *Raca* means 'worthless,' and it is, indeed, immoral for us to call one another worthless. You needn't believe in the Judeo-Christian-Islamic God to believe that—it's a universal tenet, closely aligned with the Golden Rule. Another biblical argument, reflected in Ephesians 5:4, reminds us that we only have so much time for speech, and it would be better to spend that time praising God than cursing.

The Reverend Gee's judgments of one or another profanity are fairly conventional and unsurprising. Of *Fuck you!* he writes, "This expression succinctly presents insult and repudiation. To utter this to someone is to say that you totally and bitterly reject his or her presence." He analyzes *Motherfucker!* somewhat more literally than many of us would: "[T]his phrase basically means that the person in reference has forceful and violent sex with his own mother.... The forceful and violent reference can be eliminated and the rest is still utterly repugnant and immoral." We must consider that Matthew doesn't quite proscribe *Fuck you!* because the repudiation could be justified by a "cause." Also, while *Fuck you!* certainly can be an insult, it's not always simply an insult, and, in fact, in some indeterminable number of cases it isn't an insult at all.

This book, *In Praise of Profanity*, is full of examples that undermine the referential theory on which the Reverend Gee's argument—and indeed a lot of common-sense condemnation of profanity—depends, that is, it depends on certain misunderstandings about how language works. Sometimes *fucking* literally means a sexual act—the vocative *Fuck me harder*—but usually *motherfucker* is not similarly referential—it's psychomythological, as in the Oedipus complex— and while it can indeed be repugnant and a word of anger, at least one fictional example described below suggests that constructive uses are not beyond the powers of human imagination. A great deal of our profanity is meaningful, not lexically, as in a dictionary definition, but expressively, as a matter of context.

Reverend Gee is aware of this problem, the moral distraction to which we succumb all too easily when focused on profanity. Profanity announces itself in ways ordinary bad language does not. *Fuck you!*, Gee writes, "is insulting, disrespectful, and not to mention

[sic] deprecating to the receiver. But so are the phrases 'Forget you!' and 'Away with you!' With the same intentions, they have identical meanings." The meanings are not quite identical, of course, but different shades of a meaning. According to Matthew, it's not *Raca* that leads to hellfire after all but *You fool!*, which, on the face of it—in colloquial English, anyway—is less offensive than [*You are*] *worthless!*

Maybe profanity is a legitimate target of disapproval, but the problems it supposedly signifies and enacts aren't solved by prohibiting it, even with the strongest measures. The Reverend Gee introduces an imaginary and possibly self-righteous interlocutor, who says, "I'm a Christian and I don't use those words. The Lord is displeased when people speak to each other like that." He questions this variety of Christian rhetoric: "Here the speaker automatically insinuates the popular expletives by verbalizing the phrase 'those words.' Whenever we hear the word 'cursing' our minds automatically register the four-lettered and other words that fit the socially created construct of swearing. The Christian should ask himself/herself whether or not they use any language that displays harmful intentions." The Reverend Gee has no solutions to the inconsistencies he observes, except to say that just because profanity isn't the only bad language doesn't mean it isn't bad, and there's a point there, but it doesn't capture the linguistic, social, or aesthetic benefits of profanity. Well, I can say that, but the proof of the pudding is in the eating—we'll chew that proof throughout the book.

Concern with our use or misuse or overuse of profanity need not derive from religion. For James V. O'Connor, "who has been a public relations professional and a writer in the Chicago area his entire career," according to the back cover of *Cuss Control: The Complete Book on How to Curb Your Cursing* (2000), the problem with profanity is its incivility. O'Connor's position is moderate—I'm still on the back cover—for the book "doesn't call for the total elimination of swearing, just for its confinement to situations where extreme emotion (think hammer, think thumb) demand [sic] it." O'Connor takes the position exactly opposite to mine, for "*Cuss Control* is a refreshing celebration of the joys of a civil tongue." I think civility is worth celebrating, too, and celebrating profanity need not valorize incivility but rather the myriad other uses to which profanity can be put.

O'Connor presumes a couple of things I wish he wouldn't. First, he links profanity to ineptitude of one kind or another. Still on the back cover, I can't help but notice that the book purports to teach us "ways to communicate clearly rather than use lazy language." Inside the book, he goes into more detail: "[T]he S word and several other obscenities have many applications. When we get mentally and verbally lazy, these words are always on call, sparing us the task of scanning our brain and downloading even the most simple noun or adjective. There seems to be no need to make the effort when talking intelligently is rarely a social requirement, and curse words are as common as bad grammar." Now, I don't know Mr. O'Connor, and he's probably a nice guy who means well, but I am always put off by pronouncements about everyone else's talk not being intelligent enough. Applying McKean's law—Any correction of the speech or writing of others will contain at least one grammatical, spelling, or typographical error—rather broadly, I wonder whether Mr. O'Connor means we all share a brain or that we scan our plural brains. An innocuous error? Could there be similarly innocuous profanity?

O'Connor points out, and he's right, that "It's rare to hear anyone described as *eloquent*" these days—but he may not be so right when he suggests that *eloquent* is "a word reserved for the great orators of the past." Perhaps we should overcome our rhetorical modesty and admit that we are hella eloquent at times, and further that profanity contributes to that eloquence, not on every occasion but often enough. Sometimes, as in a frustrated or pained exclamation—hammer, thumb—it's existentially eloquent, but when fine authors choose it for their literary purposes—as we'll see in later chapters they do—it's eloquent in exactly the sense O'Connor denies us. All too often, we overlook eloquent profanity because, like O'Connor, we've already assumed that profanity is the opposite of eloquent, a very mistaken view.

Second, O'Connor assumes an editorial prerogative to tell people how to say what they mean. As an editor of books and journals, I have certainly exercised this prerogative myself, and I wouldn't say that anyone's speech or writing—including mine, of course—is beyond intelligent critical commentary. In most publishing contexts, given various constraints that only publishers and editors feel, an editor will decide ultimately what stays in and what gets cut. But editorial principles are often barely defensible, especially when they take the form of this bit of O'Connor's advice: "Don't use cuss words when you can make a point without them." This is a bit like the "rule" that one should always "make a point" in the fewest possible words. Most of our communication isn't "making a point"—or, at least, isn't *only* making a point—and in the many-layered meaning of speech in context, "extra" words and "superfluous" profanity may, in fact, participate crucially.

Arguably, because profanity is expressive speech, you can't be as expressive—expressive on the precise terms—as you mean to be if you settle for alternatives. O'Connor insists that you can, but he ignores the particularity of expression, for it's just not true that one synonym is as good as another, that *Geez, Louise!* and *Holy shit!* mean the same thing. As O'Connor acknowledges, cussing isn't about points but about attitudes. He has a whole chapter about it, McKeanly titled "Causal Cussing: It's Not the Words, It's the Attitude," or, if you prefer the Table of Contents' rendering, "Casual Cussing." Profanity, O'Connor argues, "matters precisely because there is a message, and swearing conveys secondary messages that say much more about you as a person" than, I guess, you want people to know. But the secondary messages in turn convey meaning that can't be conveyed straightforwardly, so in order to avoid some secondary messages, O'Connor would like to trim away some of a speaker's intentional meaning. It's not clear why he feels he has a right to do so, or how we communicate more clearly by meaning less in the interest of somebody else's idea of good taste.

O'Connor was not "inspired by religious beliefs," he notes, but by PR, "by a desire to help people improve their image and their relationships and, in the process, restore a degree of civility." And so he "created the Cuss Control Academy as a division of [his] public relations firm in August of 1998. It seemed like a natural extension of the PR business, which strives to create a positive image and favorable reputation for companies and their products. People need to project a favorable image as well." In order to project that image, you'll need to express less, or at least differently, and the value of the image is such, supposedly, that meaning differently will be worth it. PR, we discover, will save us from language that, while "liberating and fun and sexy...would contribute to the deterioration of the English language and the growing crassness of society," which, I admit, is more than I ever expected PR to do, and, besides, I'd like my freedom and fun back. If I can feel sexy, I'd like that back, too.

Defending profanity, however, doesn't permit us to overlook its cruel and harmful uses. O'Connor has chapters about how "Names Can Really Hurt" and "The Hard Part: Controlling Anger." McKay Hatch, another interesting anti-profanity crusader, took up his shield and sword upon encountering profanity in middle school. At the age of fourteen, Hatch established the No Cussing Club, convinced that, if we could stop profanity, we would stop bullying and the world would be a better, safer place. We are all for that world, even if some of us doubt that profanity is what keeps us from it or that ridding the world of profanity will contribute to our safety. Hatch, however, is convinced, because when he started out, he explains, "Really, I was just a regular kid.... Except, now, my dad, my teachers, even the mayor of my city and people from all different countries tell me that I've made a difference. Sometimes, they even say I changed the world."

Hatch doesn't stop to consider that profanity, while potentially harmful, also can enhance expression, that its social uses are complicated, and that swearing not to swear misses the point several times over. I mean no disrespect to fourteen-year-olds when I say that the book Hatch wrote about his movement, *The No Cussing Club: How I Fought Against Peer Pressure and How You Can Too!* (2009), is written with the linguistic awareness and social experience of a fourteen-year-old. It uncritically indulges every stereotype about profanity, for instance, "Cussing is seen as language of the lower class," which I guess puts the lower class in its place, and "Cussing affects your outlook on yourself and the world," which it certainly doesn't, at least not so naively, and overlooks the important and possibly prior fact that "Cussing expresses your outlook on yourself and the world," which is the alternative, perhaps complementary, focus adopted in this book.

"Rudy Ruettiger, former football player for Notre Dame, from the movie 'Rudy'" is quoted on the back cover of Hatch's book: "McKay's story of the No Cussing Club is one of courage. It's an inspiration to us all to never give up and to stand up for what you believe in." Mark Victor Hansen—"Co-creator, #1 New York Times best-selling series 'Chicken Soup for the Soul'®"—we learn, is "cheering McKay on, as you will when you read his inspired book." The book includes lots of testimonial letters from people whose No Cussing Club experience has changed their lives, a photo of Hatch with Dr. Phil, and a photo of the City of South Pasadena proclamation of No Cussing Week, March 3–7, 2008. For me the book was less inspirational and more self-promotional, more about how "All the T-shirt wearing and the talking was helping the No Cussing Club grow at school." There are 38 pages about profanity and 125 pages about the No Cussing Club, and I'd subtract the 7 pages on cyberbullying—I'm against cyberbullying and see writing about it by someone who was cyberbullied as a public service—except that the cyberbullying was in response to Hatch's stand against profanity, which doesn't justify it, of course, but does frame it as part of Hatch's heroic story.

It's not clear to me that we need saving from profanity. The suggestion that we do is easily parodied, as for instance in "It Hits the Fan," an episode of the animated television series *South Park* described more fully later in this chapter. The Reverend Gee and Messrs. O'Connor and Hatch undoubtedly and sincerely believe that profanity does more harm than good, that it should be avoided if not banned, that we can do without it because there are other ways of saying what we say with profanity, and I disagree with all of those positions, but I think that before praising profanity, we ought to consider the cultural debate about its dangers and pleasures.

Perhaps I'd take O'Connor's and Hatch's closely related positions more seriously if O'Connor hadn't "addressed the downside of swearing on more than 100 TV shows—including Oprah—and in more than 600 newspapers and magazines" and if Hatch weren't giving "Language that Lifts" presentations and selling "No Cussing Club wristbands, T-shirts, [and] other No Cussing Club items, as well as additional copies of [his] book" at www.nocussing.com, and if "The No Cussing Club" weren't a registered trademark. I'm not against money or fame or making the most of an opportunity or organizing good works, but I am worried that, at some level, O'Connor and Hatch aren't actually writing about profanity. And one must admit that selling cuss cards or faux fucking picture books is no less opportunistic. There's a cultural debate about profanity going on out there, I'm sure, but the way it makes money distracts us from it as well as perpetuates it. Perhaps it's this book's only virtue, but here, by way of contrast, I'll stick to the subject.

WHAT IS PROFANITY, EVEN?

In addition to the cultural question, "Is profanity good for us?" we debate—or should debate—what we even mean when we use the word *profanity*, or words apparently related to it, like *obscenity*, or *curse*. If the first debate sometimes rages, this debate is peace. There are no showdowns between the swearers and those pledging not to swear, no battles between moralists and freethinkers, no intersection, really, with the encompassing and vitriolic culture wars fought in America since the 1980s over matters—abortion, affirmative action, voting rights, multiculturalism, and the like—more significant in most of the warriors' minds even than "bad" language, though "bad" language is, for them, a symptom of encompassing moral decline. Disputes over terminology are academic skirmishes on the edge of larger cultural conflict.

Nevertheless, this second debate is important, insofar as it's related to the first—it's the linguistic side of the cultural debate. Anyone firmly against profanity believes that a profanity is obviously just that—if I say *fuck* it's a profanity, or it might be an obscenity, but why quibble over categories because it's obviously wrong. A careful look at what we call profanity, however, suggests that not only isn't it obviously wrong, it isn't even obviously profanity, at least not in some contexts. The anti-profanity forces put all of their faith in the word form. If you put the letters *f-u-c-k* together in that order, voilà, it's a profanity. But that's to indulge in word magic, as though the word has a sort of power independent of its use. It doesn't. There is no such thing as Profanity, in the abstract; instead, there is only profanity in context.

The way people use words makes them profane or vulgar, but, more often than not—as this book will tell over and over—context and use complicate what we call profanity beyond what a category like *profane* conveys. Words aren't profane just because some of us attach them irremovably to the category. When someone says of language they've heard, "Well, that's just profanity," they're probably wrong—it probably isn't *just* anything. Exploring how profanity works—or, as a concept, doesn't quite work—really matters, because oversimplifying what's complex—linguistically, morally, politically, aesthetically—has consequences, and we need to take responsibility for them. We can't do that if we misunderstand the very phenomenon of profanity.

Even when pressed, most of us don't distinguish among profanity, obscenity, lewdness, swearing, and cursing—recall the imprecision of the *Cuss Cards* and the *Creative Cursing…Profanity Generator*. We know the borders aren't clearly drawn, and, linguistic entrepreneurs that we are, we take it as an opportunity. If I tell you, "Go fuck yourself" because I'm angry with you, because I'm trying to offend you with my indecency—even if fucking someone else isn't indecent, fucking yourself surely is—then I might be using *fuck* as profanity, insofar as what's obscene is profane. But if I'm dismissive of something you've just said, if I think affectionately that you're an idiot—not always, but just at this moment—and then say, "Go fuck yourself," I'm not talking about sex, not trying to be offensive, not being profane. Rather, I'm showing you how, in our familiar relationship, I currently occupy the higher ground and am not putting up with any of your shit. In the second case, "Go fuck yourself" playfully acknowledges our solidarity even as I'm dismissive—I'm not less dismissive, we're no less solid—which arguably makes *fuck* slang rather than profanity.

You can see the developing problem, I'm sure: profanity, obscenity, or slang—which is it, and how would you even know? Profanity's detractors assume that words like *profanity* and *obscenity* have crisply distinct or reliable meanings. Those who make the most of profanity prefer roguish categories, categories that intersect and overlap and, while identifiable, are not necessarily reliable. For them, disagreement isn't a problem to be fought and resolved, but rather an opportunity to speak more expressively than when they're confined to standard English vocabulary. If much of our profanity is slang and some of our slang serves the same expressive functions as profanity, then we have room to maneuver among language attitudes in achieving our expressive and social goals.

The words *profanity* and *obscenity* and the speech categories they represent are vague. If we're insecure about vagueness, we hope that dictionaries will tidy up all of the meaning mess, sorting through it authoritatively and repairing one-to-one correspondences between words and concepts that we've somehow broken through misunderstanding. Use of vague words, however, doesn't imply sloppy thinking; vagueness is a justified component of meaning, built right into semantics. In *Not Exactly: In Praise of Vagueness* (2010), Kees van Deemter points out that we depend—absolutely depend—on vagueness, especially in the semantics of adjectives. All sorts of adjectives—*short* and *tall*, *smart* and *cool*, and the like—*must* be vague, their specific meanings within specific utterances settled by specific contexts. In a room of short people, I'm tall; in a room of tall people, I'm short; in a room of people, I'm not cool. The meanings of such adjectives are outlined lexically but colored in pragmatically.

Van Deemter insists on the difference between vagueness and ambiguity, the former usually semantic, the latter usually syntactic, that is, a problem of sentence structure—think of all dangling modifiers. Well, he claims, vagueness may be somewhat more than semantic: it's "not just a linguistic concept, but a deeply ingrained psychological mechanism." That's why I suggested above that vagueness is a semantic opportunity, and that when it comes to profanity, we are often opportunists. Because vagueness is an element of language structure, it comes naturally, and we know how to interpret it and use it without thinking much about it, but we know we can do it, that we can be justifiably vague in the same way we're sure we can throw a ball, even though we're not sure how.

Our motives for this vagueness and the ways in which we exploit it are thus often below the level of consciousness, but sometimes they're well above it—we can use profanity to our advantage intuitively or artfully. The motive for vagueness can be primarily linguistic, just trying to calibrate our internal metric for gradable antonyms, like *tall* and *short* or *light* and *heavy*. Or, it can be cultural—attempting to negotiate what counts as profanity or obscenity or slang or mere exclamation in a particular context—how we mean it and how people will take it—in order to maximize expressiveness and minimize social alarm, which is exactly what happens in certain types of euphemism for profanity, presented in Chapter 3, although sometimes—as in the literature we'll examine in Chapter 4—it's social alarm we're trying to raise.

The governing example of van Deemter's book is the sorites paradox, which we know from the ancient Greek philosopher, Eubulides of Miletus, who flourished in the sixth century BCE. The paradox takes its name from the Greek word *soros* 'stone heap,' and paradox nerds will see that it's related to but distinct from Zeno's paradox: if I shoot an arrow toward a target, Zeno argued, and in flight the arrow constantly halves its distance to the target, then the arrow never actually hits the target. This sort of paradox is a "limit" paradox. The sorites paradox, in contrast, is a "threshold" paradox. One stone does not a stone heap make, Eubulides observed, and neither do two, or three, or four, or five, or…when does a group of stones cross the threshold to become a heap? Vagueness, van Deemter argues, is a sorites paradox problem: When does tall become tall or cool cool? When we use the words *tall* and *cool*, we aren't pointing to a particular value but to a range of values that eventually overlap— the tallest short is the shortest tall, and the most indecent slang is probably the least indecent profanity. Context is thus the final guide to what's what with use of a particular adjective.

We hope that dictionary definitions of terms like *profanity* and *obscenity* will establish bright, sharp parameters for their use, but they don't. The noun *profanity* derives from the adjective *profane*, so we don't learn much from the *Oxford English Dictionary*'s definition of *profanity*: "The fact, quality, or condition of being profane; profane conduct or speech; (also) an instance of this, a profane or obscene act or word." We'll have to consult the entry for *profane* to clarify matters, but the *profanity* definition is important, because it links profanity and obscenity—arguably not the same thing—such that, if it's obscene, it could also be profane. How does one know when it's one and not the other? Do they amount to the same thing in discourse, even if, as the *OED* implies, they're distinct in some features?

So, we are sent back—alphabetically and etymologically—to *profane*, which the *OED* defines as follows: first, in a purely religious sense—"Of persons or things: unholy, or desecrating what is holy or sacred; unhallowed; ritually unclean or polluted"—some bad shit; second, by way of contrast, in a neutral sense, just the opposite of *sacred*, no aspersions cast—there's sacred literature, like the Bible,

and profane literature, like this book; but third, in the most important sense for our purposes, as the definition itself makes clear—"Of
persons, behaviour, etc.: characterized by, exhibiting, or expressive
of a disregard or contempt for sacred things (esp. in later use, by the
taking of God's name in vain); not respectful of religious practice;
irreverent, blasphemous, impious; (hence, more generally) ribald,
coarse, indecent. Now the most common sense."

It's possible to argue, if you like very fine points, that words like
fuck and *shit* are "true" profanities, even though not so obviously
as *goddam*. They're impious, the argument would go, because God
doesn't want us to say them, and when we do what God doesn't want,
we're expressing disregard for sacred things. The biblical basis for
this supposed disapproval is less explicit than "Thou shalt not steal"
and "Thou shalt not take the name of the Lord thy God in vain"—
even *Geez, Louise* is more clearly proscribed than *cunt* or *prick*. If
fuck and *shit* were ever taboo, however, it wasn't because they were
blasphemies or impieties but words about sex and feces. In Western
culture, we've been more squeamish about those two subjects and
their supposed relations than we have been about cursing our neighbors or otherwise enlisting God in our verbal misbehavior. But
wouldn't that make *fuck* and *shit* obscene rather than profane?

When we consult the *OED*'s definition for *profanity*, however,
we learn that the apt formula is not "rather than" but "as well as," because "coarse, indecent" in the definition for *profane* opens the way
to "obscenity"—which is also coarse, or "lewd," and indecent—in that
for *profanity*. Sometimes, evaluating what's profane or what's obscene is like looking at the Gestalt figure of the duck-rabbit—it's the
same figure, regardless, but when you look at it one way, it's a rabbit,
another way, a duck. You can't see the duck and the rabbit at the same
time—you select which you'll see. And, importantly, when you say
a rabbit, someone can hear a duck. In this way, in the opportunity to

decide rather freely whether *obscenity* or *profanity* is the right word for what you're doing or hearing, language attitudes infiltrate semantics, and semantics inform our language attitudes.

Since it's implicated in profanity, then, what about *obscenity*? The *OED* defines it in two senses: "The character or quality of being offensively indecent, lewdness; an instance of this, esp. an obscene expression" and "The character or quality of being horrible, offensive, or morally repugnant, etc. Also (as a count noun): an extremely offensive or objectionable gesture, statement, event, etc." If, in talking with friends about my hostile work environment, I say, "I can't take this shit anymore," would those friends judge the statement as "offensive" or "indecent"? While the offense of *shit* doubtless depends on its supposed reference to feces, I don't think they'd hear it as "indecent" or take the *shit* as even obliquely referential. I would be coarse, I suppose, if I said "I'm going to take a shit." I might be judged coarse even if I resorted to the artful euphemism, "I need to drop a deuce," though surely most people would consider either of these coarse slang rather than profanity or obscenity. "I can't take this shit," however, wouldn't sound coarse or indecent or lewd or offensive—let alone morally repugnant—to anyone I know. After all, it's the work situation that's offensive and indecent, in the face of which "I can't take this shit anymore" sounds appropriately frustrated.

Profanity, returning to van Deemter and vagueness, poses a sorites paradox, though, given the subject, stones may not be the most appropriately descriptive commodity. *Profanity* is the right word for language when, in some combination, (1) it disregards or exhibits contempt for sacred things, (2) it disrespects religious practice, or (3) it's irreverent, blasphemous, impious, ribald, coarse, or indecent. Is (2) sufficient for profanity, or should it combine with some other elements of the definition in order to cross the profanity threshold? We'd probably accept that (1) or (2) is sufficient, but then how do we deal with (3)? Is my language profane at the first possibility (irreverent) for (3), or if (3) is the criterion, must my language satisfy two or three of the conditions? This is important, because *fuck* uttered as a frustrated exclamation may be coarse enough, but it's not indecent—no one's pants are down—and certainly isn't blasphemous.

Most people would consider *fuck* in any context "a profanity." Even I would use the word *profanity* to describe *fuck*—it refers to what I praise in this book, which is, after all, titled *In Praise of Profanity*, not *In Praise of Some Other Thing*. But that doesn't mean I think it's the right word, at least not for the conventional reasons. Later, in Chapter 3, I'll argue that angry or frustrated exclamatory *fuck* isn't dictionary profanity. If it's profanity at all, it must be for some other reason, and we'll turn to one later in this section. In contrast, some euphemisms—*go f*** yourself* or the supposedly innocent brand name *FCUK*—bring to mind indecencies while trying hard not to be coarse. If we just tick off the number of dictionary conditions they satisfy, they are at least as much profanities as exclamatory *fuck*. So, how many stones do we need for a stone heap? How many pieces of shit—irreverence, indecency, coarseness, etc.— do we need before we have a steaming pile?

Let's explore a second sorites problem arising from these definitions by agreeing, for the sake of argument, that it takes just one kind of shit to make profanity. So, if "coarse" is enough to qualify a word as profanity, then how much "coarse" do we need for a pile of shit? Let's say someone accuses me of saying something obscene, and I reply, "No effin way!" My *effin* certainly makes the utterance coarser than a simple "No way!" but is that enough coarseness for my euphemism to be a profanity? Or do we have to go as far as *fuckin'* to reach the threshold of enough coarseness to reach the profanity threshold? If people say *fuck* regularly enough—and nearly every page of this book suggests they do—is one *fuckin'* sufficient to make a pile of coarseness? If it's not, it's certainly not sufficient to make a pile of shit, that is to say, profanity.

We can classify language as profanity on the basis of straightforward coarseness, but according to the definition of *profane*, indecency is a straightforward path to profanity, too. But is it really? A third way into profanity is via obscenity, as we've noted before. Is *No fuckin' way!* an obscenity? Indecency leads to obscenity, but is any old indecency obscene? Some sticklers would argue that 1% indecency is the threshold. Most of us, however, prefer more indecency before we judge—how much more? In some senses, *fuck* is itself an indecent word, so a profanity candidate. When it's part of *fucked up*, though, as in *Dude, your language attitudes are fucked up*, how obscene is that? Not as obscene as the *fuck* in *Fuck me harder*, surely. Is *Fuck me harder* a really big heap of indecency and *Your language attitudes are fucked up* a less impressive but still sufficient heap of it? Or is *fucked up* indecent but not indecent enough for shit, let alone a heap of it?

The *OED* definition of *obscenity* both clarifies and complicates the problem. Mere indecency is no heap of indecency, and you need a heap of indecency to make obscenity. Or, on the definition's terms, a word or statement must be "offensively indecent" before it qualifies as an obscenity. That language sets a higher bar than the entry for *profane*. So, you can't get to profanity without a heap of indecency, unless for some reason it's easier to get to profanity directly with ordinary indecency—the indecency we encounter in the definition for *profane*—but twice as hard to get there by means of offensive indecency via the definition of *obscenity*. What accounts for the difference? In any event, it's clear that *indecent*—like *tall, short,* and *cool*—is vague, because it requires modification to amount to anything. *Offensively* is perhaps not the best modifier, partly because it might indicate either amount or quality—there could be just a whole lot of offense, or there could be offensive indecency, acceptable indecency, and a range of intermediate indecencies, with profanity achievable only at one extreme.

The second sense of *obscenity* is no less slippery. For a statement to be "an obscenity," it can't be just everyday offensive, the entry suggests, but must be "extremely offensive," which allows for a lot of offensiveness before we get to the heap of it required before crossing obscenity's threshold—a threshold merely preliminary to the profanity threshold! The sorites-like vagueness between the two senses admits no relief: in the first sense, in order to achieve obscenity, a statement's indecency must be offensive; in the second, a statement's offensiveness must be extreme. On balance, however, if what's extremely offensive is obscene, then the first sense really requires an obscene indecency—we are caught in a loop of sorites-like paradoxes, in which we never really achieve either obscenity or profanity, because we cannot judge how much of any subordinate attribute ensures that we've crossed either threshold.

In other words, we're rarely sure whether we're speaking or hearing profanity. We might be in the grey region of "acceptably profane," or we might be speaking or hearing slang, albeit especially emotionally charged, vivid, or evocative slang. We also run into the converse problem: according to the *OED* definitions, in context much slang might actually be profanity. For instance, *douchebag* has got to count as coarse; perhaps it's also offensively indecent, but is it profanity? Obviously, it isn't *profane* in the sense "not respectful of religious practices," but then neither is *fuck*. It isn't "expressive of a disregard or contempt for sacred things," but neither is *prick*, in spite of male self-regard. It doesn't take God's name in vain, but then neither does *damn*, at least, not directly. So maybe it's just obscene. But if it's obscene, the entry for *profanity* suggests, it can also be profanity—as long as the shit is piled so high that everyone agrees it's a shit heap. Generally, in cases like *douchebag*, we acknowledge some indecency, but not offensive indecency or extremely offensive obscenity.

Agreeing on where the thresholds lie and whether they've been exceeded is exactly the problem of context. You can set thresholds wherever you like in the abstract; there, you can have a zero-tolerance response to profanity, if you like. But is profanity ever distinct enough for you to engage your policy in the world of real discourse? How can it be, if the barrier between profanity and slang is permeable in both directions? A speaker might intend to cross the profanity threshold, but might assess that heap of dirty meaning as dirty, all right, but not profane. Or, it could work the other way around: the speaker could mean no offense, believing a form we call profanity so usual and so mild in its indecency that it's merely slang—yet on-hearers of the putative slang might nonetheless interpret it as profanity.

Because it trades on various types of vagueness—especially sorites-like vagueness—we negotiate the relative status of profanity speech act by speech act, given the context of each act. We don't carry around a magic measuring stick that tells us what's tall and what's short, what's cool and what's un-, what's full-on profane or only tentatively so. We judge their gradual values in the relevant contexts. Because profanity is risky language, and because much of the time it's socially useful to us precisely because of that risk—the subject of Chapter 2—we figure out ways of embracing the risk without going too far. Often with profanity, we try to get away with something— often, we succeed. The vagueness of the very concept, demonstrated by the best dictionary definitions of the relevant terms, makes it possible for us to do so. On the basis of common knowledge, then— what we all think we know about profanity—none of us really knows what we're talking about when we're talking about profanity. This doesn't bother people on the pro-profanity side of the first great profanity debate—they can use and enjoy profanity not in spite of the vagueness but because of it. Those on the anti-profanity side, however, are up a heap without any obvious defense.

This doesn't mean there's no such thing as profanity, but it does mean that we make profanity up as we go along, not according to some formula, but by the elastic negotiation of social meaning. A word's form doesn't guarantee its profanity—*fuck* and *shit* and *bitch* all regularly cross the profanity threshold, but they're also often slangy. A word's meaning doesn't guarantee its profanity, either, unless one writes that meaning out in all its detail. The shorthand, denotative sexual meanings of *copulate, fuck, swive, screw*, and *boink* are remarkably similar. One of those alternatives is usually considered profanity, some of the others also qualify at times, but adequate definitions would have to take all of the pragmatics into account, too. They wouldn't be definitions so much as essays. It all comes down, not to form or lexical meaning, but to affect, and affect is usually—though, I'll admit in Chapter 3, not always and only—a matter of context.

In an important article, "On Swearwords and Slang," Robert L. Moore (2012) attempts to distinguish slang from profanity. He explains that, in the Stroop test, subjects are rapidly shown cards with words on them, but they don't call out the words they see—they call out the colors in which the words are printed. When the words are profane, the responses slow—subjects can't resist taking a longer or second look. As Moore puts it, "The affective charge of taboo words or swearwords is obligatory." This doesn't mean that "Swearing is . . . a merely automatic response that blasts its way out of the limbic system through our vocal apparatus"—and I say, "Phew!" Still, Moore argues, profanity is an essential part of language—every language has profanity, because Language has Profanity embedded into its structure. In any given language, we depend on a set of words and phrases conventionally assigned to do what profanity does.

While I propose that context is everything, Moore argues that "functional prototypes" distinguish profanity and slang before context is even a question. As humans, we have a hard-wired need for profoundly expressive language; or, somewhere in our neuroanatomy, there's a "place" for profanity. We can't "disregard or neutralize the emotionality that swearwords index," Moore insists. If you've got a healthy brain, you've got profanity, so that you can express extreme emotion. Every language has its own profanity, and what counts as profane in one might not count as profane in others, though words for sex and other bodily functions tend to fall in the category regardless of language. Most important, however, the prototype doesn't require certain words, and if a word isn't busy satisfying the prototype, it's not profanity—*Go fuck yourself* 'you're an idiot and I'm not putting up with any of your shit' does not satisfy my need to express extreme emotion, just my need to tell you that you're an idiot, which probably doesn't have its own prototype. In Moore's theory, profanity is exactly the language that satisfies the prototype.

Slang lives in the same brain neighborhood as profanity, but it lives down the street, in a different prototype, one that satisfies our social need to establish "egalitarian solidarity." Moore considers the possibility that playfulness and inventiveness make up the prototype underlying slang—my choice of prototype, in fact—but he goes for social affect, instead. On occasion, slang and profanity are confused in use: "Of course," Moore writes, "slang can be used aggressively, just as swearwords can be used playfully," but these, he argues, are extensions of their core functions. Satisfying the core functions is like flipping a switch—language either does or doesn't fit the prototype. Consider exclamations: if you need to fire off something to relieve your profound frustration, it will be profanity, by definition; if the word you use misfires, or if it fires but fails to express the profundity of your emotion, it doesn't matter what the word is, it's not profanity. However, in use, profanity—or more precisely, what we call profanity—is a much vaguer category of speech than what responds directly to Moore's prototype, and there's no way, really, to flip profanity or obscenity or slang on or off.

I accept Moore's prototype theory, but it's the kind of theory that only satisfies linguists. The first profanity debate isn't about what's described by the profanity prototype. The prototype is descriptively lean, but definitions for *profane* and *obscenity* are stuffed with qualities profanity is supposed to have, qualities that respond to culture, not neuroanatomy. The cultural baggage is irrelevant in Moore's account of profanity—well, almost irrelevant. Moore's theory assumes that swear words—words adequate to serve the prototype—are taboo. In other words, language has to be "bad" *before* it can be profanity. That may put the cart before the horse. And I doubt that *taboo* is the right word for the badness of what we call profanity, but I admit I don't have a better one at hand.

Originally, taboo speech and behaviors were forbidden, unlawful. The word *taboo* was borrowed from Tongan into English, and it's first recorded in 1777, by Captain James Cook. First thing to note: taboo is a religious and political concept of the Pacific Islands. There's no parallel in Anglophone culture except, at some times and in some places, profanity that violates sanctity. So, pre-1777, no one thought of describing language on the edge of propriety with the word *taboo*. In fact, as Geoffrey Hughes and Melissa Mohr in their histories of profanity amply illustrate, Western cultures have had profanity for as long as we can remember, and people have used that profanity in various ways—literary, conversational, exclamatory—regardless of its disfavored status. At times, bad language was unlawful, but not unlawful enough to keep speech clean, the evidence proves.

Second thing to note: our use of the term *taboo* in Western linguistics essentially agrees that no taboos are in question. The *OED* provides two specifically linguistic definitions: "With reference to an expression or topic considered offensive and hence avoided or prohibited by social custom" and "A total or partial prohibition of the use of certain words, expressions, topics, etc., esp. in social intercourse." The first evidence in both cases is from Leonard Bloomfield's *Language* (1933), the late date of which suggests how little influence the idea of taboo has had on the history of Western ideas generally and language attitudes particularly. Prohibition sounds serious, but what is a partial prohibition? Who decides what part? Or who decides when the prohibition is in force? What does it mean that we "avoid" offensive topics and expressions—*avoid* also signals the relevance of context. So, given these definitions of *taboo*, there's a lot of taboo language that won't serve the prototype that profanity supposedly serves; or, most of what we call taboo isn't really taboo, since it exceeds what's prohibited—the horns of a dilemma and it's kind of uncomfortable to sit on either one. English profanity has at times been outlawed and has been dispreferred socially in many contexts, but if it's ever been taboo, it certainly isn't so nowadays.

In the end, you could say that *profanity* means 'words we aren't supposed to use but are expected to use anyway, for any number of legitimate reasons, and of course we do.' The rest of this book goes into some of the legitimate reasons. A curious fact about profanity, even if you add obscenity and other bad words to it, is that it's not a large vocabulary. In fact, it's very small—*Green's Dictionary of Slang*, which only includes slang, is nonetheless much bigger than *The F-Word*. A lot of slang is older and longer-lived than most of us realize, but a lot of it, too, is ephemeral, and we're always making new slang up—slang is a very active site of our linguistic creativity. Profanity, on the other hand, is a very intense site of creativity, because what counts as profanity—even if we're not really sure where to draw the lines—is severely limited. So, speaking profanity, in many cases, is both profoundly emotional speech and language play, which is why some people have made games out of it—not just for their own amusement, but because they're convinced that there's something so irresistibly human about profanity that people will pay to play.

VULGARITY

The debate over the morality of swearing seems like the big one to most people, but it isn't the most important, in my view. Or, rather, we can peel away the morality question, and then peel away the question of profanity's linguistic status, and finally arrive at the question: Even if profanity isn't immoral, and even if it isn't really taboo, shouldn't we avoid it because it's vulgar? No one wants to be immoral, and few of us willfully violate honest-to-goodness taboos, but mostly we shrink from the social evaluation of being "vulgar." As more of us have become middle class—or believe we are middle class—the more we've resisted seeming rough, unlettered, impolite, base, and any number of other qualities that mark the so-called lower classes. At the same time, as more of us clambered into the middle class, some of our lower-class behaviors also ascended a rung or two. The first profanity debate is noisy, and the second is academic, but the third is insidious—largely unremarked, but dehumanizing. Here's an idea: maybe it's time to stop thinking about language in terms of class.

I've asked myself on occasion why I'm writing a book about profanity, what makes my perspective so clear and informative, if that's what it is. It's occurred to me—not as a precondition, but while writing—that I've witnessed the devulgarization of most profanity during my lifetime. Were I a bit older, I might find it hard to shake off earlier attitudes toward swearing, and were I younger, I might not think to examine the problem of vulgarity at all, because I wouldn't see it—it really isn't there anymore. Who talks about people as vulgar nowadays? "No, he can't come to my soirée—he's vulgar." Since *Animal House* (1978), at least, we're all a little vulgar. Just twenty years later, another movie opened with a guy fucking an apple pie baked by his mother—in an affluent suburb! First World problems.

Not swearing was central to my identity growing up. My parents insisted that gentlemen don't swear, and since I was being brought up one, that meant me. My father would have put it something like this: "Jesus Christ, Michael, you ought to know better than to swear. Shit." My mother was a less confusing model. Actually, I took the whole thing seriously and never swore, not even mentally, until I was in junior high school. Even then, it didn't take. I'm sure I thought profanity was vulgar—*vulgar* is a word I'd have used back then—and I'm sure that verdict merely confirmed a general commitment to middle-class propriety. Like all of us, I acted out linguistically in my adolescence, but my rebellion was sarcasm, which I think, in retrospect, was morally more corrosive—and socially less productive—than simple swearing would have been. But I'll go into all of that when I get around to writing my autobiography.

In the meantime, we are living through a transitional period, when what was once absolutely vulgar isn't assuredly vulgar any more. Some cultural institutions haven't caught up with this fact. For instance, some dictionaries still label four-letter words as morally or socially objectionable. In entries for words like *fuck*, *The Encarta World English Dictionary* (1999) uses the labels "taboo" and "offensive" together and repeatedly in the same entry, in various shades of bold and sizes of small capital letters. The labels are meant to arrest the reader's attention, and there's a benefit given the supposedly "world" nature of the dictionary—those for whom English is a foreign language might want to know what they're getting into before using *fuck* or a similar word. When I say that *fuck* is devulgarized, I don't mean for everyone, but generally—you still have to watch your language in mixed company.

At the risk of being word-picky, consider what *taboo* and *offensive* mean. *Taboo* means 'off limits' or 'out of bounds,' and *offensive* merely implies that some unknown number of people will find a word like *fuck* or *shit* or *bitch* or *cunt* offensively indecent. When reading a dictionary entry, I know, one might take a label like "offensive" as a universal restriction—always and only offensive to everybody—but on a little reflection, most readers realize it isn't, and the rest of this book goes on to show how often such words aren't offensive but rather useful, expressive, and even artful. Still, and importantly, if someone *is* offended, that's the end of the matter. One can say whether a word is or isn't taboo more or less objectively—when lots of people use it without losing life or limb, or being locked up or shunned, it isn't taboo. But one can't insist to one who finds a word offensive that it isn't. One can argue that it *shouldn't* be offensive, but that's a losing argument—the judgment that a word is offensive is personal.

My favorite publisher, the publisher of this book, has a fine general-purpose dictionary, *The New Oxford American Dictionary* or *NOAD* (three editions so far, in 2001, 2005, and 2010, and pronounced as an acronym, *NO + AD*). *NOAD* labels some words—words in which we're especially interested—as "vulgar," and it's important to recognize that "vulgar" evaluates words very differently from "offensive." "Vulgar" is without doubt a social evaluation rather than a personal one. We associate vulgarity with certain types of people, and arguably we carry our evaluation of the people over into our evaluation of the language they supposedly use. Well, "they" probably use it, but "we" probably do, too, by which we mean some, not all, of them and us. Later on, we'll see this hypocrisy at work, the notion that it's okay for people of an upper class to swear—they'll exercise discretion—but when people of a lower class swear, it's vulgar. The words aren't the problem, then; the people who speak them are the problem. And I have a problem with that, with the war between vulgarity and gentility.

Supposedly, clear thinking—rational, educated thinking—is genteel thinking, and vice versa. You know this from school. If you wrote slang—let alone profanity—into an essay, your English teacher would object in brightest red, echoing O'Connor. Using such words, you were told, is sloppy or lazy—it's an escape from finding the "right" word, the one with a precise meaning. "We all love Holden Caulfield, but his narrative, which we know as *Catcher in the Rye*, is a fucking shambles." Note from teacher: "What kind of shambles, Michael? *Fucking* is such an imprecise word. I'm not even sure if it functions as an adjective in your sentence. Try to find a more descriptive word." Never mind that Holden and Salinger would *love* my sentence—they're just a troubled kid and a reclusive writer, not English teachers. "Clean language is superior to 'bad' language"— it's just an opinion, but we've accepted it as a universal and immutable truth.

We stigmatize "bad" language as coarse and confused, and a "bad" word uttered, like a tattoo or piercing, seems to many, as it did to the Italian criminologist Cesare Lombroso, a mark of atavism and criminality. Lombroso wanted to lock pierced, tattooed swearers up before they committed even more heinous crimes. My grandmother, who thought all Italian Americans were in the Mafia, often said that people use profanity because they don't know any better, by which she really meant "better," but she felt sorry for them—ignorance was an excuse, and we should thank the God in which she didn't believe that we were morally aware and disciplined. She didn't want to send people to prison just because they swore. Unless they were also in the Mafia. Like Lombroso, though, she suspected that swearing predicted character.

What do we mean when we label speech "vulgar"? It's a misleadingly simple question. For one thing, we didn't mean what we mean today until fairly recently, and that alone should make us wary of the term. English borrowed it from Latin *vulgāris* 'of the *vulgus*, that is, of the ordinary people,' not the senatorial or imperial families, in other words, but pretty much everyone else. I know most of us struggle to be anything but ordinary, but sociologically, ordinary is what most of us are. So, in English, *vulgar* meant "in common or general use; common, customary or ordinary." The *OED*'s anthology of quotations for this meaning includes one from Edmund Burke's *Thoughts on Scarcity* (1795) about how conditions might be "compelling us to diminish the quantity of labour which in the vulgar course we actually employ." No hint of stigma, and this had been the vulgar sense of the word from roughly 1430 to 1826, according to the *OED*'s evidence.

Eventually, that meaning extended to language: "commonly or customarily used by the people of a country; ordinary, vernacular." Latin isn't a vulgar tongue in England or America because it isn't and never has been "customarily used by the people"; by definition, it isn't the vernacular in those countries—English is. For a while, French held sway in literary England, but by the late fifteenth century—earlier really—English had overtaken it, and when William Caxton, England's first printer, published *The Book of the Knight of the Tower* (1484), he promised in his preface "to translate & reduce this said book out of frenssh in to our vulgar English," by which he did not mean slang or profanity, and he didn't mean that English in itself was somehow disreputable, either. The substance of Caxton's statement is less important than that he spoke to a mass audience, the one printing was itself creating. It only makes sense to print books for the vulgar people in the vulgar language. In 1484, from the lofty perspectives of lawyers and churchmen, *vulgar* meant 'uneducated, lewd,' but you didn't study English in school because everyone already knew it! The medieval literati could look down their noses at people without Latin or French, but the printing press and mass education would eventually make their scorn irrelevant.

The lexicographers behind the *OED* entry for *vulgar* were careful. Eventually, at sense II.9, they turned to how the word applies "of persons," and they write: "Belonging to the ordinary or common class in the community; not distinguished or marked off from this in any way; plebeian." The entry was written in a century when schoolchildren still learned Latin, *plebeian* rang a precise bell, meaning just the Roman people, basically—it wouldn't be so useful in an entry written today. But the definition's remarkable feature is the editorial comment stuck in between the two defining terms: "not distinguished or marked off from this in any way," for instance, by moral characteristics. The lexicographers knew that *vulgar* had recently taken on a moralizing meaning—they had to know, because it comes up later in the entry—and they wanted to ensure that readers not misinterpret II.9 or the preceding senses as partaking of that meaning.

How recently the moralizing meaning emerged should shock us, though it plays into familiar stereotypes of Victorian prudery and the elevated status of the middle class in nineteenth-century England. At II.13 in the *OED*'s entry for *vulgar*, we read: "Having a common and offensively mean character; coarsely commonplace; lacking in refinement or good taste; uncultured, ill-bred"—one notices how the definition shares terms like "offensive" and "coarse" with definitions of *obscene* and *profane*. The first quotation recorded under that sense of *vulgar* is from Milton, in 1643. No one thought to moralize *vulgar* until the seventeenth century, and most people were using the word in its neutral meaning into the nineteenth century. So, this is the story: moralizing *vulgar* only gradually overtook neutral *vulgar*. Moralizing *vulgar* was possible in the seventeenth and eighteenth centuries, but it wasn't the vulgar usage until it aligned with other social attitudes and finally elbowed neutral *vulgar* to the margins of Anglophone culture where, the Victorians decided, it belonged.[1] As far as we can tell, no one disparaged words as vulgar until Matthew Arnold did in his *Essays in Criticism* (1865): "*Saugrenu* is a rather vulgar French word, but, like many other vulgar words, very expressive."[2] I see that Arnold agrees with this book's fundamental point.

Consider, then, what it means to call profanity "vulgar." For a long swath of history, it's just to say that ordinary people customarily swore—not all of them, not all of the time, many of them on occasion, and some of them abundantly. No one said that swearing was good. Indeed, *bona fide* profanity, taking God's name in vain, was then and is now sinful for those who believe in sin. But what we now call obscenity's a different thing. You can use *ass, bitch, prick,* and *shit* when you're angry with someone—"You little shit!"—or when you just want to devalue him—"You little prick!" Of course, devaluing is *not* good, but we devalue others in language minus profanity all the time without calling such verbal behavior "vulgar," and while *bitch* and *motherfucker* can be used pejoratively, they are "bad" words with "good" meanings today, at least, in some contexts (see Chapter 2).

[1] "Victorians" here is crude shorthand. No great author of the period assumed the moral inferiority of working people, or even the unemployed. Dickens's Jo, the crossing sweeper in *Bleak House* (1853), is a vulgar but sympathetic character, whereas the middle-class characters, from the scrivenerage to the baronetage, are a mixed lot at best. Then, as now, thought-leaders affected thought a lot less than thought-leaders think.

[2] I have no idea why *saugrenu* 'ludicrous, preposterous' was vulgar in the nineteenth century, but of course such evaluations change, as when the once vulgar *asshole* is no longer quite vulgar.

So, what happened to change things, to make *vulgar* the go-to adjective for really bad things, things you, as a middle-class person or an aspiring person, wouldn't want to do or be? In the end, that's the word's power, the way it influences our self-estimations. Scofflaws that we are, we might speed down residential streets and make California stops daily and still feel righteous. We might cause offense—be offensive—on occasion and then apologize, and we don't have to think of ourselves as having offensive natures. Acts and words are offensive, not people—we can say "Michael is bad to the core," but not "Michael is offensive to the core"; "Michael is often offensive because he's bad to the core" makes better sense. But we never want to be vulgar, which is more like being bad than being offensive. No, more precisely, we never want to be *seen* as vulgar, which we take to be an essential rather than a contingent judgment, Henry Higgins and Eliza Doolittle notwithstanding. Criticize what I do but not who I am.

In the Middle Ages, swearing was all over the place, so prevalent that law had to intervene. The most proscribed swearing was real swearing, the swearing of oaths: *Zounds!* 'God's wounds' or *For Christ's sake*—we have no business using God's names disrespectfully, said the medieval church and, to be fair, many a subsequent church, as well. I often say to my son, "For the love of God, Oliver" or "For God's sake, Oliver," which, when he was younger, he transposed to "For the sake of God, Daddy!" We both have to work on this, but I'm glad we won't be branded or put in stocks, or fined some number of shillings, all medieval inducements to better speech. Other words we consider profane—our obscenities—were vulgar, not vulgar. Latin-into-English glossaries of the late fifteenth century often proposed 'cunt' as the appropriate translation of *vulva*. Jenny and I have taught anatomical vocabulary to our daughter, Amelia, on the principle that she should know what to call her own body, but we certainly haven't introduced her to *cunt*—she knows *vulva*, instead. Imagine how uncool she'd feel at a fifteenth-century sleepover, when the talk was all about cunts and pintels, rather than vulvas and penises.

Terms like these were vulgar in the fifteenth century because everyone used them, but they weren't vulgar in the modern sense, because people of high status used them. A century earlier, John Bromyard, a celebrated preacher, wrote about fashionable swearing among the upper classes:

> These inventors of new oaths, who inanely glory in such things count themselves more noble for swearing thus. This is to be seen among those who consider themselves of high breeding, or are proud. Just as they invent and delight in everything of the nature of outward apparel, so do they also in the case of vows and oaths.... Strange vows and swear-words invented by them are already so common that they may be found daily in the mouth of any ribald or rascal you please.

So they didn't just use profanity, these aristocrats and four-lettered men; in part, they based social performance on profanity, relying on their linguistic creativity. The degree to which this is still true and the nature of profane performances today, whether in conversation or on latrine walls or in literature, are central concerns of this book.

What happened was the Renaissance, in which, on the one hand, profanity flourished—and language on the edge of profanity, bawdy, even more so—while at the same time, on the other hand, it was developing a bad reputation. Lexicographers started to exclude the four-letter words, and translators sought euphemisms in order to save their favorite antique authors—English, Greek, Latin, or French—from embarrassment and public criticism. It's in these centuries—the sixteenth and seventeenth centuries—that profanity as we understand it was invented, because before it had just been vulgar language and after it was increasingly considered vulgarity. In her excellent history of swearing, *Holy Shit* (2013), Melissa Mohr notes the rise in this period of "The New Obscenity," followed in the eighteenth and nineteenth centuries by what she proclaims "The Age of Euphemism," because obscenity had become vulgar, and vulgarity needed to be avoided at all f***ing costs.

Consolidated, central authority was on the rise during the early modern period, and it liked to exercise control, because that's what it was made to do, so it focused on profanity as language that needed to be controlled. With middle classes emerging from out of the mass of vulgar persons and new distinctions to be drawn socially and politically as a result, language came to matter more—it began to mark status or class as it had not before. English developed levels to accommodate social stratification, especially in the rise of a standard variety of English, though this is a complicated process—social change motivates standardization and the negative evaluation of nonstandard English, but social change also takes advantage of language change motivated by other forces. The result, however, was significant and pithily well expressed by Tony McEnery: "Broadly speaking, the discourse of power excludes bad language, the discourse of the disempowered includes it." The point is so perfectly true that we'll see it operate in much of the profanity, as well as reactions to it, discussed in this book.

By the twentieth century, more or less, profanity's vulgarity was taken as given, yet some were simultaneously questioning not only the assumption that profanity belongs to the lower social orders but of "bad" language generally, however the discourse of power decides to define it. "Great purity of speech," Thorstein Veblen observes in *The Theory of the Leisure Class* (1899), "is presumptive evidence of

several successive lives spent in other than vulgarly useful occupations." Veblen is being sarcastic. The useful occupations, he's well
aware, are vulgar in the old sense, but not in the new. Veblen respects
usefulness over leisure. But his formulation hints at its obverse: several successive lives spent in vulgarly useful occupations implies
generations of "impure" speech. So speech becomes destiny, and we
find it difficult to untangle the respective characters of language and
the people who speak it.

After the Second World War, things changed yet again, as they
always do. Workers became middle class, and while there was still
plenty of aspiration to exceed social "destinies," other forces in-
truded to promote linguistic freedom, everything from civil rights
to rejection of the Establishment over Vietnam, feminism—coun-
tercultures challenged the mainstream, and it was no longer easy to
identify what was normal, let alone what was "better." Besides, there
was a lot of anger and a lot of rebellion, and I hope most Americans
appreciate that the rebellion, which from my grandparents' perspective was foul-mouthed, was nonetheless much less violent than many
had feared—I'll take honest profanity over violence, any day. The
Culture Wars perpetrated by the political Right in America in the
1980s attempted to counteract what it identified as cultural relativism,
the kind of wrong-thinking in which profanity is supposedly neither
good nor bad. Those cultural warriors, whatever they thought about
"good," wanted "bad" back—you can't fight culture wars without
enemies, and so we return to our narrative of the first debate over
profanity.

Attitudes about profanity changed profoundly in the second
half of the twentieth century. What was unprintable before the
Second World War became printable—we could even say suddenly
printable. D. H. Lawrence's novel *Lady Chatterley's Lover* (1928) was
banned for obscenity in the United States until 1960. The ban would

have been hard to sustain after James Jones published *fuck* in *From Here to Eternity* (1951). By 1960, Lawrence's novels—though not *Lady Chatterley's Lover*—were being taught in university courses, and Lawrence was generally regarded as one of the great modern writers. Jones's book won the National Book Award. So, it's not that *shit* and *ass* and *fuck* appear in pulp fiction—not that there's anything wrong with pulp fiction—but that it appears in prestigious literature, in the case of *Lady Chatterley* and James Joyce's *Ulysses* somewhat earlier, literature that people would fight in the courts to read. Plenty of award-winning works, works we consider classics of fiction, poetry, drama, and essay, have been published in spite of or maybe even because of their profanity ever since—several figure in this book.

One measure of profanity's devulgarization is how willing people are to publish and read it. Another test is latent resistance to the change. *The New Yorker* was notoriously reluctant to print four-letter words for decades, even after other magazines were doing so regularly— *Harper's* had published *fuck* in 1968. *The New Yorker* was at the time and still is an arbiter of literary taste, and its profanity standard was meant and taken seriously. The story has been told often enough, but it bears repeating briefly in this context. Harold Ross founded the magazine with, according to Brendan Gill, "the stipulation that it was *not* to be edited for the old lady in Dubuque." This did not mean, however, that Ross could handle profanity. Gill reports, "Ross was a notorious coward, in matters spiritual as well as physical," and as a result, claims to the contrary notwithstanding, "He said it was his intention to publish nothing that would bring a blush to the cheek of a twelve-year-old girl." Writers and editors performed all kinds of verbal gymnastics to satisfy both standards at the same time.

Ross's successor, William Shawn, was just as resistant, and— given his lack of interest in sports—an unexpectedly talented gymnast. Throughout his tenure, writers sought to include profanity in their work, but Shawn would outmaneuver them. According to Ved Mehta, a longtime contributor to *The New Yorker*, Pauline Kael, who reviewed movies for the magazine from 1968 to 1991, proved a particular challenge for Shawn, because he trusted her critical instinct absolutely, yet could not accept her "penchant for scatology." Kael "was fairly amenable to having her copy improved," Mehta recalls, "but fierce when she spotted changes that might curtail her frank, conversational writing style, as when Mr. Shawn would suggest that she change 'ass' to 'derrière,' or 'crap' to 'ordure,'" the former risible by the 1980s, the latter sophisticated beyond the reach even of many a *New Yorker* reader, I'm sure.

Another great *New Yorker* writer, Renata Adler, gives the story a slightly different spin. "By the sixties," she writes, "everyone was using obscenities of all kinds. The strongest Anglo-Saxon words in the language were so common that their power was nearly gone. Still, Mr. Shawn, in his words, 'held the line.' The first use of 'shit' occurred in a piece by Anthony Lewis, in a quotation of President Nixon from a transcript of the White House tapes," which, in a sense, means no one was saying it—it was an archival fact, said by a president, but then taped and saved, and printed, and reprinted in *The New Yorker*, which was thus at a safe distance from the profanity of the profanity. But still, Adler continues, "Mr. Shawn went on, in my view like Horton the elephant, nurturing, amid all the pressures and distractions, the egg of civil discourse, or whatever he thought it was. Nothing came of it, I think, except perhaps the touching spectacle of faithfulness itself." Calvin Trillin and Bobbie Ann Mason finally convinced Shawn to allow them a *fuck* or two, and a *goddam*, as well, all in 1985. But Shawn's caution cost the magazine something, not a lot, but a bit of stylistic authenticity it has yet to recover. As Adler puts it—beautifully—"Rough speech in *The New Yorker* still seems so alien that it leaps off the page—not powerfully, however, and not purely, but most often dully, as a shattering of something already in smithereens."

Just as profanity appears in prestigious literary works, it appears in Academy Award–nominated films, such as *Fargo*, in which Steve Buscemi's character, Carl Showalter, after he's been shot and retreated to a safe house, hurls so many hateful F-bombs at Gaear Grismund that Gaear feeds him to the wood chipper. Everyone remembers the wood chipper scene, but the extreme profanity is memorable, too: "Hold on! No fuckin' way! You fuckin' notice this? I got fuckin' shot! I got fuckin' shot in the face! I went and got the fuckin' money. I got shot fuckin' picking it up! I've been up for thirty-six fuckin' hours! I'm taking' that fuckin' car! That fucker's mine, you fuckin' asshole!" It's not the first time Carl has sworn a blue streak in the film, and Carl is far from the only character in first-rate films to go on a cursing rant.

Similarly, profanity doesn't occur any more in raunchy rock-and-roll songs than it does in alternative music, the music of college radio station playlists—consider one refrain of Aimee Mann's "How Am I Different": "Just one question before I pack/ when you fuck it up later/ Do I get my money back?" It's just one example of profanity that appeals to cool, educated people, and since anyone reading this book is probably one of those, she's probably already thought of an even better example. It makes little difference whether social acceptance of profanity derives from realism—people talk this way, and reporting and art need to convey how people actually speak— or from a new appreciation of profanity's expressiveness. The big questions are: Can profanity be both vulgar and sophisticated, or can a poem or film, award-winning or not, be vulgar yet also art? Whether we simply accept such paradoxes or decide that profanity at least doesn't get in fine art's way, nevertheless, it's hardly vulgar, let alone taboo.

In fact, far from being taboo, profanity is prestige language. The media have gone a step further even than devulgarization—they have begun to develop a meta-profanity. An interviewer for the men's magazine *Stuff* can ask actress Jaime Pressly, of *My Name Is Earl* fame: "What's your favorite curse word and how often do you use it?" and she can answer, "Fuck, and quite frequently. I love saying fuck. It seems to be the universal code word in Hollywood, where it can't be overused. It is such a fucking release to say fuck. I say fuck all day long, but not around kids," a scruple we've already challenged and will challenge some more. Pressly hasn't done fieldwork to support her assertion that *fuck* is Hollywood's code word, but others corroborate her intuition:

> Judging from her buttoned-down work as an ADA on *Law & Order*....Kring didn't think [Jill Hennessy] could cut it as feisty, salt-of-the-earth medical examiner Jordan Cavanaugh. But he agreed to meet her for breakfast, only to arrive and discover that the restaurant wasn't open yet. "She comes walking up, and I start apologizing," Kring says, "The first words out of her mouth were, 'Dude, f— it. Who gives a s—? We'll go someplace else.'" Those turned out to be the magic four-letter words. Kring was instantly sold.

Once upon a time you couldn't say the bad words, but now you can talk about them with impunity and rack up social points, score for the bad words, triple score for the impunity.

And, of course, nowadays, you can find plenty of profanity in *The New Yorker*. For evidence, turn to a recent profile of notorious potty mouth Seth MacFarlane, who has been trying to invest vulgarity with new meaning in animated situation comedies like *Family Guy* and *American Dad* for over a decade now —"In a world where vulgarity was virtually extinct," you can hear his impression of a movie trailer running through his mind in yours, which is creepy, "one man gave voice to as many vulgar characters as he could without developing a personality disorder." McFarlane is quoted as saying, before a live audience in a jazz club where he was singing, "I'm a little under the weather tonight, so forgive me if I sound a little like Joy Behar.... We are just fucking winging it." The article prints MacFarlane's free-wheeling profanity but doesn't mention that anyone in the club booed when he used bad words, which suggests that *fuck* is devulgarized in many contexts.

Worrying about profanity has become a joke. The television show *South Park* satirized attitudes toward taboo words in 2001 in the episode "It Hits the Fan." Residents of South Park, including the elementary school children who "star" in the half-hour animated show, use *shit* 162 times in the episode, epochal "bad" language use that calls forth world destruction, from which we are all saved by the timely entrance of the Knights of Standards and Practices. Twenty years ago, the Knights would have rescued us from *bitch*, but major television networks now regularly broadcast that word, so the writers of *South Park* resorted to another. Eventually, we won't need knights to defend Standards and Practices, because there won't be any standards, just practices, and the practices will take care of themselves. It gets harder and harder for anyone to say, "Ooh, that's a bad word" with a straight face. If that's because we've got past sorting people and language by the vulgarity standard, that's fine by me. If there is no vulgarity, I'm not sure it can win, but I'm pretty sure, if I'm right, that gentility loses the third profanity debate.

THE AGE OF PROFANITY

The taboo surrounding profanity— supposedly an ancient cultural and semantic structure—has, like so many ancient structures, tumbled into ruins. Vulgarity, once a solid attribute of profanity, is vapor in the air. Already in the 1960s, Renata Adler claims, "the strongest Anglo-Saxon words in the language were so common that their power was nearly gone." If Moore is right about the prototypical functions of profanity, Adler has to be wrong, because the functional need to express powerful emotion is inherently human. As Timothy Jay points out with such clarity, "a 'language' without emotions is no more normal than a person without emotions." But we must consider the possibility, too, that Adler is right, that Moore and Jay are wrong, if only in a sense, for we wouldn't say that the prototypical function *expression of powerful emotion* can be supplied only by profanity. We would need a different function, something like *expression of powerful emotion that other language can't handle*. Profanity supplies this function, but we have to keep in mind—as both Moore and Jay do to their credit—that profanity performs other functions, profanity is an opportunity rather than a necessity.

Jay also insists: "Curse words are normal because they obey semantic and syntactic rules. Curse words are unique because they provide emotional intensity to speech that non–curse words cannot achieve. Curse words have so much power that they become words that, once learned, must be suppressed in formal contexts." This formulation, too, is only partly correct. Profanity does, against its inclinations, follow the rules, more or less. And profanities are unique among words in conveying emotional intensity, but, critically, intensity need not be conveyed in words. Menace, for instance, is often conveyed without profanity—perhaps even more effectively conveyed without it—so profanity is not, like a neurotransmitter, specifically keyed to unlock its supposed function. Finally, the current power of profanity is just what Adler questions, and it simply isn't true that profanity must be suppressed in formal contexts, though perhaps we live in fewer formal contexts than we did half a century ago.

If profanity is so weak today, it seems unlikely that I would triumphantly declare this, our own time, to be "The Age of Profanity"—but I do, because we can use profanity to satisfy multiple human and linguistic needs better now than at any previous time in history, without much constraint. Some institutions—schools, for instance—still operate as though swearing were taboo, and profanity cannot achieve its cultural moment without interference. If we want talking dirty to improve our sex lives, if we want the extra edge profanity gives us in forming group solidarity or in performing certain identities, if we want profanity's keen blade to cut through lazy assumptions to philosophical truth, or any of the other purposes this book claims that profanity satisfies, it has to be mostly free of taboo and even of vulgarity, but "mostly" is the important word—to reach the zenith of its value, profanity has to be used as freely as possible while still carrying the vestiges of taboo and vulgarity. In The Age of Profanity, maximum freedom and necessary constraint are optimally balanced; so, paradoxically, while this is new, it's also just another phase in its history when profanity is like no other language.

How long can we maintain this finely suspended state of affairs? When will the thread of constraint snap and profanity fall into the heap of usual words? If profanity becomes too usual, then how can it also be special? Of course, the words won't go away. Given the usual historical processes, in which words do become obsolete on occasion, *shit* and *fuck* and *bitch* will probably survive for centuries; they'll probably continue to generate derivative forms, like our own *shitfaced*, *fuckwad*, and *bitchslap*, though we can't predict what the new words will be. Our emotional needs probably won't change significantly, either, and just because they're useful as exclamations of frustration or anger, some profanities will continue in their current roles, but all of the obscenity we consider profanity will lose the cachet of either—perhaps nothing will be obscene, nothing profane, and nothing taboo, the signal of frustration in *Shit!* or *Fuck!* merely a matter of phonetics, not of attitudes towards those terms.

For now, at this moment, we can experience a mishap—break an ankle, for instance—and release our frustration physically—with violent mouth gestures—in a psychologically effective series of sounds. When we do so, we are also saying, implicitly, that it hurts so bad that we don't give a fuck about what other people think about what we say. But people will still help us rather than shun us, because profanity alone is not enough to discourage their sympathy—it may, in fact, in The Age of Profanity, deepen it. It's possible that this pragmatic meaning—that is, meaning arising from context rather than the definitions of words—could become implausible, unproduceable, though we still produce the words conventionally associated with it. The exclamatory release, on one hand, and other people's opinions, on the other, aren't inextricably linked. *Aaagh!* works reasonably well in such situations, I've found—the emptying of air requiring a focusing big breath to follow—though it lacks all the layers of pragmatic meaning that accompany *fuck.* As English stands now, anyway.

Were there ever a time to admire profanity, it would be now, in The Age of Profanity, when it accomplishes more than it's ever otherwise been able to do; it would be now, when our attitudes toward it are elastic enough to ensure its free and frequent and productive use even while we trade on its negative social value. If it differs functionally from slang, as Moore argues, then we should celebrate it now before it loses its distinguishing power and becomes "mere" slang. If it is already just particularly powerful slang, then we should celebrate it now before it loses *that* distinguishing power. As much as some detractors of profanity would like to see the profanity debates end in a profanity Armageddon, that's unlikely to happen. Given the many attitudes toward it, profanity won't be brought down by its most histrionic antagonists.

Melissa Mohr reminds us that "Just as there has always been swearing, there have always been attempts to top or control it." But what if we're running out of always? What if profanity becomes obsolete, not with a bang, but with a whimper, not because McKay Hatch or others are against it, but because it's semantically, pragmatically fatigued from overuse? For all of the reasons outlined in this book, I hope The Age of Profanity lasts a long time. We humans will always be expressive, but we can't assume that the means of expression will remain the same forever, that expressing strong emotion will always be so easy or so much fun, as we skirt vulgarity in order to have our say. In the meantime, if we admire profanity, we should praise it. Soon, age will pass into age, and our praise will be too late. We can't reasonably praise "the smashing of something already in smithereens."

REFERENCES

In the Preface, I quote Timothy Jay from *Why We Curse: A Neuro-Psycho-Social Theory of Speech* (Amsterdam and Philadelphia: John Benjamins, 2000), p. 10. James D. McCawley wrote on one occasion as Quan Phúc Đông, a professor at the South Hanoi Institute of Technology—figure it out on your own—contributing "English Sentences without Overt Grammatical Subject" (3–10) and "A Note on Conjoined Noun Phrases" (11–18)—serious articles heavily laden with profane examples—to *Studies Out in Left Field: Defamatory Essays Presented to James D. McCawley on His 33rd or 34th Birthday*, originally published in Edmonton, Alberta, by Linguistic Research in 1971, but since reprinted by John Benjamins (1992). Jay is author also of the foundational work *Cursing in America: A Psycholinguistic Study of Dirty Language in the Courts, in the Movies, in the Schoolyards, and on the Streets* (Amsterdam: John Benjamins, 1992). The Classics, new and old, are: Geoffrey Hughes's *Swearing: A Social History of Foul Language, Oaths and Profanity in English* (London: Penguin, 1998), first published in Oxford, by Blackwell, in 1991; Steven Pinker's "The Seven Words You Can't Say on Television," in *The Stuff of Thought: Language as a Window into Nature* (New York: Penguin, 2007), pp. 323–372; Tony McEnery's *Swearing in English: Bad Language, Purity, and Power from 1586 to the Present* (London: Routledge, 2006);

and Melissa Mohr's *Holy Shit: A Brief History of Swearing* (New York: Oxford University Press, 2013). The books of mine to which *In Praise of Profanity* is connected are *Slayer Slang: A Buffy the Vampire Slayer Lexicon* (New York: Oxford University Press, 2003), *Slang: The People's Poetry* (New York: Oxford University Press, 2009), and *From Elvish to Klingon: Exploring Invented Languages*, of which I was editor (Oxford: Oxford University Press, 2011). I will acknowledge here, but not throughout the book, the debts I owe to Jonathon Green and his *Green's Dictionary of Slang*, in three robust volumes (London: Chambers, 2010), and to the *Oxford English Dictionary*. In the latter, I quote from entries written by subeditors and editors of the nineteenth century; later entries were edited under the ultimate supervision of John Simpson, until lately—but when this book was conceived and much of it written—the dictionary's Chief Editor; now, the Chief Editor is Michael Proffitt, and Victorian entries bearing on profanity will doubtless be revised under his regime. In any event, you can see how hard it would be write a concise bibliographical note for each entry consulted, and I leave it at this.

Chapter 1 begins with an account of "Little Bo Bleep," an episode of the ABC series *Modern Family* (2009–), aired on January 18, 2012, directed by Chris Koch and written by Christopher Lloyd, Steven Levitan, and Cindy Chupac. Eric Stonestreet plays Cameron Tucker on the show, and Jesse Tyler Ferguson plays Mitchell Pritchett, but Ms. Anderson-Emmons is deservedly the star of the episode. Adam Mansbach and Ricardo Cortés's *Go the Fuck to Sleep*, and all of the related books, are published by Akashic Books of New York, in the years indicated. The novelty firm Know Questions Asked LLC advises "Play dirty. No cheating" on every box of their *Cuss Cards: European Edition* (2006), place of publication as yet undetermined. Sarah Royal and Jillian Panarese's *Creative Cursing: A Mix 'n' Match Profanity Generator*, as well as *Creative Cussin'*, were published in Philadelphia and London by Running Press, in 2009 and 2010, respectively. Jesse Sheidlower's now classic *The F-Word*, 3d ed. (New York: Oxford University Press, 2009) is arranged alphabetically, so we can do without page numbers. Green accounts for the distribution of obscene terms in just a little bit of the introduction to his massive *Green's Dictionary of Slang*. I quote from Christopher C. Gee's *Swear Not at All: An Overview of the Constructs and Consequences of Foul Language* (Bloomington, IN: AuthorHouse, 2005), pp. 40, 41, 20, 22, 20 again, and 59, in series. I quote the Bible from *The Bible: Authorized King James Version with Apocrypha*, edited by Robert Carroll and Stephen Prickett (Oxford: Oxford University Press, 1997), rather than the Reverend Gee's text, in order to achieve biblical consistency throughout this book. James V. O'Connor's *Cuss Control: The Complete Book on How to Curb Your Cursing* was originally published by Three Rivers Press of New York, in 2000, but my copy was published by iUniverse (New York; Lincoln, Nebraska; and Shanghai) in 2006; I quote it from pp. 18 twice, 171, 49, xvii, and xvi, in series. McKay Hatch is quoted from *The No Cussing Club: How I Fought Against Peer Pressure and How You Can Too!* (South Pasadena, CA: Dawson Publishing, 2009), pp. 6, 19, 30, and 71, in series. O'Connor's appearances are enumerated in the biographical note on the back cover of his book; No Cussing Club Swag and Hatch's uplifting presentations are mentioned in the end papers of his. I borrow a big idea from Kees van Deemter's *Not Exactly: In Praise of Vagueness* (Oxford: Oxford University Press, 2010), refer to the distinction between vagueness and ambiguity he draws on p. 113, and quote a bit from p. 109. I also trade rather freely on Robert Moore's "On Swearwords and Slang," which appeared in *American Speech* 87 (2012): 170–189, but I quote it from pp. 172 twice, then p. 173, p. 177 for egalitarian solidarity, and pp. 178–79, in series. My alternative prototype explanation is the subject of Chapter 4 of *Slang: The People's Poetry* (New York: Oxford University Press, 2009), pp. 163–212. *Animal House* was directed by John Landis, written by Chris Miller, Harold Ramis, and Douglas Kenney, and released by Universal Pictures in 1978. *American Pie* was directed by Paul and Chris Weitz, written by Adam Herz, and released, once again, by Universal Pictures. In the same year that *American Pie* celebrated American raunch, *The Encarta World English Dictionary*, edited by Kathy Rooney and Anne Soukhanov (London: Bloomsbury and New York: St. Martin's, 1999) attempted to make the world safe for people with "fragile sensibilities" (see Chapter 3). In his critical review of *Encarta in Dictionaries: Journal of the Dictionary Society of North America* 21 (2000): 112–124, Sidney I. Landau, one of America's great lexicographers, guides us through the dictionary's problems. I wrote somewhat more about the labeling in "Teaching 'Bad' American English: Profanity and Other 'Bad' Words in the Liberal Arts Setting," *Journal of English Linguistics* 30 (2002): 353–365, on p. 153—I have revised sections of this article and inserted them into the current chapter. The *New Oxford American Dictionary* (New York: Oxford University Press) has appeared in three editions so far: the first edition (2001) was edited principally by Elizabeth J. Jewell and Frank Abate; the second edition (2005) by Erin McKean; and the third edition (2010) by Angus Stevenson and Christine A. Lindberg. One wonders who needs an introduction to J. D. Salinger's *Catcher in the Rye*, but for the record, it's been published in New York, by Little, Brown and Company, since its release in 1951. For the Lombroso story, see Stephen Jay Gould, *The Mismeasure of Man* (New York: W. W. Norton, 1981), p. 132. The quotation from John Bromyard's *Summa Prædicantium* is taken from Geoffrey Hughes's *Swearing*, pp. 60–61. Melissa Mohr's book includes a section on "The New Obscenity" (pp. 165–172); "The Age of Euphemism" is the title of her Chapter 5. McEnery is quoted from *Swearing in English*, p. 12. Thorstein Veblen's *The Theory of the Leisure Class*, originally published in 1899, is quoted here from my Modern Library edition (1931), p. 399. The stories of *Ulysses* and *Lady Chatterley's Lover* and American courts have been told many times, but there is a useful synopsis in *The F-Word* (2009), pp. xx–xxi, and Mohr does well by them, too, on pp. 239–244. Brendan

Gill on Harold Ross and *The New Yorker* is quoted from *Here at* The New Yorker (New York: Random House, 1975), pp. 32–33. Ved Mehta's *Remembering Mr. Shawn's* New Yorker (Woodstock, NY: The Overlook Press, 1998) is quoted from p. 281; Renata Adler is quoted from *Gone: The Last Days of* The New Yorker (New York: Simon & Schuster, 1999), twice from p. 165, and then p. 166. *Fargo* was directed and written by Joel and Ethan Coen, released by PolyGram in 1996. Sheidlower mentions other notable movies in the same vein in *The F-Word* (2009), pp. xxvi–xxvii; and Jay presents a synopsis of his research into American films, 1939–1989, in *Cursing in America*, pp. 222–234. Aimee Mann's "How Am I Different" appears on her album, *Bachelor No. 2, or the Last Remains of the Dodo* (New York: SuperEgo Records, 1999). Mann's seventh album was titled *@#%&*! Smilers* (New York: SuperEgo Records, 2008) and is usually called *Fucking Smilers*, but I think there's a spelling problem. Jaime Pressly's theory of profanity is taken from Stuart Matranga, "May We Check Your Coat?" *Stuff* (June 2001), p. 64—the article covers pp. 62–67. The Jill Hennessey story comes from Bruce Fretts, "Crossing Jordan," *Entertainment Weekly* (September 7, 2001), p. 52. Seth McFarlane is quoted from p. 42 of Claire Hoffman's profile, "No. 1 Offender," in *The New Yorker* (June 18, 2012), pp. 38–43. "It Hits the Fan," which aired on June 20, 2001, kicked off the fifth season of *South Park* and was written and directed by Trey Parker. Timothy Jay is quoted twice from *Why We Curse*, p. 11. Mohr's *Holy Shit* is quoted once again, from p. 254.

Chapter 2

Intimacy, Exceptionalism, and Having It Both Ways

The whole point of taboo is that if you break it, you are an outlaw, literally outside the law, not worthy of protection—in fact, anyone who protects an outlaw is guilty by association, and so, to the extent that profanity is taboo and those who use it outlaws, we are supposed to shun those who swear. Some shun them, most don't, and that's good, because them is us. More surprising than our toleration, however, is the way that swearing—far from putting us asunder—brings us together. While we establish intimacy with friends, family, and lovers by other means, and while profanity isn't necessary to the social work of maintaining somewhat larger groups, profanity nonetheless plays constructive roles in group and interpersonal relationships. Of course, because profanity occurs in abusive speech, it can destroy as well as build relationships—it can cause considerable harm, as its adversaries rightly point out. But abuse no more depends on profanity than intimacy does. Is profanity, then, merely a neutral marker that follows the overall morality of speech in which it occurs, or is it especially well suited for some of our mutually rewarding social activity?

In this age, The Age of Profanity, bad words are unexpectedly useful in fostering human relations because they carry risk—so that use of them demands trust—but not the traditional risk of taboo. We like to get away with things, and sometimes we do so with like-minded people. But how do we know that they're like-minded? How do we know we can trust them with our tender emotions or our sexual self-esteem? How do we know that we can rely on them or that they know they can rely on us? With whom can we be so casual that profanity doesn't matter? Or, rather than not mattering, profanity in such relationships matters a lot precisely because it doesn't, because the participants feel such complete comfort with each other that they can be impolite together—that's one of the many paradoxes accompanying our use of profanity.

We deploy profanity carefully in close relationships so that there's no misunderstanding, but the closer the relationship, the less likely misunderstanding is—successful use of profanity proves that. Some close friends, spouses, lovers will use a lot, some will use it occasionally, but the value of profanity in either case is much the same. The amount, frequency, and specific items of profanity spoken are matters of style. In groups, we constantly negotiate our credibility, and the warrant to curse among others—and sometimes *at* others— puts us and others in their respective places, or sometimes it helps us achieve a place, to take the upper hand. Most often, though, we use profanity so that we can agree that we can use it, and once we're sure of that, we can move on to playing with it, having fun with it in the way we do with slang or other types of poetic language.

In the digital age, we're told, face-to-face interaction will be less and less common—the machines we use to communicate, our social media, keep us constantly engaged but at a distance. From that distance, our relationships require intense attention. Our messages to one another can be clever, but not too subtle, so we figure out how to swear minimally (*OMG, WTF, ROTFLMAO*), preserving as many of our 140 characters as possible for other news, a little more content, a little less attitude. Really, though, we have all been distant from one another for some time—since the beginning of time, in fact. We work incredibly hard to establish and maintain what relationships we can. The urge to connect with others is specific, local, focused on a social group we can see and hear and touch, but it's also existential, one of the fundamental problems of being human. Profanity figures in human connection at every scale, from dyadic relationships to others both hopelessly and hopefully diffuse.

INTIMACY AND SOLIDARITY

In a sense, this section's case is easily proved: we use profanity to foster intimacy with those closest to us and to promote solidarity in groups to which we're committed. Profanity is an effective way of marking and developing intimacy, because, in using it, you can speak things with one or two other people as though you are talking to yourself, things you can't say outside of an intimacy without paying some sort of social cost, and if a relationship passes the profanity test, the parties conclude a pact that whatever they say in their intimate relationship stays in their intimate relationship. Though it isn't part of everyone's sexual repertoire, "talking dirty" is nonetheless sometimes intimacy's handmaiden. Profanity is extreme slang used to map the limits of affiliation and social relationship. Perhaps profanity isn't in the strictest sense necessary to explore regions of intimacy, but if it's ready, we're likely to use it.

While profanity functions in ways that other slang can't, often it operates as no more than slang and serves the same social purposes. So, it can mark in-groups from out-groups. Not everyone says, as an interjection, *What the fuck?!* and not all of those who do so use *WTF* in tweets, etc. Profanity, because it's supposedly forbidden, can enact rebellion, too, and like other slang thus mark dissenters off from the mainstream. On the other hand, the back cover of *Go the Fuck to*

Sleep recommends, "You probably should not read it to your children," and of course adults wouldn't, partly to protect their children's virgin ears, but also because adults, though ostracized by their children's slang, are warranted to use a certain amount of profanity among themselves—it's one of the verbal behaviors that identifies the mainstream adult in-group—and the book is their joke, it belongs to them, not the damn kids.

I suppose, dear reader, that you may be one of the very few of us never to have used profanity at any time in your life, under any circumstance. But you probably have used a little profanity, not when you were grade-school sweet and innocent and not later once you'd taken a side in one or more of the profanity wars, but when you were a teenager—walking around the neighborhood with your gang, at a sleepover, in a locker room—you used some. Or, if you didn't utter the profanities yourself, a friend did and you observed it, tolerated it, even enjoyed it—you knew right from wrong, but you were no McKay Hatch. Well, you're not off the profanity hook, my friend, and your experience makes my argument for me. Even if you believe intimacy shouldn't depend on profanity, you must concede that it can and does, that you've seen it in operation.

First, it's a test. Someone—a leader or aspiring leader—uses a bad word. She feels comfortable in the group, but she wants herself and the others to commit yet more firmly to the relationship. Can they break the rules together, forging the bond of mutual reliance and secrecy necessary to the fully formed adolescent clique? Such relationship affirming criminality isn't confined to bad language— friends induce one another to shoplift, drive recklessly, loft toilet paper into the neighbors' trees. Of all of these, swearing is perhaps the least obnoxious. The circle of friends that swears together stays together. You can't swear in front of your parents, teachers, or other adults—except as an act of rebellion—but you can swear in front of your friends. You can do it because you're intimate, and doing it only fortifies that intimacy. In this regard, one can barely distinguish between profanity and slang, though the stakes are slightly higher with profanity—there's more proof of commitment.

The Showtime comedy series *Californication* (2007–2014) illustrates—in a very stylized way—how profanity promotes group solidarity and intimacy The central character in the series is Hank Moody, an alcoholic, almost washed-up writer sometimes working in Hollywood, trying rather haphazardly to dig himself out of many holes. Hank is a bad boy, and his on-again off-again partner but forever love, Karen, and his friend and agent, Charlie Runkle, and Charlie's wife Marcy are also bad, and frankly just about everyone else on the show is pretty bad—bad in the sense that they flout social mores and official laws, and profanity is almost as ubiquitous in the mix as the sex and drugs. Solidarity among the core group of characters is built as much on profanity as anything else. Although the loose morals and bad language are taken as symptomatic of Hollywood, Hank is always at the extreme even of that abnormal normality. Hank and his compatriots are too cool for school—literally, it turns out in Season 3, when Hank embarks on a short-lived teaching career, during which he manages to copulate with the Dean's wife, his teaching assistant, and a student—and those are just the women at the college.

Charlie and Hank share an exemplary bromance. It's true love, with all the trimmings. The bros aren't just profane together, in the way of delinquent juveniles—they love to play with the profanity, kids who can't leave their feces alone. For instance, at one point in the episode titled "The Way of the Fist," from Season 5, Hank calls Charlie out with: "You're a real twatty fucking cunt, you know that?" That's an unusual amount of profanity for one sentence in real life, but in *Californication* not so much. Though Hank is by all accounts a romantic, he's also usually in trouble with women, partly because he uses language like *twatty* and *cunt* to demean his bro—nothing insults a man more than being called by words for women's sexual parts—and women don't especially like that.

Charlie replies, "Twat? Twat? I cunt hear you. I've got an ear infucktion. I'll finger it out later"—he attempts to save face by outclevering Hank while being no less profane. What's most revealing about their playfully competitive profanity is how what comes after it frames it. Hank responds, "You've still got some cum on your foot." Charlie looks down. "Made you look," Hanks says as he slaps Charlie. Charlie slaps him back, and then they call a truce. It's the Two Stooges and their interminable foreplay. If they were half as clever about the world as they are verbally clever, Hank and Charlie would be in a lot less trouble. But they'll never choose a lexically pure life over the profane one or any friendship over their own. Anyway, for them, profanity and friendship are inextricable.

Hank uses every profanity you can think of, but his signature is a very special version of *motherfucker*. His voice rises to falsetto at the onset and throughout the word—"Muthafucka!"—usually holding the terminal vowel past its natural, even its comfortable duration. The jubilant boy-man sound of it is a compact version of what makes Hank so irresistible to friends, male and female alike. Especially, though, when Hank raises the pitch of his voice, he raises the stakes of his profanity—he makes a spectacle of it. Later in Season 5, after Hank fires Charlie both as agent and friend, Charlie harasses him with supplication—it sounds dirtier than it is. After an attempt to win Hank back, in the episode titled "Perverts and Whores," Hank sums up the state of play from his point of view: "See you in hell"— regular voice—"muthafucka!"—falsetto. It's meant to be off-putting— or is it? "Don't say 'muthafucka' like that," Charlie wails, "it makes me miss you."

Hank Moody's example won't persuade anyone dead set against it that profanity has its virtues. Nevertheless, and as perverse as it might seem to some, Hank's *muthafucka!* is the expressive emblem of his affection. In Charlie's case, Hank knows perfectly well that he's speaking intimately with someone he appears to have written off. If Hank had said *muthafucka* in his usual voice, the sentence "See you in hell, muthafucka" would indeed mean that he was withholding friendship from Charlie. But when he cries his signature falsetto *muthafucka!* it's more complicated. Either the Moody *muthafucka!*—understood as intimate—hints that Hank intends to restore friendship, or he taunts Charlie with it, which is how Charlie hears it. If the latter case seems mean, one has to remember that Charlie betrayed Hank with another client, and Hank thinks he's entitled to make Charlie grovel for reinstatement, even if he never actually left Hank's affections. So often, profanity allows the profaner to have it both ways.

Hank and Charlie flirt with profanity, but they never use it to arouse each other sexually—they joke about such arousal, but you can't take them seriously about much of anything. Fully bromosocial, they can't really be homosexual. Others see profanity as a sex toy but also as proof of intimacy. Proving it, the story goes, heightens intimacy, which in turn heightens arousal. It makes sense, when one thinks about it, that within sexual intimacy, you would call a spade a spade and use sexual language for sexual things. You're not in the public square; you can have dirty sex talk. The thrill of taboo mingles with reassuring intimacy. You can use words you won't use—just as you can touch places you can't and get into positions you can't—with anyone other than your mutually consenting sexual partner. It's like chocolate and peanut butter and the Reese's Peanut Butter Cups of sexual intimacy.

Intimacy doesn't require profanity, and profanity certainly isn't sufficient for intimacy, yet for some, apparently, it promotes intimacy.

If you want sex advice, *Cosmopolitan* advises, turn to *Cosmopolitan*. There, you'll read, "Arousal isn't only about touch—according to experts, the sexy phrases you whisper, moan, or scream trigger a neurochemical reaction that gets him hotter for you than ever." The sweet nothings in question aren't necessarily profane, but some of us like our sex salty. In one of the article's key examples, a partner—presumably a woman who has momentarily shed her good girl—commands or entreats or suggests, "F--- me harder." *Cosmo* explains, "Pushing yourself outside of your comfort zone with words like 'tits,' 'pussy,' or 'f---' conveys that your boundaries are down and lust has taken over. You don't want to sound phony, so only drop an f-bomb if it feels right to you, and make sure your language matches your level of arousal, becoming more explicit the closer you get to orgasm." It's not clear why, so quick to give advice, *Cosmo* isn't willing to print the word you're supposed to say—I doubt that hyphens or asterisks are a turn-on, but I lack experience in these things.

Sexual satisfaction improves when partners communicate well about sex, research tells us, but surveys don't generally explore the register of sex talk, so the role of profanity in sexual intimacy is difficult to gauge—usually, in spite of Kinsey and Masters and Johnson, the researchers aren't actually in the room to hear the moans and cries of ecstasy, let alone the dirty words. Study after study explores the relationships of sexual self-esteem, sexual self-disclosure, and sexual assertiveness—if you can make your desires known to a partner, you're more likely to find satisfaction. Of course, you can do so without uttering a word, let alone a profane one, and there's evidence that nonverbal communication is more effective than talk at intimate moments. It makes sense, though, that expressive speech like profanity communicates desire more effectively than everyday speech—"Please penetrate me and move your penis in and out with greater enthusiasm" versus "Fuck me harder."

Obviously, profanity and sexual intimacy can stir up a dangerous cocktail. You should feel very sure of a partner's sexual self-esteem before you do a lot of sexual self-disclosing ("I like my sex rough") and self-asserting ("Fuck me harder"). Abusive nicknames—unwanted *slut, whore, cunt, bitch,* for instance—research tells us, decrease women's sexual satisfaction, hardly a surprise. The million-dollar question is whether they're ever wanted, but you ought to have permission before you use them—they may arouse your partner, but not in the way you hope. Profanity often expresses, not intimacy— or, in some cases, not just intimacy—but power over others, the power to call them certain things or speak to them in certain ways. In the BDSM world, issues of sexual power are overt, and Rebecca Dwyer, in *Terms of Endearment? Vocatives and Power in BDSM Erotica* (2007), concludes, "For the most part, dominants use profanity almost exclusively," and just over half of the erotica she examines includes some use of profanity and "objectifiers," which are often one and the same, as in the cases of *slut, whore, cunt,* and *bitch.* Intimacy in bondage, discipline, and sadism/masochism distributes power on terms unfamiliar to most of us, terms outside, not just of our comfort zones, but of our very notions of intimacy. In other words, you have to be intimate and confident in that intimacy before you risk using profanity to push it even further.

Beyond the intimacy of bromance or romance, profanity is frequently a component of group solidarity. Again, if you're alive, you know this already, but a couple of well-documented examples help to make the case. Jay Mechling, an anthropologist and a scoutmaster, wrote an article subtitled "Food and Feces in the Speech Play at a Boy Scout Camp" (1984). We're interested in neither food nor feces per se, but rather in the mildly profane words Scouts in his experience used for them. Mechling draws heavily on psychoanalytic theory to classify Scouts as anal-erotic, and if you believe in that stuff, the case is easily made. The Scout Law insists that they be clean, thrifty, and trustworthy; anyone who's spent any time camping knows that half of it is spent cleaning up; and Scouting involves a lot of collecting, merit badges, trail patches, and such things—it's straight from *The Boy Scout Handbook* into the psychology textbook.

Yes, I write from experience. I worked at a Boy Scout camp for a decade. I remember an epic latrine cleaning—*honey-dipping* in the jargon—during which the staff removed logs and refuse dumped there during winter camping. We memorialized the event with a photograph of our program director's head coming up through the toilet seat. As Mechling puts it,

> Knowing, as we do, that human excreta make excellent symbolic materials for a group's expression of concern about boundaries, purity, and contamination..., and knowing that symbolic links between food and feces are not uncommon in cultural rituals..., the prevalent pattern of food/feces speech play provides a useful interpretive entry into the psycho-social dynamics of a modern Boy Scout camp.

Some of my camp staff colleagues were disorderly louts, but those who set the tone, the leaders, are some of the most anal-erotic people I know, as well as my lifelong friends. They were clean and trustworthy—still are—but they were also capable of the most off-colorful joking and teasing you can imagine—still are—not always profane in the strictest sense, though the older we got together, the more straightforwardly profane our speech became. Not mine, of course, but I've been the butt of many of their anal-erotic eructations.

Speaking of which, Mechling's Scouts passed a little poem that classified farts into nine types from generation to generation:

> There's the pip and the poop and the anti-poop
> And the fizz and the fuzz and the fizzy-fuzz
> And the ring-tail, tear-ass, and the rattler.

Besides this fart typology, Mechling provides examples of the food-feces intersection. For example, the Scouts referred to their oatmeal as *scroatmeal* and, for reasons that are beyond explanation, even for Mechling, they called a particular axe handle a *high kybo floater*. To make any sense of it, you have to know that *kybo* is the camp's traditional name, also transmitted across generations, for the latrine. It's possible, though not proven, that *kybo* is an acronym for 'keep your bowels operating' or 'open'—there's some dispute about which—so you can imagine what the floater is. Whether it's a high floater or a floater in a high kybo, whatever that would be, is still a mystery. What any of it has to do with axe handles defies imagination.

Camp culture includes not just the Scouts present one summer but generations of Scouts summer after summer. Profanity—especially custom profanity—consolidates Scout identity in each Scout's here and now but also transcends anyone's experience in campfire lore. Recently, Bernie Chun Nam Mak and Carmen Lee have explored a quite different sort of interaction, that of backstage workplaces—those out of view of clients and customers—in Hong Kong businesses, where use of expletives is "strategic, rational, and business-oriented," yet profanity carries covert prestige that promotes solidarity among colleagues who text one another about business matters—usually, complaints about the behavior of supervisors or clients. Mak and Lee summarize things this way: "Researchers have noted the construction of identity and power during the swearing process." Swearing helps to build intimacy or fortify solidarity among friends at school, lovers in the bedroom—or any room they prefer—

and in various "communities of practice," as they're called, whether voluntary, like the Boy Scouts, or not quite voluntary, like the businesses in which we work. Swearing isn't necessary to these interactions, but it seems well suited to them, so perhaps we should respect profanity rather more than we tend to do.

Interaction involving profanity is still mostly face to face, though increasingly personal but mediated,—as in the Hong Kong workplaces—and sometimes very personal and proximal, though not necessarily face to face. Profanity also promotes solidarity in diffuse associations, such as a brand community. Profanity is of limited use in branding because it can't be trademarked. Sometimes, however, it serves excellently as a branding focus, for instance, in the case of Bitch Media, which among other things brings us the (excellent) quarterly magazine *Bitch*, like everything else at Bitch Media "dedicated to providing and encouraging an engaged, thoughtful feminist response to mainstream media and popular culture." Bitch Media has been criticized for using the b-word, but they defend their decision eloquently, and to my mind compellingly:

When it's being used as an insult, "bitch" is an epithet hurled at women who speak their minds, who have opinions and don't shy away from expressing them, and who don't sit by and smile uncomfortably if they're bothered or offended. If being an outspoken woman means being a bitch, we'll take that as a compliment. We know that not everyone's down with the term. Believe us, we've heard all about it. But we stand firm in our belief that if we choose to reappropriate the word, it loses its power to hurt us. And if we can get people thinking about what they're saying when they use the word, that's even better. Bitch. It's a noun. It's a verb. It's a magazine. It's a feminist media organization.

It's hard to argue with that. Bitch Media asks of women—these are my words: "In this manifesto sense, we're bitches. Are you also a bitch? Feel the solidarity." This is the branding story of Andi and Lisa, the Good Bitches of the Northwest, and their Munchkin friend, Benjamin, who founded *Bitch* together back in 1996, in Portland, Oregon, when it was a zine distributed from the back of a station wagon.

Actually, though, *bitch* had been reappropriated in hip hop culture before the first issue of *Bitch* appeared. *Bitches* appeared in lyrics as the parallel to *niggas*—male and female rappers used the term to different effects—and, before you could say *Sup, Bitches!* to your besties, it was sweeping through food courts in suburban malls. This loose and supposedly apolitical sense of *bitch* lends itself to other types of branding, the kind with scary crystal balls and flying monkeys. In February 2011, three Cornell coeds started the blog that became *Betches Love This*, now just *Betches*. The *Betches* site allows you to navigate "Celebs & Scandals," "Fashion & Beauty," and "Party & Lifestyle," etc.—there's some topical overlap, but a quick glance at the content proves that *Betches* isn't *Bitch*, and the Betches aren't *Bitch*'s bitches. Change the *i* to an *e* and you euphemize the feminism right out of the brand. You also avoid brand confusion.

The Betches used to rate universities with plenty of attention to and appreciation for their seamier sides—they are unabashedly aligned with the Raunch culture that Ariel Levy decries in *Female Chauvinist Pigs* (2005), even though the Betches characterize themselves as "brutally honest and self-aware young women." *Betches'* "About" page includes a section titled "The Brand" that extols the coven's "brand extensions." They brag:

> Our social media channels, primarily our Instagram@betches have become quite popular as our 2.7 million followers including Madonna agree that we're absolutely fucking hilarious. We've been

hailed by the New York Times (ever heard of it?), Jezebel, The London Times, Telegraph, Vogue, Rolling Stone, Cosmopolitan, and many others. Our online boutique, Shop Betches, has been putting out the betchiest tanks, tees, phone cases, sweaters, etc. for only one year and, as you probably already assumed, we're killing it. Ugh there is like so much more, but we gotta go, we're late for brunch.

Since they put it that way, you really want to join their brand community. You want solidarity with the mean girls they claim they're not. And they're okay with that. You can go to brunch, too, and they say, in a teasingly grudging invitation, "Fine, You Can Sit with Us"— but buy our betchin stuff, or you won't really be betches.

The editors at *Bitch* probably want nothing to do with the Raunch purveying Betches, and the Betches aren't much interested in feminist critique of popular culture, at which *Bitch* excels. But it makes no difference to profanity whether the Bitches and Betches of this world get along. As different as they are, both Bitch Media and Betches Brands have found profanity a means of consolidating a self-identifying following, on terms familiar in the twenty-first-century media landscape. As the media convergence guru Henry Jenkins puts it, "according to the logic of affective economics, the ideal consumer is active, emotionally engaged, and socially networked. Watching the advert or consuming the product is no longer enough; the company invites the audience inside the brand community." And so Bitch Media and *Betches* both do—the thrill of associating with profanity and the people who use it, with the political and social and cultural attitudes it represents and the people who hold them, is written right into the invitation.

Sometimes this profane branding seems more than a little opportunistic. *FCUK* is an initialism for *French Connection United Kingdom*—like *DKNY* for *Donna Karan New York*—and by accident it's more or less profanity, so—thought the FCUK people—why not use it? *FCUK* has been using *FCUK* on products since 1997, which, when you match it up with the chronology of *Bitch* and *Betches* begins to tell a story about when profanity became viable in marketing. Those in the know are inside the brand community, which is a really big brand community insofar as nearly everyone is in on it. As the linguist Ruth Wajnryb points out, "You realize the mis-ordering [of *FCUK*] only after FUCK has registered. The company has, no doubt, revelled in the association, the risqué element, the apparent avoidance through mis-ordering, the in-your-face-ness of *fuck*, which they appear to sidestep but in fact highlight," false euphemism that foreshadows our discussion of euphemism for profanity generally in Chapter 3. In cases like these, both profanity and its euphemisms help to manufacture the brand community.

We started with tight circles of friends and intimate sexual partners but end this survey with the most diffuse brand community imaginable since the Pepsi Generation—tumblr and *fuck yeah*. The brand is diffuse because there often isn't any connection among members of the brand community except the brand—they aren't wearing the same jeans; they aren't reading the same magazines. They're just all in the same place, Yahoo!'s microblogging platform tumblr, roughly 260 million of them, posting photos and memes, waiting for the future to pull up and zoom away with them. They are bound, not by politics or love of pop culture or self-justifying consumerism, but by an attitude apparently best expressed in profanity, what they can't wait to say until the future arrives—*fuck yeah*.

Tumblr didn't invent *fuck yeah* but in a strange, decentralized way, it did brand it. Many think *fuck yeah* became a thing with "America Fuck Yeah," the theme song from *Team America: World Police* (2004), a film directed by Trey Parker of *South Park* fame and written by him and Matt Stone, also of *South Park* fame, no strangers to profanity. Maybe it did, but *Urban Dictionary* records it in 2003, and rumor has it that *Humanity fuck yeah* memes showed up on *Funnyjunk*—founded in 2001—even earlier. *Team America* may have given an otherwise lonely catchphrase a boost, however, for the movie—albeit satirically—is all about solidarity, a nation that's a team, a team that saves the world from North Korea, so *fuck yeah* turns out to have some solidarity value. The very phrase is the basis for loose affiliation among so many people that they can't have much more than an attitude in common.

In 2008, journalist Ned Hepburn launched his now infamous microblog, *FUCK YEAH SHARKS because SHARKS ARE FUCK-ING RAD*, and a mass of people who shared no interests with Hepburn nonetheless shared their interests on tumblr because fuck yeah they could—their fundamentally shared interest was sharing their interests, and *fuck yeah* for anything became the verbal tie that bound them all together: *Fuck Yeah Cilantro; Fuck Yeah Aquascaping; Fuck Yeah The Beatles; Fuck Yeah Stephen Sondheim; Fuck Yeah Elliott Carter; Fuck Yeah Marxism-Leninism; Fuck Yeah Fluid Dynamics*— "Celebrating the physics of all that flows"—and my favorite, because it's truly profane, *Fuck Yeah Altars*—"Altars, shrines, and other sacred spaces from all traditions and spiritual paths." There are snarky *fuck yeahs* devoted to dislikable celebrities and such, but mostly it's about celebrating things you love, like fluid dynamics. There's a directory of *Fuck Yeah* tumblr sites called the *Fuck Yeah Directory: A Fuck Yeah of Fuck Yeahs*—it isn't comprehensive but celebrates those Fuck Yeahs that capture the essence of *fuck yeah*.

Fuck yeah is utterly undiscriminating, which is what makes its branding power so mysterious. As Sadie Smiles, the creator of fuckyeahpizza.tumblr.com recounts, "I would just type in 'f***yeah' anything that I like, trying to find the f-yeah Tumblr for it. Once you realized that there was a f-yeah blog for any obscure thing, you'd start to think I could find a f-yeah blog for anything I like." And when one does find such a thing, it resonates with one's identity, says Amanda Brennan, creator of fuckyeahmodernism.tumblr.com: "You're on Tumblr and you see something and you're like 'f*** yeah, that is me.'... The term is just so celebratory. I think Tumblr users really identify with it." And so, Julia Carpenter reports, "Tumblr corporate does, as well: 'F-Yeah' is now so much a part of the Tumblr brand that the micro-blogging platform even themed its 2015 SXSW party as 'The F*** Yeah Tumblr Party.'" Fuck yeah is basically a brand for all of us who want to celebrate things we love or find ourselves in things people celebrate, as long as they celebrate them on a tumblr micro-blog.

Just before she graduated, in the spring of 2014, Hannah, with whom I'd had class the previous term, poked her head into my office to say "Hello," and I invited her to sit and chat. She was wearing a T-shirt whose only message was *fuck yeah*, and knowing that I'd soon be writing more or less what I'm writing at the moment— I disclosed that fact—I asked her what *fuck yeah* meant to her. I should say that Hannah was a top-notch student, very active in the student writing community. That doesn't preclude her using pro-fanity, of course, but I admit I was a little surprised at the bold, public declaration. How can anyone believe that profanity is still taboo when people walk around with it emblazoned on their clothes? "I don't know," she said. "I just thought it was a great attitude." She didn't know she was a member of a brand community. She was just telling everyone that she was having a good life. She wasn't trying to prove a point and *fuck yeah* was happy-go-lucky, in her case, not risky. Her *Fuck yeah* was an invitation for anyone who saw her to join the Good Life brand community. That's a little unsettling, the way solidarity in this case precedes community, but there are worse ver-sions of solidarity, and who doesn't want a Good Life?

In the case of brand communities, profanity is a magnet that pulls members toward it until they stick, but it's instrumental—not necessarily cynically so, but it's profanity without feeling, even if it conveys an attitude. You wear your *fuck yeah* shirt on Tuesday, but you don't wear it every day; *fuck yeah* signifies something about your identity, but whatever it is, it's relatively superficial. However, profanity can enable solidarity of much greater significance than attaches to any brand community. In *The Water is Wide* (1972), Pat Conroy describes his experience teaching elementary school on what he calls Yamacraw Island in the book, actually Daufuskie Island, off the coasts of Georgia and South Carolina. White teacher, poor African American kids, dysfunctional school system in the 1960s—Conroy had to establish trust where there was none, and profanity helped him do it.

Usually, we frown on teachers swearing in the classroom. I admit to an occasional lapse, but I teach in a university, among adults. We're convinced we need to protect children from bad words. We draw a strict line between adult discourse and children's discourse in school, though we sometimes cross the line at home. Even teachers who swear a lot in their extracurricular lives know the limits. For instance, Nora Eldridge, the narrator protagonist of Claire Messud's novel *The Woman Upstairs* (2013), like Conroy an elementary school teacher (we'll encounter her again, later in the book), warns us against our assumptions about her: "Be advised that in spite of my foul mouth, I don't swear in front of the children—except once or twice when a rogue 'Shit!' has emerged, but only sotto voce, and only in extremis." Nowadays, teachers can't swear in class because we don't want to leave children behind. Swearing distracts them from what's really important. After all, there won't be any profanity on the high-stakes tests students take so that we can grade their schools.

For Conroy and his kids, there's no *sotto voce* or *in extremis* about it, partly because they're sticking to English for the time being. It starts with an argument over how to scrinch and eat squirrels, common fare on the island. When Conroy admits he hasn't eaten squirrel and probably never would, the children are incredulous. Saul and Lincoln—favorites of the author and his readers—fight over the degrading things each would eat, and you can probably guess what happens:

> "You know what you eat, Saul? You eat buzzard."
>
> The class laughed wildly again.
>
> "Fat man, you know what you eat?"
>
> "What I eat, little man?"
>
> "You know what you eat," Saul answered menacingly, his tiny frame rigid with anger.
>
> "Little man, better tell me what I eat."
>
> "Fat man eats shee-it."
>
> "Oh Gawd," half the class exclaimed simultaneously. Someone shouted, "Little man told big man he eat shee-it. He curse. He curse, Lawd, Mr. Conrack gonna do some beating now."

But there was no beating. Conroy realized the loss of classroom discipline was his fault: "Why I had let the situation totally escape me, I did not know. I had been so interested in the downward progression of gourmet foods according to the island connoisseurs that I was totally unprepared for the final plunge to unpackaged feces." Put it down to lack of experience—the result, we know, was inevitable.

Saul apologizes for using "the forbidden word" after Conroy threatens to scrinch him. When scrinching a squirrel, "You slit open the belly with a sharp knife, peel the squirrel's pelt off like the skin of

a grape, then scrape the squirrel's skin until it is white and smooth."
Saul doesn't want to be scrinched. "'White man crazy,' someone
whispered." All of this came about because Conroy had attempted
to build class-wide solidarity, but especially to demystify his role as
teacher. Before the profanity incident, he explains, "I had pulled up
a chair in the middle of the class and all the kids had drawn up their
chairs in a semi-circle around me. And we just talked. We spent the
whole day talking." And that's how the profanity happened. It was an
accident of just talking. Break down social barriers, attempt to build
new relationships, and people talk the way they talk, neglecting
self-censorship. And that's when Conroy realized he could use profanity pedagogically to nurture a sort of authenticity rarely found in
schools.

How did his students learn to trust him against all the odds of age,
race, and authority? Because he trusted them with his flouting of the
rule that says teachers don't curse—they had something on him, and
the moment they did, he and they knew they would never use it
against him. Their relationship was more important than the rules. So,
in the very next chapter, while debunking island snake lore, Conroy
calls some of it "'Bullcrap.'" The profanity does not go unnoticed:
"'He cuss,' Sam whispered." Supposedly, a snake on the island whips
people to death with its tail. Conroy doubts it: "'Who was the man
you actually saw getting the hell beat out of him by a snake?' 'He cuss
one more time.' Old Sam was keeping tabs." Through Sam, the whole
class takes Conroy's measure. Conroy didn't beat Saul for cussing;
he cusses himself, without apology. Unexpectedly, he talks to them
naturally, in vulgar, that is, "ordinary" language. Does he hope to
derive credibility from solidarity with the students rather than from
off-island authorities? That's the conflict of the whole book, and
when Conroy is forced to leave the island, it wasn't for lack of trying.

Many of the students in his class cannot read, though they range from fifth to eighth graders, so Conroy invents a game called Play and Talk meant, in some measure, to mitigate a serious problem. "It was during a session of this game," he writes,

> that Prophet electrified the class and held it unwittingly in the palm of his hand for several staggering moments. He spun the dial and landed on the letter *F*. He properly identified the letter and its sound. But naming a word that started with F proved a considerable challenge. Finally, after long and tortured deliberation, he came out with a word.
>
> "Fuck," he said rather smugly. The class and the teacher of the class were stunned. Prophet grinned.
>
> "What did you say, Prophet?" I asked inanely.
>
> "Fuck," he repeated, with bell-like clarity for Prophet.
>
> "Would you please spell that word, Prophet," I asked, praying for deliverance.
>
> "F–U–X," he spelled.
>
> "Do you mean 'fox,' Prophet?"
>
> "Yas'm. Look like dawg."
>
> The whole class erupted.

The class erupted because the dialogue proved that teacher and student could collude in the resolution of their differences. Profanity was the subject of their interaction, and solidarity among the whole class was its result.

Later, Conroy goes to great lengths to arrange a Halloween field trip for the kids on the mainland. Many of them are afraid to go and their families are reluctant to let them—they live on an island, yet few of them can swim, and all correctly fear the sea. Conroy overcomes all of the objections, or so he thinks. On the eve of departure, he confronts renewed opposition.

> "All right, gang. Listen up....As you know I am not used to the way things work around this goofy island, right?...Yesterday everyone was keyed up to stash up on candy in Beaufort. I mean, you were going wild, going absolutely ape-crap about going to town....You mean to tell me that none of your parents are going to let you go trick-or-treating? I think that's just crap."
>
> "Conrack curse," Sidney said.

In this instance, the important word isn't *crap* or *ape-crap* but *gang*, a word he uses to address them throughout the book. We watch as Conroy helps them become one—they're his gang, and they know he's on their side, but relations among the children also consolidate under his guidance. Anyway, the gang identifies the source of the opposition, and he turns the tide toward the mainland—they have their field trip, after all.

Bad language in the schoolroom, in their relationship with Conroy—not just any and all bad language—helps the kids on Yamacraw Island become something they hadn't been before, something paradoxically wholesome—they came to love Conroy and one another better partly because of profanity. And that's not the only good that comes from profanity in the Yamacraw classroom, for they not only use profanity there, they examine their use of it— they do some metalinguistics and talk about talk. Mrs. Brown, the oppressive head teacher/principal who stands in Conroy's way, presumes to lecture his class about all manner of things, and the class doesn't like her. One lecture prompts the following exchange:

> "Gang, we have been getting these talks from Mrs. Brown all year. You get too damn upset by them. Just don't listen to what she's

saying. Think about something else. If she wants to be a big talker, let her talk, just don't get involved with snapping back at her."

"She ain't talkin' to you," Frank said....

"That's a good point, Frank. She isn't talking to me but she is talking about you, and it hurts me to see you get your feelings hurt. You may not believe me yet. You may not trust me yet. But you can damn well believe that it pisses me off to hear Mrs. Brown talk to you like that."...

"Bitch woman," Richard said.

"Yeah! Bitch woman." The echo passed around the room.

"I bet you call me bitch man behind my back," I said, trying to cut through the ominous, murderous atmosphere building in the room.

"No, Conrack," Fred said.

"I call you bitches and bastards when I get mad at you sometimes."

"God Almighty Jesus!" Lincoln exclaimed.

"Everyone gets mad, gang. But we have to learn when not to show our anger."

Although the ending may seem childish, it's a moral message directed at kids, after all, a message about the moral implications of language use, and the point about anger is sound, as our later consideration of profanity in *The Sopranos* and anger according to the Roman moral philosopher Seneca will prove.

Conroy's version of events on Yamacraw Island probably doesn't represent his experience on Daufuskie Island with utter accuracy. It's lived, it's remembered, it's written, it's edited—a certain amount of fiction is bound to seep through cracks in the process. But there's no reason to doubt the tenor of the tale, that profanity unexpectedly made a difference to Conroy and his kids. Textbooks don't recommend that teachers swear in front of, let alone with their students, but maybe our pedagogy is wrong. Maybe, we learn and teach better when we come to agreement over something that requires it, and if profanity retains any of its earlier taboo, then it requires just such agreement. It's clear that Conroy's profanity and his acknowledgment of his kids' profanity did no harm. He treated them like the children they were, but he treated them like human beings, too, full of language and emotions. He did not turn his head or avert his gaze or blame it on them, as Mrs. Brown did, when they expressed themselves. Through profanity, he afforded them the respect they deserved.

EXCEPTIONALISM: AN INTERLUDE

On the face of it and according to tradition, swearing is anti-social behavior, but profanity is actually about social construction of identity by both fitting in and standing out, sometimes simultaneously. In another book, I argued that slang is used socially to fit in (a social motivation) and to stand out (an aesthetic motivation), but with profanity, the standing out is also primarily social, usually a matter of asserting the privilege to curse where others don't have it, because it means you have more power or because you don't give a good goddamn, as my father frequently used to say he didn't. So, on June 25, 2004, Vice President Dick Cheney could say to Senator Patrick Leahy on the floor of the Senate, "Go fuck yourself," because he doesn't give a good goddamn about what Pat Leahy or the rest of us think. Actually, he does give a good one because he wants us to think he's the sort of person who doesn't. Obviously, profanity's value in such interchanges depends on its outlaw status, even though it's counterintuitive in this case that the president of the Senate should be such an outlaw.

Animosity between Leahy and Cheney didn't start during Cheney's vice presidency, and it was politically visceral, regardless of how they might disagree about law and policy. Cheney had been a rising official in the Nixon White House before Watergate shook the American political landscape and succeeded Donald Rumsfeld as President Ford's chief of staff. Leahy was elected to the Senate in 1975, part of the Democratic post-Watergate surge, which lasted for decades and, as far as Cheney and his sort were concerned, changed America for the worse. Winning the presidency with George W. Bush was a reinstatement, in Cheney's eyes, and a vindication. It had to do with Republican control of everything, if possible, but also with a strand of Republican identity. With his daughter, Liz Cheney, he's written a book titled *Exceptional: Why the World Needs a Powerful America* (2015), and in his response to Leahy, he momentarily embodied American exceptionalism—a powerful America requires a powerful American leadership, not a bunch of capitalist-hating, United Nations–loving, climate change–believing, French fry–eating Democrats, and the EPA trying to save the damn ducks.

Apparently, Leahy had jokingly crossed the line at a photo session in the Senate Chamber, asking why Cheney wasn't having his picture taken with Democrats. Cheney changed the subject to recent Democratic criticism of Halliburton's sole-source contracts in Iraq. Halliburton is a huge energy services corporation, and Cheney had been chairman of the board and chief executive officer from 1995 until he became vice president, and Halliburton—partly through its onetime engineering division, Kellogg, Brown, and Root—made a lot of money reconstructing Iraq. Anyway, Cheney didn't like the criticism, and as it often does with senators, the argument escalated to judicial appointments, and before anyone knew what was happening, the vice president had crossed the profanity line.

Cheney's sense of linguistic exceptionalism is nothing new. Lots of presidents have flouted rules of usage, publicly but especially privately. It's very clear that George W. Bush operated according to his own grammar, and he's on record for profanity, too. Unaware that he was still within range of the microphones, he called Adam Clymer of *The New York Times* "a major-league asshole" and an infamous prepresidential interview with Tucker Carlson (1999) is replete with the F-word. Use of profanity is bi-partisan, by the way. President Truman, for instance, was a world-class swearer. In a *Rolling Stone* interview, John Kerry said of the president's Iraq policy that Bush had "fucked it up," and the Republicans pounced on it; so, as *The Washington Post* reported it, the Democrats were "gleeful" when Cheney emitted the same word at Leahy. Leaders of the world's most powerful nation spend a lot of time squabbling over who among them has the right to be profane, who is socially exceptional.

Vice President Cheney isn't the only exceptional person in America, nor is he the only one to mark his exceptionalism with profanity. On KTVA, Anchorage, Alaska's television station, a relatively new on-air correspondent, Charlo Greene, was reporting on the Alaska Cannabis Club, a recently founded marijuana dispensary, marginally legal in Alaska, which allows for medical use of the drug and has decriminalized recreational use. No one had noticed that the ACC appeared on the scene more or less at the same time as Charlo Greene—I'm sure lots of things happened in Anchorage when Greene started her gig there. In fact, however, she was part owner of the ACC, and you don't have to be a journalist to know that you're not supposed to report on your own business—it's a serious conflict of interest.

Greene had graduated from the University of Texas at Arlington in 2011 and worked as a reporter, honing her skills and establishing a reputation, at various other television stations across the American South before moving to Alaska and KTVA. When she did, I'm sure many of her acquaintances wondered, "Why Alaska?" without realizing that she was a budding advocate for legal weed and that Alaska's weed laws were a major draw, more important to her, it turned out, than a career in television news reporting. Greene lives on the edge, as every advocate for legal change will, but that doesn't mean she's without morals, and she found the conflict of interest between her advocacy and her reporting unsustainable, and so she did what any right thinking person in the situation would do—she quit.

That she quit isn't relevant to this book, but the manner in which she quit is totally relevant. While reporting on the ACC during the 10 p.m. news on September 21, 2014, Greene revealed her alter ego, pointed to the need for marijuana advocacy, and promised anyone watching that she would be in the vanguard of such advocacy—then she quit: "As for this job," she said, eyes riveted on her audience in the best tradition of television news presenting, "well, not that I have a choice, but fuck it, I quit." From the clip readily available on YouTube, you can tell that weekend anchor Alexis Fernandez was surprised at Greene's exit, but of course she apologized on behalf of the station as best she could at such short notice. Since then, Greene has been responding to warrants and subpoenas, as anyone running a pot dispensary/head shop so publicly should expect to do.

Many viewers were unimpressed or even angered by Greene's display, but whatever one thinks about legalization or on-air politeness—who paid this FCC fine?—or decency toward the colleagues—like Fernandez—who clean up the mess, Greene's resignation was bold and simultaneously reflected her sense that she is exceptional—you may find that delusional, if you wish—and actually made her exceptional. That is, if she wasn't exceptional before the broadcast—just another stoner with aspirations of leading a weed empire—the very act of profanity ensured that she was thenceforth. Of course, one can be exceptional on relatively small or larger scales, and in spite of subsequent media hype, Greene's profanity doesn't allow her to play in the national or international arena, alongside Vice

President Cheney, but, given the setting and the cause, she becomes exceptional through it, nonetheless.

To be fair, Greene has gained some national attention: *High Times* presented her with its Courage in Media Award in 2014. But did she need to say "Fuck it" to win the award and admiration of stoners everywhere? Arguably, she did. For such a young person it seems rather old-fashioned, but she was sticking it to the Man, and that's not something you can do politely, with deference. You have to show—and this is especially important if you want people to follow you—that you aren't scared of the Man and his repercussions. In pursuit of a worthy cause, repercussions be damned. Among comments following Laurel Andrews's same-day account of Greene's on-air resignation in the *Alaska Dispatch News* is one from Kevin Rivers, founder of Bluurp!, a social networking app, whom we might plausibly call a thought leader: "She quit like a boss."

Exceptionalism has its limits, however—it requires an audience, which means that what seems to resist solidarity actually depends on it. Vice President Cheney's contretemps with Senator Leahy took place in front of the host of Republican and Democratic senators—the vice president performed his disdain for the Democrats and, as the most exceptional among them, stood as proxy for his caucus. While some presidential profanity ends up in the news by accident, Cheney's performance appealed to tough Republicans watching from their sofas, too, and in the midst of it, the vice president was probably aware of the incident's potential and the exceptional value of his profanity. More important than setting Republicans apart from Democrats, it promoted solidarity among Republicans in just the same way it does among junior high school girls and boys. A leader—Vice President Cheney can't be a Queen Bee, so let's think of him as Chief Timber Wolf, or something like that, an animal so exceptional that it's nearly extinct—anyway, a leader swears, announces his exceptionalism, and the other wolves aspire to the same exceptionalism and swear in their turns, affirming his leadership and their solidarity, as well as projecting their sense of privilege into the world.

Charlo Greene, too, played her profanity to an audience, those who like her want to see marijuana legalized in Alaska. Greene's example thus consolidated an otherwise somewhat vague and diffuse group as they sat around watching the YouTube clip of her resignation over and over again, while planning a legalization march on Juneau—Greene used some other f-words in her speech, saying she'd be "fighting for freedom and fairness," which is, of course, exactly what Congress was doing when it renamed the French fries in their cafeteria "freedom fries." Greene was also building a clientele for the Alaska Cannabis Club, a group she needed to consolidate fast once she lost her regular paycheck. She had one chance at free television advertising and—exceptional as she is—she took it.

Profanity usually presents us with paradox, and the case of exceptionalism is no exception. Profanity proves a speaker exceptional only when an audience agrees that's what it proves. Exceptionalism—being outside of or beyond a group—requires also being inside a group. All exceptional profanity requires a social context—*exceptional* is meaningful only in relation to a group's identity. Thus, profanity supports exceptionalism only insofar as it supports group solidarity and the identity that follows from it. And you can flip the equation. McKay Hatch was exceptional—or marketed himself as exceptional—in *not* using profanity. In so doing, however, he promoted group solidarity in No Cussing Clubs all over the world and also proposed a No Cussing Club brand community, affiliation by means of wristbands, T-shirts, and "other No Cussing Club items." I'm all for human sociality, and it seems a little churlish to point this out, but Hatch couldn't have done any of it without profanity.

HAVING IT BOTH WAYS

Obviously, then, while some profane speech builds intimacy or solidarity, and other instances mark a level of social exceptionalism, very often, those who swear accomplish some measure of both at the same time. We hear it in the locker room talk of sports teams, who—especially when they're winning teams—feel that they travel above the common herd, and winning or not, within the social setting of an American school, especially, teams own the sort of prestige that licenses their swearing. No principal in my memory ever sent a starting football player to detention for an errant *shit* or *bitch*—jocks have privileges, and swearing is one of them, though I'm far from condoning the exception. Other students are liable to be punished for swearing. They are denied the jocks' circular reasoning: we are exceptional because we can swear; we can swear because we are exceptional. The *Californication* crew is the hipster parallel. Led by Hank Moody, they prove their cool by flouting all sorts of taboo—including the one against profanity—and they can flout taboo because they are already and always too cool. Nonetheless, football players and hipster Hollywood types alike groom one another in group solidarity even as they break the rules that apply outside their groups

This interaction of intimacy, solidarity, and exceptionalism makes people interesting—we're social animals and we have complex repertoires of social behavior, some elements of which are common to humanity while others are personal. For now, let's call the interaction a conflict, though it surpasses conflict, as we'll see. It pervades our everyday experience, but as a result we're likely to miss it, not so much taking it for granted as operating it subconsciously, much as we do breathing and other essential things. So, we may see it more clearly in the bright light of exaggeration. In this case, we'll illumine dark corners of the least social of spaces, the toilet stall, where the walls are covered with profane graffiti, only to discover that while it's a solitary art, such graffiti is also social, and profanity mediates its phases.

I say the toilet's the least social of spaces, but that's not entirely true. While some of us expect privies to be private, because we observe taboos about pissing and shitting in public, they can be the locus of intimate encounter, too. Until most of us got over the taboo against same-sex love, gay men, particularly, had recourse to—ironically, public—toilets as a place to meet or initiate sexual contact. In gay slang of an earlier era, toilets were sometimes called *cottages*—a domestic reinterpretation of an undomestic space—and those who used them were known as *cottagers* or *cottage-queens*, and when the stall was occupied, cottagers were busy *cottaging*. Some gay men were closeted some of the time in the WC. The shithouse in Island Park, Cedar Falls, Iowa, was anonymously renamed *Fuck House*, as the great American linguist Allen Walker Read recorded in his notebook on September 4, 1928.

Hetero sex fumbled its way into latrines, too—men have bragged about it. "Me and my wife had a fuck," one gentleman wrote on a privy wall in the Municipal Auto Camp of Red Bluff, California, Read noted on July 17, 1928. Auto camps are quite public. They aren't convenient places for sex, so some drop their britches and scratch their itches in the convenience. And, of course, one can relieve one's sexual needs without a partner. As one fellow wrote in self-explanation at Bryce Canyon National Monument, in Utah, as Read recorded on August 20, 1928:

> Some people come here to
> Shit and think & wright upon the door
> But I come here to shit and stink &
> Jack off on the floor...

and then, apparently, to write upon the door. One predilection can be as irresistible as another, and latrines afford those inclined the opportunity to satisfy as many as possible—though not this fellow, another might manage to think as well as shit and stink and jack off and write. Enclosed, cramped, and foul, the latrine is paradoxically a wide open space.

Much more social activity goes on in public toilets than such encounters, and graffiti—a sort of modern cave painting, an atavistic art we can't seem to evolve out of, any more than we've evolved out of our tonsils—is putatively an act of communication, though on such strange terms that it's paradoxically both public and private speech. Does the writer of scatological or obscene graffiti conceive of it as private? He wouldn't say in a public space what he writes in a privy, when no one is looking. And at the moment of utterance, the writer is alone; when someone else reads what he's inscribed, he's long gone. Nevertheless, he anticipates an audience—he's been that audience on any number of occasions. Does he think of the graffiti as an act of communication directed at an unknown person, transcending space and time? The graffiti is a relic re-animated in adventitious reading. Until I paid graffiti and its profanity some serious attention, I had never thought of the wilderness outhouse or the public toilet as magical spaces, as outposts of the imagination, but I do now.

Evidence of the magic comes to us from Read, who had been an editor on the *Dictionary of American English* during the 1930s and spent most of his career teaching at Columbia University in New York City, no place more urban or urbane. Read was sophisticated. He took a B.Litt. from the University of Oxford. He wore a beret, for an American surely a *coup d'éclat*. But he was born in Winnebago, Minnesota, in 1906, when Minnesota was still somewhat West in the American imagination, and he earned a B.A. from the Iowa State Teachers College and an M.A. from the University of Iowa. Though a lexicographer, Read was no drudge, nor was he pale and scrawny from office work—he was a physical man, an outdoorsman. Madeline Kripke—one of the world's greatest collectors of dictionaries and a friend of Read's—once sent me a photograph of him hanging from the side of a windmill in a cornfield somewhere, probably Iowa, by one hand and one foot, thirty feet or more in the air. It's not the pose one expects of a lexicographer. Perhaps Read was extraordinary, or perhaps we underestimate our lexicographers, or perhaps both.

During what Read described as "an extensive sight-seeing trip throughout the Western United States and Canada in the summer of 1928," he relieved himself in an untold number of public toilets. He saw a lot of graffiti on the toilet walls, and he realized "that these inscriptions are a form of folklore that should be made the subject of a scholarly study. In no case," he writes, "did I go out of the ordinary course of my trip in order to collect the material. I merely copied down whatever came to my attention as the opportunity offered." He wrote the scholarly study he imagined and published it as *Lexical Evidence from Folk Epigraphy in Western North America: A Glossarial Study of the Low Element in the English Vocabulary*, privately printed in Paris in 1935—just 100 numbered and signed copies—because in the United States, at that time, his scholarship was legally obscenity, and the graffiti unprintable as he found it.

And what epigraphy did Read find on the frontier? On July 28, in Grand Coulee State Park, Washington, he glanced on "Like a pole-cat's ass thou smelleth bad/But oh cunt thou must be had." You can tell it's poetry because of the rhyme, of course, but also the old-fashioned English and the Shakespearean apostrophe to the cunt. And I say this with my tongue only half cheeked, because, no doubt tongue in cheek themselves, the graffiti artists thought of themselves as doing something aesthetically valid—opportunistic, yes, and not particularly adept, but poetry on the fly, poetry as *jeu d'esprit*. They are "shithouse poets," according to their own lore. In Truckee, California, at an auto camp, on July 16, AWR read this advice:

> Shit here shit clear
> Wipe your ass
> And disappear
> Shakespear

Shakespeare is the toilet bard throughout the Anglophone world. From some surface—he doesn't specify—outside Ripon Cathedral, in the North Riding of Yorkshire, England, Read copied the following on August 11, 1929:

> One would think
> By all this writing
> That Shakespeare himself
> Had been here shiting.

And, though surely the writers of these inscriptions weren't known to one another, they had established a graffiti trope. "By the funny display of wit/It Look like Shakespeare had/been here to shit," wrote another latrine-wall poet in Norris Junction Camp, Yellowstone National Park, as Read transcribed on August 14. So, not really Shakespeare, but maybe the best you'll get in an auto camp outhouse. Yes, some will object to calling these vulgar verses "poetry," but they are literary expression nonetheless, and the poetics of outhouse graffiti depends on profanity.

Or, sometimes, on euphemisms for profanity. And, it turns out, in an American context, Shakespeare isn't the only bard, after all. At the Norris Junction Camp in Yellowstone National Park, Read found the following on August 14:

Some come here
to shit and stink
and scratch their
itchie balls
But I come here to
stand and think
and write upon the walls
— Longfellow

as well as a second work by the same master:

Remember the Maine
The sinking Ship
So pull the chain
And sink your shit
— Longfellow

Longfellow, of course, is not just homage to Henry Wadsworth of that name, the author of *Evangeline* and *Song of Hiawatha*, but also to the latrine poet's member—apparently, the poet is exceptional in a number of ways. *Shakespeare* may be a similar sort of euphemism. At the Anna Spring Camp, Crater Lake National Park, Oregon, on July 21, Read noticed "Piss here ***/Shake your cock/And disappear." There is, in fact, a lot of cock shaking in shithouse poetry. Though neither *spear* nor *spire* is recorded as slang for "penis," they present a wonderful opportunity to the shithouse poet, who might well have taken one in hand.

In a limited way, Read apologized for the lexical souvenirs he picked up along his route through the American West:

Judged merely as reading matter, the following work…is abominably, incredibly obscene and the compiler begs that anyone will

lay this book down who is not prepared to look at all social phe-
nomena with the dispassionate eye of the anthropologist and the
student of abnormal psychology. I believe that no emanation of
the human spirit is too vile or too despicable to come under the
record and analysis of the scientist.

Today, this seems quaint. The title page reads, "Circulation restricted
to students of linguistics, folk-lore, abnormal psychology, and allied
branches of the social sciences," as though ordinary people would
be not only offended, but harmed by what they found inside the
book. In the twenty-first century, none of it is shocking, and nothing
proves how much the profanity taboo has loosened than the contrast between attitudes of the 1930s—some of them sophisticated,
scientific attitudes—and current attitudes, even those that deplore
profanity and its uses.

I have never scratched graffiti into the metal wall of a school
toilet stall or written on one with marker, though, like pretty much
everyone else, I guess, I've spent time in stalls covered with comments about length and girth, the philosophy of life, who puts out,
pictures of various genitalia, teacher evaluations, most of which were
put in broadly profane terms—"My dick is so long it can turn corners"; "Life's a bitch and then you die"; "You-know-who fucks for
free"; "Mr. Radley is a cocksucker"; on and on. And I've read them.
I'm pretty sure I've stood in a stall at an off-peak lavatory time and
read all of the comments on all of the walls. Not a writer myself, I've
wondered, "Why would someone scribble profanity or obscenity in
a men's room stall?" which shows me at my most obtuse—the answer,
of course, is "I'm reading it."

Actually, that's only part of a much more complicated answer. It
is possible, after all, to write for the mere self-satisfaction of it, and
I don't think it's hard to imagine that in the euphoria of having

dropped a deuce or some other form of self-pleasure, one might want to write a note of congratulation, say something in praise of one's anatomy or prowess, or editorialize on the state of things in jingling rhythms and jangling rhymes, or not, but with liberating profanity either way. Read thinks folks—men in his experience and mine— write in latrines to satisfy "the well-known human yearning to leave a record of one's presence or one's existence." I'm intrigued by that way of putting it, for marking existence isn't quite the same as marking presence at one place and not another. You may not record the time of your presence, but there is one—though it's asynchronous— for the interlocutor, the one reading your latrine poetry with its privy profanity, can note the date of his encounter with it, just as Read did and does for us in his book. Do trees fall in the woods if no one hears them? Were profaners present in those latrines if no one reads their graffiti? Whatever self-pleasure is inscribed on those walls, other dimensions of the writing—of the profanity—are lost entirely if what's written is never a medium of exchange. Oddly, when we peruse *Lexical Evidence from Folk Epigraphy*, we close profane transactions initiated long ago and far away from their original places and times.

This is not to deny the private, personal pleasure of writing profane graffiti in a quiet and only partially occupied moment—surely in that moment, one can do more, and so most of us do. We read, for instance, and when we visit others, we're always pleased to find they've anticipated our need and supplied us with reading material. Off in a Western latrine on one's lonesome and with nothing to read but others' graffiti, one might indulge the impulse to write, instead. Rangers don't stock the toilets of Geyser Baths Swimming Pool, Old Faithful Camp, Yellowstone National Park with the local newspaper or trivia books or *Reader's Digest*, yet on August 11, when AWR visited, someone had thoughtfully provided him something to read: "All wishing to be sucked off get a bone on.... I will choose the best looking pricks." As information, it's about as useful as knowing that Aquafresh insured America Ferrara's—admittedly beautiful—smile for $10 million. And the sheer narcissism of the prick connoisseur elicits a guffaw. When you're alone in a toilet in Yellowstone, unwashed and hungry and desperate to swim in the Geyser Baths Pool, perhaps laughter is the best medicine.

The writer's personal pleasure derives partly from an inscription's profane element. Indeed, Read thought some "inscriptions are motivated merely by the desire to use stigmatized words." I doubt that "merely" and I also think that, while it's natural for a lexicographer to focus on the artifact—the inscription—the pleasure is actually in the inscribing of profane words, the transgressive authority of knife blade cutting into the wall, or at least the paint, if there is some—it's the act that matters, not the result, one reason, though only one, that the inscription left behind is so often unsatisfying, whether as verse or sentiment. But this is just to say that latrine graffiti belongs to the ethos of the latrine as much as anything else we do there—we do our "business" and then we leave. Some linger admiringly over the outhouse output of that business, the totem of their narcissism, but for what it all means, you'll have to ask Freud, who also has theories of why you would fuck where you shit, or write about it there, anyway.

The thrill of writing dirty little rhymes on dirty little walls isn't all positive, or a matter of what we do; it's also negative thrill—a matter of what we don't do and how—in a latrine, of all places—we are free from social constraint. Latrine literature is anonymous, and its authors can't be traced. They're responsible for putting the graffiti there, sure, and they revel in that light shade of responsibility, but they can't be held more darkly responsible—it's all agency and no consequences. Self-censorship isn't required because by the time censorship intrudes—when someone effaces an inscription, or comments on it critically, or someone cleans or paints the wall—the writer is nowhere to be found. In fact, by then, he may not remember what he wrote—he may have forgotten *that* he wrote anything of which his mother wouldn't approve. Some graffiti is cut into wood and meant to last, but most of it is ephemeral and disappears on schedule under a fresh coat of paint. You can't hold someone responsible for what isn't there.

What latrine wall readers make of the graffiti is a complicated question, too. Just as the writer enjoys profaning, so does the reader. Some readers are prompted to inscribe something in return, while others are happy just to read, simultaneously detached and engaged, the serial vicarious beneficiaries of serial impulsive potty mouths. Anyway, some of the verse isn't as bad as you'd expect. Farting, for instance, inspires some decent indecency. There are plenty of variations on the popular rhyme, a bit of folklore, "Here I sit all broken hearted/Came to shit and only farted," which Read saw in Sentinel, Arizona, on June 27. Other writers are more original and exhibit some poetic flair. So, on July 4, in Visalia Park, California, Read celebrated American independence with

> Now and then we sit in bliss
> Listening to the dropping piss
> Now and then a fart is heard
> Mingling with a dropping tird,

And he celebrated the storming of the Bastille, on 14 July, at Lake Tahoe, California, in similar style:

> Here I sit in silent bliss
> lisining to the
> trinkling piss
> now & then

a fart is heard
telling of a coming turd.

Comparing the two, one notes, as Read puts it, "the transmission of
folk material" in the *bliss/piss* rhyme, the line—however represented—
of "now and then a fart is heard," and the ultimate turd, but otherwise their poets' sensibilities are quite different—interestingly so.

For one, the turd is pending but unrealized at the poem's end, an
expectation—like so many others in the lives of those who use out-
houses—left unfulfilled. The fart, a harbinger wind, foretells the tardy,
yet inevitable turd. The other, less poetic poet hears dropping piss
and a dropping turd, which is carelessly indiscriminate—piss and
turds drop in different ways. The more poetic of the two knows this.
In the explicit silence, he listens carefully and hears what he calls a
trinkle, which the *Oxford English Dictionary* finds in Chaucer and the
Scottish poets Gavin Douglas and Robert Burns. What the better
privy poet heard is unclear, but the word he uses to describe it is
richly suggestive. It's usually thought to be a form of *trickle*, but in
Scots it can mean 'besprinkle, scatter over'—perhaps it's a blend of
trickle and *sprinkle*—which we all know piss does as well as trickle.
Anyway, it's poetic diction, and when one realizes that, one is forced
to reconsider the status of *piss*, *fart*, and *turd*. On a latrine wall, they
may count as poetic diction, too.

This issue of art, of the graffiti writer as an artist, is a not infre-
quent theme of the shithouse wall. Inscriptions on the theme are
doubly paradoxical. They are cleverly like the Cretan Liar Paradox—
"This sentence is a lie"—sometimes horribly so: "I'll kill the son of
a bitch who wrote this," which Read copied in Island Park, Cedar
Falls, Iowa, on September 4. But they are also putatively self-loathing
inscriptions by proudly profane poets, who raise themselves by
going as low as they can. For instance, one of these poets wrote what

Read noted on August 14, at the Norris Junction Camp, Yellowstone National Park:

> Of all the poets
> under the sun the shit house
> poet is worse than none
> I wish the one that first
> wrote in this place
> was lying where I could
> shit in his face.

Two days later, in Artesian Park, Ogden, Utah, Read discovered that a fellow traveler had written,

> Some people are poor
> While others are rich,
> But a shit house
> Poet is a Son of a Bitch.

I, the poet, am a son of a bitch, because I'm only good enough for the shithouse, but I'm compelled to write this verse anyway. People— like me, the shithouse poet writing this very poem—deserve to be shit on—I'd shit on myself, but I'm a writer, not an acrobat.

All of this perversity—not just the shitting, but logical perversity, poetic perversity, moral perversity—is a form of exceptionalism, and profanity participates in making it so. The poet is cleverer than most of those reading his poem; the poet is more daring than those mere readers, because he doesn't just sit there reading, he writes on latrine walls, he's a maker, a doer; the poet is a poet, and poets are exceptional by their very nature—they claim to speak in a higher register than the rest of us, except that in the case of the shithouse poets, the lowest register is paradoxically the highest. You can write bad poetry without profanity, but you cannot hit the lowest poetic register without it. If I wrote an ode or sonnet on a latrine wall, I'd still be breaking the rules, destroying property, but if I'm willing to go that far, why not go all the way, write lowdown poetry with profanity and thoroughly enjoy my transgressive moment? The setting allows me to be exceptional. I can get away with stuff there that I can't in the world outside the toilet.

I have tremendous sympathy with latrine graffiti artists and shithouse poets. They are ordinary people doing an ordinary private thing and taking the moment to be exceptional. Dick Cheney is exceptional because he's rich and powerful. When he held public office among many other exceptional people, he had to prove that he was yet more exceptional than they. As vice president he had a license to do so, and ordinary people don't have that license—to be honest, they can't even apply for that license. Charlo Greene had a big voice because she was a television news anchor, somewhat exceptional, I suppose, but she became more so because her voice was amplified through the medium—the average "Fuck it!" doesn't get the time of day, and if you say it in school you'll be exceptional like the Breakfast Club. Everyone wants—needs—to be at least occasionally exceptional, and oddly the latrine provides an opportunity to be so. I beg you not to dismiss profane but often playful and sometimes even profound evocations of a fundamental human desire. Rather, consider what it says about life in modern America that shithouse walls are a canvas for expression of authority through authorship, however low, however ephemeral, for those who lack conventional authority. AWR thought latrine graffiti evidence of neurosis, and perhaps it is, but in response to what? Don't blame the messenger.

Given this current of exceptionalism, latrine graffiti also looks for solidarity and, against the odds of time and space, often constructs it. Some comes in nods of agreement, laughter, reaction to the sense or nonsense of the graffiti one reads—"Bullshit!" you say on reading one message; "Fuckin-A!" you say on reading another. But some interaction is recorded in further graffiti, anonymous people talking back to or cooperating with other anonymous people for the record, ephemeral though it may be. Graffitists criticize one another's work: "[T]he man that drew this never saw a cunt," Read jotted in Lake Tahoe, California, on July 14. The better sort of shithouse poet values correctness—"Learn to spell kid, you big cocksucker," one advised in El Centro, California, spotted by Read on June 27—the schoolmarm in the shithouse. "I fucked my girl here last night," someone bragged in the latrine at Island Park, Cedar Falls, Iowa; "I don't think there is anybody that can fuck a girl better than he can," someone else insists—Read recorded these on September 4. The writer of that second comment may be expressing solidarity with the original fucker, or he may be attempting to establish it with any readers of the two pendant inscriptions, or both—desperate for solidarity, one might say.

It surprises me how many of Read's inscriptions reach out from one to another, or many others—some of them attempt to construct intimacy, some of them group solidarity. Sure, they can be creepy, especially the ones that go for intimacy. So, in Yosemite National Park, California, on July 11, Read encountered "OKFICUPP Honey?" Voyeur much? "No," you say, cringing, "you may not see me pee-pee." But this initialism isn't just a warning—though any reader will undoubtedly be on his guard—nor is it just a joke. The bid for intimacy in "Honey" is overt, and it's not just "pissing" our graffitist wants to watch, but "pee-pee," which, as child's talk and out of register in a men's latrine is framed as intimate, too. Though clever—a sort of showing off, really—it's also coy and asks the reader to come find the writer behind those initials—there's a reveal, though it's of something we'd rather not see. And you can't escape the uncomfortable fact: if you are sitting on the stool and read the inscription, it means you, honey.

Read may have sat on the stool, the object of attempted intimacy. Or, he may have stepped in as a scientist recording lexical and folkloric data, in which case he's not "Honey," but perhaps still brought closer to intimacy than he would like, as are we. *OKFICUPP* is not *WTF, STFU,* or *MILF*—it's not conventional; you have to figure it out. And as you do, you join in an intimacy exercise, a coming to a-greement over something private and mutual with the inscription's author. Detached readers—you, me, Read, at one or two ironic removes from the original material—are implicated in graffiti intimacy as well as engaged readers, whether they like it or not, and probably not. This sense of irresistible implication explains why I keep bringing Read into the story—the lexicographer may not have been a graffitist's expected audience, but each inscription is read when recorded, read again in *Lexical Evidence,* and read yet again by this book's readers, in a series of increasingly remote shithouse encounters.

At other times, graffitists seek solidarity, either because they'd find comfort in knowing others like them were out there, or because they want to consolidate a group by means of graffiti, as in Grants Pass Oregon, noted on July 21: "Other degenerates sign here/Jack Hoff (Shithouse Poet)." On August 10, in the Madison River Camp of Yellowstone, Read copied a similar inscription: "All cocksuckers Register here." These aren't meant literally, at least not necessarily— one need not be a degenerate or a cocksucker—but invite all comers to play the name game, like the one Jack Hoff started, another iteration of which Read found in Cedar City, Utah, on August 18, "Ivan Jackoff [among a list of names, as *Who Flung Dung, Lotta Cocks,* etc.]." Some of us are born to organize the rest of us into games and other activities. In the shithouse, they bring isolated people together— notionally, but sometimes that's as good as it gets.

At the Kicking Horse Auto Camp, in Yoho National Park, British Columbia, on August 2, Read noticed what may be the most important bit of graffiti included in *Lexical Evidence*: "A thing that never should be done at all / Is to write your name on the backhouse wall." The fundamental principle in latrine writing is anonymity. Of course, anonymity can be used to hide, but it is also potentially empowering—it enables certain types of performance. Some of these are awful, as when hiding and terrorizing are part and parcel of each other in the Ku Klux Klan. Mostly, the backhouse is free from terrorism, though one finds plenty of sexual aggression. Privy performance is mostly sexual—various scholarly studies, undertaken at different times and in different places, agree that 80% of it is, and most of the 80% is homosexual in interest.

The writers are well aware that latrine graffiti is performance, and some acknowledge it directly, by playing the game in character:

> I suck cocks eat cunt suck pussys
> skin pricks tickle cunts play with balls...
> signed SLIPPERY SLIM

No mother, surely, not even Ms. Slim, named her son *Slippery*, let alone *SLIPPERY*—we must assume that the name is assumed for the purposes of writing this particular message. Slippery Slim does all of the things itemized in it, but what about the writer who invented the slippery persona? Performance experiments with imaginary possibilities—it implies no commitment outside of itself. If you read Slippery's message and have your balls at the ready, they may turn blue. *Slippery* is a meaningful name, in the sense that you, the reader, can't count on anything. If it's as exciting as Read thought just to play with profanity, then perhaps such verbal play substitutes for sexual play—perhaps it's not substitution, but sufficient to itself.

Some of the performance is revealed in improbability. Undoubtedly, dates were made on latrine walls. Gay men had ways of figuring out whether the person in the stall was the date, ways of avoiding third parties accidentally present at an assignation. But not all of the dates proposed were authentic, and one fears that some might have been gay-hating traps. It's hard to take seriously an invitation like that recorded by Read in Yosemite National Park on July 11: "My cock is only 10 inc long so if any one would/like to suck meet me here 9 PM at eny night/welcome." Eventually, some authority against gay assignation would read it and know that whoever showed up there at that time, night after night was likely to be the writer—the supposed promise undermines the required anonymity. Such fiction is more clearly exposed in a message left at the Geyser Baths Swimming Pool privy, Old Faithful Camp, Yellowstone, which AWR read on August 11:

> NoticeI will suck off 2 boys' (over 16) cocks
> next Sunday—July 25th at 12 p.m.
>> All wishing to be sucked off get a bone on and
> wait. I will choose the best looking pricks
>> My friend will jerk off the rest
>>> Chief Ranger Martindale

In spite of the legal and even occasional punctuation niceties—I didn't expect the correctly marked plural possessive—this probably wasn't left by the Chief, but someone who knew that he could perform the role—the message is an official "notice"—and simultaneously undermine it—that's not the way Chief Rangers lay out their official notices.

These are conspicuous performances—well, more conspicuous than the rest of the graffiti, which are nonetheless more conspicuous than the continuous performance by which we maintain our identities. We perform all of the time, just one thing of which conspicuous performance reminds us. We perform because we resist the way things are without the performance, the preperformance status quo, in which we aren't as expressive as we'd like to be or in the ways we'd like to be. This is where profanity enters the shithouse performance. When stigmatized, gay men, for instance, need a way of talking that's revealing within the consolidated group but inaccessible to the straight world—especially the hostile straight world. After all, an out-group is an out-group, and the in-group distinguishes itself from it—from all of them—for reasons of its very groupness. Language—profanity in particular—constructs and maintains the necessary social boundaries.

What gay men required was an anti-language, a concept introduced by Michael Halliday—as, looking at my own span of days, I must ruefully admit—a long time ago. Paul Baker sums up Halliday's view neatly: "For Halliday, anti-language was to anti-society what language was to society. An anti-society is a counter-culture, a society within a society, a conscious alternative to society, existing by resisting either passively or by more hostile, destructive means." Baker thus reformulates Halliday in *Polari—The Lost Language of Gay Men* (2002), an engaging and especially well-informed view into what might be considered quite extreme anti-language, extreme because, unlike everyday slang, it's not intelligible outside the in-group. Profanity on latrine walls is not as extreme as Polari—not in terms of linguistic structure—but it is extreme in the sense that it taunts the mainstream taboo, and, while writing on latrine walls is relatively passive resistance, the profane element is overtly hostile.

Recently, Scott Herring has argued in *Another Country: Queer Anti-Urbanism* (2010) what the subtitle implies, that we locate queer culture in the metropolis and overlook the variety of queer experience in America, especially that which is committedly anti-urban.

Herring blazes trails into Appalachia, the Deep South, and the Heart-land, but Read's collection of graffiti allows us to go further west with the idea, and when we arrive at the Left Cost with Read, we aren't in San Francisco, but in the wilderness, reading latrine-wall declara-tions of gay men—explicit, strangely intimate but distant declara-tions to one another; implicit "fuck-off" confrontations with those who stigmatize and harass them, boldly uttered from a safe distance; gay identity projected to the world, to anyone who needs to relieve himself at that place. Profanity enforces the borders between in- and out-groups, welcoming citizens of the anti-society, reassuring them with the intimacy of transgression, but—in the very same words—unquietly provoking and excluding those who don't belong.

Except that, as voyeurs, they aren't excluded. Readers can look into other people's business—in fact, by the nature of the medium are invited to do so—without belonging. And, if they want to, they can experiment with identities they encounter only on latrine walls. Anthropologists and folklorists who write about latrine graffiti—what Alan Dundes calls *latrinalia*, a term for all the writing we find in the toilet stall—carefully analyze graffiti as having homosexual content or heterosexual content, because the anonymity inherent to *latrinalia* blocks our view of the writer and his authentic sexual iden-tity—authenticity is relevant in some cases, but not in all. As Read points out, "The content is not trustworthy for fact," and so we cannot take as fact what's communicated in *latrinalia*—in many cases, it's communicating something else.

Finally, it isn't about cock size or sexual opportunism or poetry, but about human existence—the underlying message is existential, as Read partly guessed, but it goes beyond recording presence, be-cause just as recording presence is a motive for the graffiti, recording presence itself must have a motive, too. There you are, by a canyon at night, under the biggest sky, bigger than you had ever imagined.

You've never felt so at one with creation. You've never felt so alone. We are all equal under the stars, under the immense canopy of stars by which we measure our own significance. Remember man that thou art stardust, and unto dust thou shalt return. So, we seek to connect, even or maybe especially at the most awkward times, in the least sociable places, but we are also, despite all contact, ultimately alone. Because it mingles "come hither" with "go away," "I need you" with "I am exceptional, self-sufficient," profanity expresses the existential paradox—we are conflicted, yes, but about something above and beyond mere conflict.

Somehow, belonging can't be without longing, and when you walk through the latrine door, you are going in and out, for once in the confined space of the stall you are out of society—not just "part of a society within a society"—and you can imagine and gesture toward new connections with your anti-language, in search of your anti-society. Every in-group is an out-group, and in the outhouse we can be alone with company, intimate but distant, ourselves but not really, isolated yet engaged, connected but not then and there. Profanity is thus the language of our several dualities—our many-splendored paradox is immanent in every shithouse *fuck*, *cunt*, and *cocksucker*—and it signifies our longing for belonging though we know belonging will never fill the hole of existing. When we go out of common space and time when we go into the latrine, what we read there—profanity included—is the writing on the wall.

IN PRAISE OF PROFANITY

We construct networks of social connections. In a sense, they're given to us. We're introduced to a friend of a friend or a cousin's college roommate, and it's impossible to avoid the neighbors. However, beyond these introductions, beyond proximities for which we're not responsible, we work to be friends. Well, we say we "make" friends for a reason; it's far from just happening. It's not necessarily hard work, making friends, because we're hard-wired to do it—like many animal species, *Homo sapiens* is naturally social, and language is at once the proof of our specifically human sociality and its mechanism. Like other primates, humans groom one another—foot rubs, nit-picking—usually in dyadic sessions, during which we gossip about the rest of our group, forming and fostering intimacies all the while. Sometimes, three's a crowd, but actually, socially, we need the crowd as much as we need intimacy, and so we promote the solidarity of relatively large groups, too. Fantastic as it seems, in the era of mass culture, we consolidate relationships with people we'll never meet except through social media, and brands are busy consolidating us into brand communities without expecting personal interaction—we have some sort of relationship to those carrying the same bag or wearing the same shoes or microblogging under *fuck yeah*. We shouldn't look down, I guess, on our looser affiliations.

I realize that some reading this chapter will never accept its premise, that profanity helps us do things we need or want to do and to that extent is good for us—at least, it's useful. Those who disagree will point out that everything that supposedly benefits from profanity can be achieved or managed without it, and I agree, that's true. We disagree on whether the effort to manage without profanity is necessary and whether what's achieved without it is qualitatively the same as what it achieves. Some are more comfortable with reducing the complexity of experience than I am. I think experience is complex in its very nature, and I doubt it's our job to fix the complexity just because it bothers us. Profanity plays a role in some intimacies and not others, across the various associations of a lifetime.

It may facilitate solidarity among the soccer team, but not the Bible study group—you can belong to both.

I suppose, too, I've only proved that profanity keeps bad company. When magazines give sex advice, it's dirty talk for dirty sex; when Charlo Greene uses it, it's in the interest of promoting drug use; when it's written on latrine walls it's like the shit children supposedly smear in the anal phase of psychosexual development—research makes the connection. Never mind that Greene thinks it's about freedom or that what goes on in the bedroom is, according to the Supreme Court, nobody's business. In saying that bad words help us to achieve good ends, I'm not saying that's all they do, or that good ends are only achievable with profanity—these are all corners into which those on one side of one or more of the debates over profanity want to push me, and I won't be pushed. Actually, I will say later in the book that some good emotional and aesthetic ends are achievable only with profanity, but that's not part of this chapter's argument. And that's just to insist, in response, that while some are very sure they know what constitutes good and bad, I'm not sure they do, and I am willing to suspend judgment, to allow folks to figure out what works for them according to their own social intuitions and experience, what's good for them according to their own consciences. Profanity is a stubborn fact of speech and cannot be disregarded simply because some people disapprove of it.

As hard as life is, I'm in favor of anything that makes it possible to connect with others over whatever times and spaces will satisfy us—or probably not satisfy us, when it comes to it, but we have to try. I know the struggle involved in trust, the distances we impose against our interests and, in a sense, even against our wills. So, we take a risk—we reach out with a hand, or a smile, or a profanity, depending on the situation, depending on whose eye we can catch. I could not have made up the relationships between profanity and friendship, profanity and desire, profanity and trust. At first blush, they seem like a philosophical fiction. They amaze me, and I respect and celebrate them as a big human conundrum, one I can't solve, indeed, for which I suspect there is no solution. So, against my better judgment, I write in praise of profanity. Profanity fuck yeah!

REFERENCES

Go the Fuck to Sleep! (New York: Akashic Books, 2011) was written by Adam Mansbach and illustrated by Ricardo Cortés. Mackay Hatch appears in Chapter 1, and reference to his work can be found there. *Californication*, created by Tom Kapinos, ran on Showtime from 2007 to 2014 and starred David Duchovny as Hank Moody, Natasha McElhone as Karen, Evan Handler as Charlie Runkle, Pamela Adlon as Marcy Runkle, and Madeleine Martin as Hank and Karen's daughter, Becca, who grows into profanity as the series progresses. "The Way of the Fist" (Season 5, episode 2) aired on January 15, 2012, directed by David Duchovny, and written by Tom Kapinos and Mike Metz. "Perverts and Whores" (Season 5, episode 10) aired on March 18, 2012, directed by Bart Freundlich, and written by Tom Kapinos. Molly Triffin writes about "How to Talk Dirty" in *Cosmopolitan* at http://www.cosmopolitan.com/sex-love/advice/g2074/ dirty-talk-he-loves/. Beware: This isn't the only *Cosmopolitan* slideshow available on this topic. It isn't difficult to find sex research relevant to the issues discussed here, including the following: E. Sandra Byers and Stephanie Demmons, "Sexual Satisfaction and Sexual Self-Disclosure within Dating Relationships," *The Journal of Sex Research* 36 (1999): 180–189; Leslie A. Baxter and William W. Wilmot, "Taboo Topics in Close Relationships," *Journal of Social and Personal Relationships* 2 (1985): 253–269; Kathryn Quina, Lisa L. Harlow, Patricia J. Morokoff, and Gary Burkholder, "Sexual Communication in Relationships: When Words Speak Louder than Actions," *Sex Roles* 42 (2000): 523–549; Elizabeth A. Babin, "An Examination of Predictors of Nonverbal and Verbal Communication of Pleasure during Sex and Sexual Satisfaction," *Journal of Social and Personal Relationships* 30 (2012): 270–292. Rebecca A. Dwyer's *Terms of Endearment? Vocatives and Power in BDSM Erotica* was her MSc. thesis at the University of Edinburgh (2007). Jay Mechling's "High Kybo Floater: Food and Feces in the Speech Play at a Boy Scout Camp" appeared in the *Journal of Psychoanalytic Anthropology* 7 (1984): 256–268. His point about anal-eroticism and the Scout Law appears on p. 261; the quotation is taken from p. 260; the fart classification appears on p. 263, *scroatmeal* on p. 259, and *kybo* on p. 258, with the etymological speculation at

p. 266n2. Bernie Chun Nam Mak and Carmen Lee contributed their "Swearing Is E-Business: Expletives in Instant Messaging in Hong Kong Workplaces," to *Digital Business Discourse*, edited by Erika Darics (London: Palgrave Macmillan, 2015), pp. 124–143. *Bitch* was founded by Andi Zeisler, Lisa Jervis, and Benjamin Shaykin in 1996 and is still going strong. I quote Bitch Media from their site https://bitchmedia.org. Geoffrey Nunberg, in *Ascent of the A-Word: Assholism, The First Sixty Years* (New York: PublicAffairs, 2012), pp. 132–136, discusses the political dangers of *bitch*. On partially re-appropriated *bitch*, see Geneva Smitherman, *Black Talk: Words and Phrases from the Hood to the Amen Corner*, 2d ed. (Boston: Houghton Mifflin, 2000), p. 69. The Betches can be found at http://www.betches.com, whence I quote them. While *Bitch* is far from prudish, *Betches* is often casually profane, which is why I bring up Ariel Levy's *Female Chauvinist Pigs: Women and the Rise of Raunch Culture* (New York: Free Press, 2006)—the profanity is only one symptom of a much larger problem, in Levy's view, but you can find all of the other symptoms on *Betches*, too. Henry Jenkins is quoted from *Convergence Culture: Where Old and New Media Collide* (New York: New York University Press, 2006), p. 20, and Ruth Wajnryb from *C U Next Tuesday: A Good Look at Bad Language* (London: Aurum Press, 2005), pp. 139–140. *Team America: World Police*—directed by Trey Parker and written by Parker, Matt Stone, and Pam Brady —was released by Paramount in 2004. Julia Carpenter provides "A Complete History of "F*** yeah" Tumblrs, the Happiest Blogs on the Web" in *The Washington Post* (April 8, 2015), and the several quotations about tumblr and *fuck yeah* are taken from the same. Smiles is not alone in her experience of infinite manifestations of a linguistic pattern; see my *Slang: The People's Poetry* (New York: Oxford University Press, 2009), pp. 166–169, and "Slang in New Media: A Case Study," in *Global English Slang: Methodologies and Perspectives*, edited by Julie Coleman (London: Routledge, 2014), pp. 175–185, for additional examples. Nora Eldridge protests her innocence in Claire Messud's *The Woman Upstairs* (New York: Knopf, 2013), p. 5. Pat Conroy's delightful and deeply affecting *The Water is Wide: A Memoir* (New York: Dial Press, 2000) is quoted from pp. 42 (twice), 41 (twice), 48, 64–65, 128–129, and 161–162, in series. Vice President Cheney's profanity received considerable notice, as befits his exceptional status, but see especially Helen Dewar and Dana Milbank, "Cheney Dismisses Critic with Obscenity," *The Washington Post* (June 25, 2005): A4. You can read Cheney's views on the world in Dick Cheney and Liz Cheney, *Exceptional: Why the World Needs a Powerful America* (New York: Threshold Editions/ Simon & Schuster, 2015). On some of President George W. Bush's linguistic exceptionalism, see my "Nicknames, Interpellation, and Dubya's Theory of the State," *Names: A Journal of Onomastics* 56 (2008): 206–220. For more on the Clymer incident, see Nunberg, pp. 35–38, and on the Leahy incident, p. 104; regarding President Truman and subsequent presidents and profanity, see Allan Metcalf's *Presidential Voices: Speaking Styles from George Washington to George W. Bush*

(Boston: Houghton Mifflin, 2004), pp. 89–90. As for Charlo Greene, enter her name in your search field and see what comes up! The resignation clip is available at https://www.youtube.com/watch?v=eRPYaWLtgWg, and Kevin Rivers's comment can be found underneath Laurel Andrews's account of the affair, "KTVA Reporter Quits On-Air after Saying She Owns Alaska Cannabis Club" in the *Alaska Dispatch News* (September 21, 2014), http://www.adn.com/article/20140921/ktva-reporter-quits-air-after-saying-she-owns-alaska-cannabis-club. Allen Walker Read's *Lexical Evidence from Folk Epigraphy in Western North America: A Glossarial Study of the Low Element in the English Vocabulary* was printed privately in Paris in 1935, and I am not lucky enough to own a copy, but fortunately the book was reprinted as *Classic American Graffiti* (Waukesha, WI: Maledicta Press, 1977) and is more readily available. I have quoted Read's text from pp. 55 (twice), 60, 17, 31 (twice), 72, 73, 60, 75, 42, 5–6, 17, 38, 20, 50, 51 (twice), 73, 38, 46, 43, 52 (twice), 65, 61, 44, 62, 33, 71, 78, and 79, in series. You can find out about America Ferrara's smile in Ben Schott's *Schott's Miscellany 2009: An Almanac* (New York: Bloomsbury, 2008), p. 126. You can find out more about Allen Walker Read in a collection of his work, *Milestones in the History of English in America*, Publication of the American Dialect Society 86, edited by Richard W. Bailey (Durham, NC: Duke University Press). Those who want to explore the folkloric value of latrine graffiti, see Alan Dundes, "Here I Sit: A Study of American Latrinalia," in *The Meaning of Folklore: The Analytical Essays of Alan Dundes*, edited by Simon J. Bronner (Logan: Utah State University Press, 2007), pp. 360–374. For some commentary on the differences between graffiti by men and women, see Flora S. Kaplan, "Privies, Privacy, and the Political Process: Some Thoughts on Bathroom Graffiti and Group Identity," in *Group Cohesion: Theoretical and Clinical Perspectives*, edited by Henry Kellerman (New York: Grune & Stratton, 1981), pp. 393–410, on pp. 401–403. Kaplan (p. 394) said it best: latrine graffiti "express shared ideas and values even as they violate ideal and conventional behavior... [and] segments of society [are] formed and reformed through this dialogue." For the comment on anti-language, see Paul Baker, *Polari: The Lost Language of Gay Men* (London: Routledge, 2002), p. 13. I highly recommend Scott Herring's *Another Country: Queer Anti-Urbanism* (Chicago: University of Chicago, 2010), whose sophisticated and wide-ranging argument kept coming to mind as I was writing my plainer, narrower one.

Chapter 3

Expletive and Euphemism

Occasionally, in her masterpiece *H Is for Hawk* (2014), profanity helps Helen McDonald manage her anger. Her father has died unexpectedly and she is having trouble training her goshawk, and she writes in her journal, "rest of day terrible because I had to see people, have to pretend everything fine. On and on. Wish they would FUCK OFF AND LEAVE ME ALONE." She ruminates on the anger that justifies the profanity in that entry:

> The anger was vast and it came out of nowhere. It was the rage of something not fitting; the frustration of trying to put something in a box that is slightly too small. You try moving the shape around in the hope that some angle will make it fit in the box. Slowly comes an apprehension that this might not, after all, be possible. And finally you know it won't fit, know there is no way it can fit, but this doesn't stop you using brute force to try to crush it in, punishing the thing for not fitting properly. That was what it was like: but I was the box, I was the thing that didn't fit, and I was the person smashing it, over and over again, with bruised and bleeding hands.

I especially admire McDonald's decision to employ *apprehension* in this context. On the one hand, *apprehension* means "understanding," a grasping of the uncomfortable or vexing truth of things. On the other hand, however, it can mean "anxiety or fear of something bad," and McDonald has it both ways. Apprehension lends itself to the tragic dimension of experience; it's a point at which we are likely to employ profanity.

Some would insist that profanity is no solution to anger, and I heartily agree. Anger, they say, is morally and spiritually bad, and we must discipline ourselves in order to be rid of it. If you believe that, then profanity, insofar as it indulges anger, must be proscribed. We could argue about whether there's such a thing as righteous anger, in which case there would be no need to suppress it. We could argue about whether anger is a natural or inevitable emotion, bound to find expression, in which case we might prefer profanity to alternatives like violence. I'd rather have someone who is angry with me swear at me than poison me—I think superpolite poisoners are morally inferior to harmless people who swear. McDonald's rage is not only righteous and inevitable but ultimate, in her case an apprehension of human limitations. Whether anger is a product of the human condition, or a moral failing, or a moral failing that's a product of the human condition, anger is the issue, not profanity. You can't save humanity from emotional fire by dousing profanity, though arguably the release accomplished in exclamatory profanity may dampen the anger it expresses.

Exclamations are not easy to account for on linguistic terms. They are a sort of interjection, such as *oh*, which is why *Oh shit!* makes so much sense—it's half expletive but 100% interjection. Erving Goffman, in *Forms of Talk* (1981), argued that an interjection is a "ritualized act," and thus not part of language per se. That seems wrong to me. It's true that *Shit!* isn't "a statement in the linguistic sense," and it's true, too, that when used as an exclamation, it can't be defined in a dictionary way—its meaning isn't lexical or syntactic, a linguist would say, but pragmatic. Pragmatics is the aspect of meaning that depends on context, and even though Goffman is wrong to take exclamation out of language, he has a point: the meanings of exclamations and other interjections respond immediately to the circumstances in which they are uttered: Goffman classifies *Ouch!* as a "pain cry" and exclamatory profanity as a "response cry"—these are no more linguistic, he thinks, than the cries of animals, communication but not language. Or, we might propose as an alternative to Goffman's view, that atavistic cries—cries that originated in our prehistory and perhaps before language evolved—have been absorbed into human language.

Anyway, when you exclaim *Fuck!* there's no fucking in it. If you prefer *Shit!* there isn't a whiff of excrement in the air. The pragmatic meanings have overtaken the lexical meanings of those words; how they sound matters as much as what they mean, or it might be more precise to say that how they sound participates in their meaning. That's why McDonald puts her profanity in CAPITAL LETTERS, so that you can hear her frustration. The meaning is in the very act of exclaiming, which leads to a problem in characterizing profanity. If *fuck* and *cunt* are supposedly taboo because they're vulgarly sexual, and if we avoid *shit* because it's about defecation, and these associations are the bases for their profanity, then how can *Fuck!* or *No shit, Sherlock!* or *Fuckin'-A!* count as profanity? The supposed basis for profanity has been lost in the pragmatics of expletive exclamation. Could it be that expletive exclamation is not, in fact, profanity?

Anger may be justified and profanity its apt expression, but we have covered our shame since the beginning of human nature. At the opposite pole from profane exclamation is profanity's fig leaf, euphemism. Euphemism is a most curious phenomenon. As Keith Allan and Kate Burridge, two very impressive linguists, put it in *Euphemism & Dysphemism* (1991), "Euphemistic expressions trade on illusion: the bluntly profane (and therefore in some eyes blasphemous)

'Jesus Christ!' is euphemistically transmuted into 'Jeepers Creepers!' but the same person is referred to by both, and if the former is profane, even blasphemous, so should the latter be, too." God knows all, knows what's underneath *Jeepers Creepers*, so it's just as offensive to God and those who love God as any other blasphemous rendering of one of God's names.

But there's a difference between *Jeepers Creepers* and *Oh, Fudge!* for *Fuck!* and *c**t* for *cunt*, because the latter profanities aren't blasphemous, and their euphemisms don't work in quite the way of *Jeepers Creepers*. In fact, while some euphemisms aren't recognized as euphemisms by those who use them—the euphemism has lost its connection to its historical referent—in other cases, the euphemism isn't even an illusion, or it's a terrifically fucked-up illusion, because the profanity is still transparently present—really, it's like a see-through fig leaf. Add to this a twenty-first-century irony that plays with the wink-wink obviousness of some euphemism, and clearly euphemism isn't what it once was—euphemism is just another word for profanity, which is obviously the opposite of what we expect it to be, much as expletive exclamation also overturns expectations. You recall, from Chapter 1, that Robert L. Moore's prototype theory explains how exclamation is exactly when profanity is profanity, but that theory may suffer from the lack of taboo in modern times, or from circularity in determining which words are taboo enough to serve the prototype. In any event, profanity and its relationship to euphemism are more complicated than most of us realize.

SHIT-SLINGING CHIMPANZEES

When chimpanzees are in captivity, living in zoos and whatnot, they occasionally sling shit at their captors, the well-meaning zoo personnel who are just trying to run a zoo and take the best care possible of the animals—given that they are captive in a zoo. They do not throw feces at one another in their natural habitat—that would be gross, and no chimp deserves a faceful of another chimp's shit. But zookeepers are a different matter. If I were a chimpanzee in a zoo, even if I more or less liked my keepers, I'd be royally pissed off and inclined to take it out on people who are, after all, not chimpanzees, and don't deserve a chimpanzee's dignity. Also, I imagine, it wears on you. There's not a lot to do, so when you see the shit just sitting there, you think, "I could sling this at what's his name," and before you know it, that's exactly what you've done. The other chimpanzees all pitch in.

Helen McDonald felt that she was the box so full of rage that it burst into expletive and other manifestations of anger. But the chimps are much more literally in a box than McDonald, and the zoo "rooms" in which they live are much more than slightly too small, you know, if your natural habitat is the equatorial rain forest belt. When you think about it, captive chimps respond to their less-than-ideal situation with a sense of humor, and you can't deny that shit slinging is funny—people who visit zoos love to watch. It's as though the chimpanzee in question, having suppressed a lot of frustration at zoo life, cries "Go fuck yourself, zookeeper!" Of course, it can't *say* that, because it doesn't have language. It slings shit instead. But shit slinging can be quite meaningful, even if it isn't linguistic, and the meaning has to be in the very doing of it, in the act, because the chimp won't get anything but satisfaction from it. As William D. Hopkins and his colleagues at Yerkes National Primate Research Center point out, "In captivity, it is difficult to imagine that human caretakers would overtly reward a chimpanzee with food immediately after they had just been soiled with faeces by the very same ape."

Hopkins is recently famous for a study about chimps and throwing. After a battery of experiments, he and his colleagues, Jamie L. Russell and Jennifer A. Schaeffer, concluded that chimpanzee throwing—of anything, not just feces—is positively correlated with certain types of intelligence, both intellectual and social. For instance, "chimpanzees that throw"—it's actually a rare behavior—"exhibit a considerable degree of planning in their actions and seem to know that they can use their throwing actions to manipulate or change the behaviors of other social beings, notably naïve human observers." Clever. It turns out, too, that "chimpanzees that have learned to throw are better at communication tasks than chimpanzees that have not," which "suggest[s] an explicit association between the cognitive foundations for throwing and the ability to engage in successful intraspecies communication," and perhaps interspecies communication, too, since anyone hit by a flying fistful of chimp feces probably gets the point.

Hopkins and his colleagues didn't come to their conclusions by mere observation of behavior. They are neuroscientists, and they examined the neuroanatomy, the brain activity, associated with chimpanzee throwing, and this is where the results get really interesting, because they confirm that, for chimpanzees, learning to throw is like learning to gesture, which suggests that, as far as the brain is concerned, throwing and communication are related. Indeed, the brain centers responsible for the motor control throwing requires are also intimately connected to speech and language in humans—we may have developed speech and language after the fact of learning how to throw. One newspaper account of Hopkins's study claimed, "The researchers . . . are still unclear as to why hurling your own filth might be a crucial evolutionary step towards speech." But readers of this book, I'm sure, can fill in that blank: perhaps obscene gestures are implicated in the evolution of language.

LANGUAGE AS GESTURE

The notion that language "originates" in some oblique way from gesture is not new, and the chimpanzee study doesn't prove that human language comes from or is necessarily related to the human ability to throw, even if it proves something about chimps. Nevertheless, the throwing scenario is suggestive. What if, before our early ancestors, Grandma and Grandpa Hominin, emerged from the prehominin primates, some of those primates, just a few, had a baseball team? Those primates could throw. And they also had the cognitive capacity to call pitches; they had the infield chatter, and it really sounded like chatter, because there weren't any words; they used knowing looks and sly finger gestures to communicate plays among themselves. They lacked but one thing—another team. Under this adaptational pressure, the Hominins—both of them, according to the cave paintings, phenomenal players—separated from the other *Hominini* into their own subtribe, with a few friendly australopithecenes, leaving their chimpanzee relations behind in the genus *Pan*. A few chimps, as we've learned, can throw, but humans specialized in throwing and eventually in speech and language, too. The descendants of the Hominins multiplied until they had not only enough teams for baseball games, but indeed whole baseball leagues. Chimpanzees in captivity get satisfaction in slinging shit, while humans get it making double plays. After we realized we could have language as well as play ball, profanity made its way into baseball as in every bipedal walk of human life. So, human language developed out of baseball. True story.

Throwing requires finely controlled motor skills. The shortstop grips the ball and flings it—overhand, sidearm?—to hit the base player's mitt. The throw involves calculations of distance and velocity, as well as manual technique. Throwing is complicated. And so is speech, and, like throwing, speech—whether signed with hands or articulated in the mouth and related spaces of the body—requires very fine motor control. For one sound, the tip of the tongue strikes the alveolar ridge; for another, the tongue trills against the hard palate. Almost no animal brain has developed to support such control—just ours. What baseball proves is that where there's throwing there's chatter, that once the relevant areas of the brain grow to accommodate the throwing, language is also possible—though not inevitable, the throwing chimps remind us. Brain science has begun to map the connection between throwing and language, which light up some of the same brain centers.

Brains can't throw, and they don't talk on their own outside of science fiction. The human brain's capacity for either activity is accompanied by other evolutionary developments. We can date "accurate throwing... as far back as *Praeanthropus africanus* (previously known as *Australopithicus afarensis*) over 3 million years ago," Michael Corballis informs us in his cleverly titled *From Hand to Mouth: The Origins of Language* (2002). "Not only did the structure of the hand change in ways consistent with holding and hurling rocks or other fist-sized objects, like modern-day baseballs or cricket balls, but the bipedal posture would have supplied extra leverage"—you can't play baseball on all fours. Although Corballis considers the possible role of throwing in human language, he thinks it is too specific a connection and prefers instead to bring language out of gesture more generally, with throwing one particular kind of gesture among many related to language. "Save for the hurling of insults," he quips, "people do not throw well with their mouths."

But here, in this book, we are interested in just that exception: we may not throw all words, but we do throw invective. Chimps sling shit, and we sling some of our expletives, and neither is entirely metaphorical. Language may derive from or be associated with gesture, but speech is actually gesture—in the mouth, each articulation is a gesture, each word is a set of gestures, and use of some expletives includes a hurling gesture. We are confused by this because when we hear "gesture," we're not thinking in the right scale: obscene gesture for us means flipping the bird—the arm is out, the middle finger erect, it's hard to move the finger into that position and hold it, and the gesture isn't—for most of us, at least—automatic. That's gesture on one scale. Think of producing speech sounds as gesture on a Lilliputian scale.

All words, not just profane ones, are complex gestures, then, but what does it mean to hurl an expletive? Why are expletives different in their hurlability? The sound structure of expletives may help to explain why we can hurl relatively few words. *Slush* is a pretty good word, and you can yell *Slush!* in pain or frustration, but it lacks the force of expletive. Say it as many ways as you like, it will never sound as though it's being hurled at someone. I know people who shout *Asshole!* at drivers who pass on the right, cut into your carefully maintained safe driving distance, and all that, and *asshole* is okay, but the assholes are out of hearing by the time I—such people—get to the *o*, and that *l* is just a fucking disappointment. *Bitch* and *cunt* are more easily and reliably thrown at others. When someone on a bike bumps into you and your bag falls into the puddle that always seems to be there, you can't hurl your bag at the ground in frustration, because it's already there, so you let loose with *Fuck!*—you throw *fuck* to the ground. *Fuck* is admirably expletive, in part because of its sound structure. What follow aren't rules, so much as the terms on which we prefer to sling certain expletives like so much lexical feces.

Vowels play a role in expletive slinging, but the consonants matter even more. To begin, expletives suitable for hurling will be short with two consonants. A word is better suited when both consonants are unvoiced, so *f* rather than *v* and *k* rather than *g*—*fuck* is better than *fug* is better than *vug. If you want to make an expletive point, keep your vocal cords out of it as much as possible—you'll have a vowel in there, anyway. Further, it's best when at least one of the expletive's consonants is velar, that is, produced by striking the soft palate, at the back of the mouth, with the tongue—*k* and *g* are both velar consonants. It's second best when at least one of the consonants is alveolar, produced at the gum line behind the top front teeth—*d* and *t* are alveolar—thus *damn* is pretty good for throwing, but *damn it* is better. Simple consonants are expletively better than consonant clusters: the initial cluster *fr* is one reason *frick* works as a euphemism for *fuck*. *Frick* is still expletive—it's an expletive euphemism—but the *r* mitigates its force. Which is the better expletive for slinging, *shit* or *crap*, *bitch* or *cunt*?

Once we've noticed what's typical of expletives that throw well, we can isolate a principle or two. Expletives are thrown hardest, most accurately, when they have both propelling and stopping consonants, one to hurl sound forward in the word and the other to register the force that builds in the course of the word—the force builds until the final consonant, itself often a striking gesture, releases the pent up force. So, in *fuck*, there is a propelling *f* and a stopping *k*, and in *shit* a propelling *sh* and a stopping *t*. Both *f* and *sh* are great propelling consonants because you can build up a lot force with them. They are fricatives, so obstruct airflow but don't stop it—you let off a certain amount of steam as you say them. Sounds like *b* and *p* stop the air flow, which isn't ideal for building force, because you can't hold them for long. *Bitch* can use a little wind up to compensate for its *b*—as in *Son of a bitch!* And, again, because the *mn* in *damn* absorbs rather than releases the force initiated by *d*, it serves better as a propelling consonant—or perhaps as a booster of the original force—in *Damn it!*

This is where vowels come in. Not every vowel makes for a good throw. In baseball, a good throw leaves the hand with enough force on a straight enough line, and you hear the ball smack hard against the waiting glove. When hurling an expletive, you want the propelling consonant to provide that force and guide the throw, and you want to hear the force smack up against the stopping consonant. For all of this to sound right, the word needs to move fast, so you need a short vowel. The *ea* of *freak* makes for a slower throw than the *u* in *fuck*, and the *oo* of *shoot* suggests less urgency than the *i* of *shit*—a ball tossed from a short distance to tag a slow runner rather than one fired at a base player's glove to make the double play. With vowels like those and "softer" initial consonants and consonant clusters, *freak* and *shoot* are relatively euphemistic gestures.

Speech of this kind—exclamatory *fuck, shit, cunt, crap, bitch*, and the like—is the violent expression of emotion, though violence miniaturized and concentrated in the mouth. In some cases, we are simply flinging our frustration out upon the world, but in others we are spitting, biting, and striking out at others—*fuck* has both biting and striking, *bitch* arguably has all three, since *ch* is a strange sound, what linguists call an affricate, both fricative and stop, where the fricative aspect spits and the stop aspect strikes. Words like exclamatory *fuck* and *bitch* represent social wisdom and enact a social strategy of venting anger, for it's much better to swear than strike out, marginally better to swear than use a broader gesture—that is, you're less likely to end up in fisticuffs if you say *fuck you* than if you flip the bird—and if you swear under your breath, violence satisfies your emotional needs, and you may invite no response at all. Profanity didn't evolve separately from the rest of language to mediate violence and social responses to it. One prehistoric day, someone uttered the first profanity. Like flint fire, it enacted the subconscious connection between language and gesture, perhaps specifically language and throwing. The uses of profanity were repeatedly demonstrated in social situations and entered the repertoire of human language.

PRAGMATIC PROFANITY

Obviously, to say that certain phonetic features help exclamatory profanity work as well as it does is not the same as saying that all words with those features are expletives—we have more explaining to do. The principles underlying exclamatory *fuck*, *shit*, and *cunt* apply to other words—not a lot of them, but enough to spoil the theory. For instance, *shut* has the same vowel as *fuck* and otherwise the same structure as *shit*, so why isn't *shut* on a profanity par with those other words? The furthest we can go is that *Shut up!* is a very mildly expletive alternative for *No way! Puck* and *buck* ought to have some expletive meanings, and *bunt* and *runt* ought to be in the profane pantheon alongside *cunt*. But again, although the sounds and patterns of sounds we considered enable the force of exclaimed profanities, we aren't claiming here that they cause *fuck* (copulate), for instance, to be used as *Fuck!*

In fact, a few linguists out there, reading the previous section, may have unleashed a few profanities of their own, because what I said there sounded to them like naïve sound symbolism, meanings of words deriving from or somehow associated with the way the words sound, words like *fizz*, *slush*, and perhaps Lewis Carroll's *galumph*—instances of onomatopoeia—that actually sprang to life, etymologically, as imitations of one or another phenomenon's sound. I don't reject sound symbolic etymologies out of hand, even beyond the obviously onomatopoeic cases, and there is an interesting argument from sound symbolism later in this chapter. Sound symbolism can't explain everything about etymology and lexical meaning (indeed, it doesn't explain very much at all), but sound may have a profound role in pragmatic meaning.

Here, though, I'm not interested in sound symbolism. Rather, I'm trying to put words back into the mouth, as gestures with pragmatic meanings that go well beyond what the words in question are supposed to mean, meanings that correspond to the physical nature of the gestures without our generally being aware of the connection. We perform language gesturally, and if we don't acknowledge that,

then our notion of language and how it works becomes too idealized, too much a matter of the mind but not the body, though, of
course, neuroscience is posing all kinds of new problems for any distinction between the two. As Steven Pinker suggests in *The Stuff of
Thought* (2007)—in a section titled "The Blaspheming Brain," not
"The Blaspheming Mouth" or "The Blaspheming Hand"—"The
ubiquity and power of swearing suggest that taboo words may tap
into deep and ancient parts of the emotional brain." Pinker tries to
find profanity in the brain and it's surely there, but only because it
developed together with abilities, like throwing and speaking, that
responded to physical and social demands of early human environments—the prehistoric brains weren't in vats, and, except postmortem, the twenty-first-century ones aren't either. Whether you
follow traces of it in the brain or mouth, however, our use of profanity is atavistic, a very old part of ourselves we've kept a long time,
in spite of the social risks entailed in its use.

But back to the problem of why we prefer *Fuck!* and *Shit!* to
Puck! and *Shut!* as exclamations in times of great stress, because in
certain respects they aren't exceptional. As Pinker puts it, "angry
expletives are conventional. Like our other words and formulas,
they depend on a memorized pairing between a sound and a meaning
which is shared throughout a language community." *Lamp* doesn't
mean "lamp" because *lamp* sounds like it would mean "lamp"; *lamp*
means "lamp" because we've agreed that it does. Even though we
use expletives in some situations to avoid sounding conventional, to
defy social conventions like being polite or being subordinate, a
profanity is just as conventional as any other word. Not only do we
know what the expletives mean, we know that they don't all apply in
all situations. So, Pinker continues, "When we bump our heads, we
don't shout *Cunt!* or *Whore!* or *Prick!*, though these words are just as
taboo as *shit, fuck,* and *damn.*" As a speech community, over time, we

select which lexical and pragmatic meanings apply to each profanity. Similarly, we have to choose which among the profanities will work best when we need to exclaim or cry out.

Some profanities fit the bill especially well, and not just because of their sounds or the meanings we ascribe to them conventionally. Though I've argued against "taboo" as a currently relevant label for words like *fuck* and *shit*, they were once more taboo than they are today, and we still agree that they are risky words. There is no prohibition against using words like *puck* or *trap* to mean just what they do. They are everyday words doing their everyday business. Politeness usually isn't an issue with them, and they are very useful for the meanings they convey. When we use *fuck* or *crap*, on the other hand, we challenge standards of politeness because we conventionally associate such words with sex and excrement, the very reason they've been taboo, and why they are so often still risky to use. This is the point at which they might serve the prototype somewhere in the brain—the inherent human need to express profound emotion—that Moore identifies as underlying profanity. It's unclear whether the prototype responds to conventional or contextual meanings, but as exclamations or cries, *Fuck!* and *Crap!* and *Shit!* are bleached of their conventional meanings, which allows them to take on colorful pragmatic ones.

Because, obviously, when my lunch falls out of my bag into the ubiquitous puddle, and I cry *Fuck!* I'm not thinking about sex, I'm thinking about my lunch. The person who says *Go fuck yourself* clearly can't mean that in any literal way; it's as anatomically unlikely as when one says, in surprise, *Fuck me!* to oneself. When we say *don't shit where you eat*, we really mean shit; when someone asks us why we can't do something fun, we say it's because we have a lot of *shit* to do, and we don't mean excrement, but we mean something that draws on the excremental meaning. When we say, *Shit!* in surprise or for any other emotional reason, actual shit doesn't even come to mind. *Bitch* is a bad thing to call someone, and *son of a bitch* is arguably worse, in the way it further objectifies the target of the b-word. When we say to someone, *Stop bitching!* that's truly bad because using *bitch* (complain) is a slight against all women, *bitch* already having been turned against them. But when something takes us by surprise, and we say *Son of a bitch!* mothers and sons don't come to mind. We call these words profanity even in exclamatory contexts, but what made them profanity in the first place is no longer in the words, nor is it implied in their use.

We have difficulty making sense of this paradox. While I was at Albright College two decades ago, in Reading, Pennsylvania, I occasionally taught a course in the college's January term titled "Maledicta: Profanity and Other Bad Words." We had many students from private Roman Catholic schools in New Jersey and the Philadelphia area, and those students reported the same detention formula for profanity—*bitch* was a one-day detention word, but you were in the pokey for five days if authority overheard you use *fuck* or one of the hundreds of words derived from it. But surely, we thought at the time, the schools had it backwards. You were likely to use *bitch* at someone—as a verbal weapon, to cause harm—but exclamatory *fuck* was tossed into the air, no target in view but life itself. *Fuck* should have been the one-day word, while *bitch* probably deserved five days. It should be noted that detentions did not treat girls and boys equally, a morally and intellectually shabby story we'll pick up again in the next chapter.

None of this means that profanity exclaimed is meaningless. Sometimes, we can even identify synonyms for the profanity in question, for instance, *Go fuck yourself—rot in hell, have a lousy day, eat shit and die.* The synonyms could, I suppose, be fulfilled more literally than the original profanity, but really their lexical meanings dim and their pragmatic ones shine in use, too. Further, any synonym or definition will underestimate the exclamation's social meaning. *Go fuck yourself* doesn't just indicate a desired result, like rotting in hell. It also means things like 'I am more powerful than you and saying this to you proves it' and 'I do not respect you,' meanings just as important in the social context as any others. It's safe to say that these are the meanings people in the situation hear; if they have the spare time, they may also think about the potential lexical meanings and synonyms—but probably not. Pinker notes what he calls the "swappability" of profanity in this register—the specific terms aren't important, but only the pragmatic outcomes.

What allows us to use *fuck* and *shit* in this lexically bleached but colorfully pragmatic, exclamatory way? We could just all agree that *puck* should serve this function, as well as meaning 'disk you hit with sticks in hockey' and 'blackleg, a disease afflicting cattle' and 'mischievous spirit,' as in Shakespeare's character thus named. Most English words have more than one lexical meaning, and we often twist meaning to accomplish pragmatic goals. *Pit* could just as well substitute for *shit*. We prefer to use *fuck* and *shit*, though, for a few reasons, and those reasons cooperate: first, their sound structures, which depend on hurling or flinging gestures, make them eligible; second, we have no other legitimate use for them, because their more obviously profane uses are excluded from speech, or at least they were more so when they shifted into exclamatory uses; yet, third, as Pinker says, "Taboo status itself gives a word an emotional zing"; and fourth, because the riskiness of using what in other instances is lexically profane corresponds to the event causing our anger, anxiety, or frustration—extraordinary events call for extraordinary measures. We need ultimate exclamations, and profanity supplies them.

Infixing illustrates especially well how pragmatics overwhelms the supposed meaning content of profanity. Basic infixing is familiar to all Americans, even though we don't use it often, not nearly as much as other types of profanity. In infixing, at a stress-appropriate point in a base word (or matrix), like *absolutely*, we can insert an expletive infix (or insert, like a prefix or a suffix, but attached in the middle of a word), like *-fucking-*, thus yielding *absofuckinglutely*. As with exclamatory expletive, the *-fucking-* here has got no sex in it, and though there are cases of infixing with lexically meaningful inserts, they serve quite different pragmatic purposes from this classic variety. The infix provides an emphatic quality difficult to achieve by any other process of forming words or phrases, because of the gestural properties of the inserts.

Of course, what someone supposedly means by *absofuckinglutely* is 'really, seriously absolutely,' and eventually anyone who hears it will figure that out. But the emphasis, and the sense that an unusual word is answering an unusual situation, and the status claimed by a speaker who resorts to fancy profanity maneuvers—all the pragmatic meanings—are understood by hearers before the meaning of the matrix, because the sounds constituting *fuck* are processed by the brain much more quickly than word meanings—the whole pragmatic load has been interpreted before the word is completely articulated. Pinker expresses this result nicely: "Thanks to the automatic nature of speech perception, a taboo word kidnaps our attention." In infixing, this is all the more dramatic, because our attention is kidnapped mid-word.

Cries of pain or anguish or fear are so effective because there's no lexical semantic information to be processed for those hearing them, just pragmatic meaning conveyed by the sound itself. Thus, Goffman's point: we do not need to hear all sounds in a word's structure before we recognize the word and its meaning, but the infix overtakes the base and we register its meaning more rapidly than the base's meaning because it's expressive. Exclamatory *Fuck!* works in more or less the same way—expressive or affective meaning conveyed principally by the word's sound short-circuits any search within memory for lexical meanings, which, after all, wouldn't apply to the situation, anyway.

People who watch the CBS situation comedy *How I Met Your Mother* (2005–2014) are perhaps aware of the processing problem of infixing, but in reverse. It lies at the heart of Barney Stinson's infamous infixing, oft repeated during the series, that something will be *legen-wait for it-dary*. After a few episodes, you don't have to wait for it because it's become all too familiar—you are already processing *legen-wait for it-dary* when you hear "X will be." At first, though, you can be overwhelmed by all that's going on in that one little infixing. Barney likes attention, and the infixing is a means of getting some— he kidnaps our attention just as Pinker suggests profanity will but without the profanity. Saying that his newest scheme will be legendary won't capture nearly as much attention as saying it will be legen-wait for it-dary. The infixing is performative, in the sense that it enacts what it's describing. When Barney says *-wait for it-*, you are in fact waiting for *-dary* all the while. Because the insert is primarily lexically rather than emotionally meaningful, because it lacks every phonetic and semantic feature we've discussed as useful in profane exclamation, processing slows down and Barney achieves the opposite effect of classic infixing—that's the joke.

Barney wants us to wait for it, but he wants something more. He wants us to be invested in the legendariness of Barney, but aside from laughing at his quirk—both the attitude and its linguistics— we aren't as interested as he would like us to be. Barney is all talk. In contrast, the fundamentally pragmatic nature of exclamatory swearing is clear in our interest in other people's profane cries. Whenever profanity comes up in one of my courses, someone raises the issue of sympathetic response to it. We all know what it feels like to be angry enough to yell an expletive. Most of us know the catharsis that attends on actually uttering one. And we notice that when we hear and especially when we see and hear someone yell *Fuck!* or *Shit!* we feel something, a little shiver of emotional recognition—a sort of secondhand pain that momentarily draws us to the sufferer—as well as a more intellectual assessment of the provoking circumstance.

Exclamatory profanity may engage our mirror neurons. These specialized neurons are essential to human learning and what we call "theory of mind"—other people's minds, where we're pretty sure something is going on—because, as V. S. Ramachandran tells us in *The Tell-Tale Brain* (2011): "The main computation done by mirror neurons is to transform a map in one dimension, such as the visual appearance of someone else's movement, into another dimension, such as the motor maps in the observer's brain, which contain programs for muscle movements (including lip and tongue movements)," which may allow us speech and language in the first place. Once monkeys or humans have figured out how to gesture, with either hand or mouth, they have to come to an understanding of what those gestures mean, and because of mirror neurons, as Ramachandran puts it, when we watch another monkey, we are "for all intents and purposes reading the other monkey's mind, figuring out what it was up to." When we swear, certain neurons in our brain leap into action; when we witness someone else swearing, the same neurons light up.

None of this grasping of what others are up to when they exclaim profanity has to do with what *Fuck!* or *Shit!* means, but rather with what it means to say them in that way. The Epistle of James warns Christians to keep themselves "unspotted from the world," not be stained by it, and many think of profanity—when it's not outright blasphemy—as just such worldly stain. Wash away the world and be pure, we're told. Stop swearing. Oddly, though, when the

profanity isn't really profanity, when the word form—a shell historically full of sex and excrement and disease—is emptied of its former
semantic content and left to pragmatic uses, we can hear the sea of
human feeling ebb and flow when we hold the shell to our ear, and
what was uttered in anger or frustration invites sympathy and understanding and fellow-feeling, all of them good things. Profanity is
more paradox than verbal pestilence.

In cases such as those considered here—exclamatory uses of
fuck, shit, son of a bitch, the meanings of which are affective and pragmatic—what we call profanity is not really profanity. We are stuck
on word form rather than word meaning or pragmatic function. If it
quacks like a *fuck* and waddles like a *fuck,* we think, it's a *fuck,* and, of
course, it is, but not the *fuck* many of us think we're talking about.
This paradox isn't new and hasn't gone unnoticed, because when
courts and executive agencies like the Federal Communications
Commission proscribe "indecent" speech, they have to have some
rational basis for doing so. Some jurists insist that exclamatory expletives can't escape an underlying indecency on account of the sex
or bodily waste associated with the terms originally, though that's
not the same as saying that originally such words were always seen
as indecent or profane.

Prompted by the decision in *Federal Communications Commission
v. Fox Television Stations, Inc.* (2009), W. Wat Hopkins has proposed
an "Emotive Speech Doctrine" that would protect "fleeting profanity" bleached of its objectionable content and used on the pragmatic terms illustrated here. The FCC need not punish Bono for
saying that receiving a Golden Globe was "really, really fucking bril-
liant." The doctrine is rooted in a decision written by Justice Harlan
in *Cohen v. California* (1971), in which he noted the difference between "cognitive" and "emotive" aspects of speech—corresponding
to our distinction between lexical and pragmatic meaning—and

supported protection of the latter as well as the former. Bono wasn't just happy to receive the award, he was excited, he was more than happy, and that "more" is not conveyed in an FCC-approved sentence like "I am more than happy to receive this award." Some Supreme Court justices have grasped the significance of the distinction and some have not, a disagreement Hopkins hopes to resolve.

Justice Harlan refused to accept the *fuck* of *Fuck the Draft*— which was written across the back of Paul Robert Cohen's jacket, the speech that caused *Cohen v. California*—as obscene, because it wasn't erotic: "It cannot plausibly be maintained," Harlan wrote, "that this vulgar allusion to the Selective Service System would conjure up…psychic stimulation in anyone likely to be confronted with Cohen's crudely defaced jacket." In other words, despite the fact that *fuck* often carries sexual meanings, in this case, it doesn't, so it hasn't violated any laws. Later, in a dissenting opinion in *FCC v. Pacifica Foundation* (1978)—the case about the broadcast of George Carlin's famous monologue "Filthy Words"—Justice William Brennan would remark that what seemed taboo to the FCC and the Supreme Court might be "the stuff of everyday conversation in some, if not many of the innumerable subcultures that compose this Nation," a point Justice Ruth Bader Ginsburg reiterated in her dissent in *FCC v. Fox Television Stations, Inc.* Indeed, in 2016, we might agree that it's the stuff of everyday conversation in mainstream American culture. Unless you want to dismiss all of those speakers as vulgar, you might have to consider the profanity devulgarized, at least to some extent, at least in some situations. You might have to consider that sometimes a profanity is not a profanity, however much it looks or sounds like one.

The FCC, some Supreme Court justices, and, frankly, a lot of us, are convinced that *fuck* can't lose its sexual meaning and that shit sticks to *shit* however hard history and pragmatics try to shake it off. In its order following Bono's on-air expletive, the FCC insisted that "given the core meaning of the 'F-word'... its use invariably invokes a coarse sexual image," which is false on both sexual and linguistic terms, or at least depends on the FCC deciding what images are "coarse." Justice Antonin Scalia's subsequent opinion in the case supported the FCC's claim and quoted more than once its assertion that *fuck* is "one of the most vulgar, graphic, and explicit words for sexual activity in the English language," which nobody denies is true enough in some contexts, but which is not thereby true in all of them. Hopkins concludes that "[t]herein lies the conundrum—the word is always sexual, even when it is not, which may explain the inconsistent and schizophrenic way it is treated in society and in the law." Undoubtedly, it does, but I don't agree that *fuck* is always sexual—I think the supposed paradox is resolved by clear linguistic thinking. Reconsidering it might lead to good results in law, our attitudes toward language, and the ways in which we understand and value one another.

PROFANITY AND THE END OF LANGUAGE

HBO's series *The Wire* aired from June 2, 2002, until March 9, 2008—just sixty episodes, which, regardless of universal admiration for the show, might have been all its viewers could take, because in spite of its art and the humor that occasionally relieves the show's depressing tension, *The Wire* is hard to watch. Drake Bennet, in *Slate* (March 24, 2010), recalls the series' "grim subject matter" and its "fatalistic worldview," how "the show was meant to be a Greek tragedy but with institutions like the police department or the school system taking the place of the gods: the immortal forces that toy with and blithely destroy the mortals below." Unlike *The Sopranos*, for instance, in which profanity marks moral agency and there is no tragedy, because the characters more or less get what they deserve,

The Wire is metaphysical and proposes that the world is beyond human influence. Its use of profanity corresponds to that dramatic purpose.

A scene in "Old Cases" (Season 1, episode 4) is particularly memorable for its profanity because, throughout its three minutes and thirty-two seconds, *fuck* or words based on *fuck*—*fucking, fuckity-fuck-fuck-fuck, motherfuck, motherfucker, fuckin'-A*—are essentially the only words spoken. There are thirty-eight of them, and that's a lot of *fuck*ing. In the scene, detectives Jimmy McNulty and Bunk Moreland re-investigate a murder that might be connected to characters central to the current story. On entering the crime scene, they look at gruesome postmortem pictures, and there's little else to say but *fuck*. On the surface, other *fucks* and *fuck*-derived words do their usual business. When McNulty gets snapped by a retracting tape measure, he says *fuck*, as many of us would—nothing could be more ordinary. When they succeed where the previous investigation had failed, *fuckin'-A* seems a normal expletive way of registering that success. There are wry *fucks* and surprised *fucks*, but they all sound normal within the apartment where they're uttered.

Our experience of these *fucks* is ironic, however—we're outside the apartment listening in, aware of the relationship between the scene inside the apartment and the world of *The Wire*, as well as the relationship of the *Wire* world to our own. That ironic distance gives significance to profanity in the scene different from what it means to the characters and also unavailable to them—they are not Cassandra, the Trojan princess who was doomed to know the future and tell about it in prophecy that no one else would believe, and who figures profoundly in Aeschylus's tragedy, *Agamemnon*. Instead, McNulty and Bunk are among those with whom the immortal forces toy, and so often in *The Wire*, we sense impending destruction. The *fucks* in "Old Cases" are part of that story, but they are part of a larger story, as well, one that includes us, one perhaps just as grim.

Reliance not only on profanity but only on profanity in "Old Cases" is interesting partly because, in police procedurals, detectives always seem to have something to say. They look at disfigured or rotten corpses, blood on the walls, vomit, shit and urine, industrious bugs enjoying their postmortem feast; but with mortality splayed on the floor, they still have something to say, whether it's the firm-jawed, steely eyed investigator evaluating the scene in dispassionate jargon—"Could I have a grid please? C-6 enlarge please. Zoom times four and hold. Zoom eight times and hold"—or Lenny Briscoe cracking wise on *Law & Order*. Television detectives expertly deflect intimations of mortality; they do so in order to get the job done. It's very professional and also strangely inhumane. Superficially realists, these detectives don't deal with certain realities.

McNulty and Bunk are unusual because, faced with the tragic scenario of *The Wire*, they struggle to acknowledge it, respond to it, resist it. When things are so grim, not just at this crime scene but at every crime scene, in every scene of life, ordinary words fail even the most seasoned detectives. It's not that McNulty and Bunk don't know more words—there just isn't anything else to say but *fuck*, or *Aw, fuck*, or *motherfuck*, nothing that's apt to the purpose. Rather than ignore or deflect mortality and the fragility of life, and all of that, they confront it with expletive, which, it turns out, is sufficient, even eloquent. They are on the edge of experience, but they keep it real. They swear without regard for us, but the profanity is meant for us nonetheless—it proves the very limits of language.

Usually, when we are dissatisfied with our language, we make something up. We make up a word to fill a lexical gap, or perhaps we invent some slangy way of saying something, an ephemeral fix for the sake of style. If we just can't live in this world with its languages, we can construct a language—Esperanto, Quenya, Dothraki—and a world in which to speak it, or, at least, we can hope for such a world. But at the limits of language, it doesn't matter how many words English or any other language has or what we could create—there, we would be inarticulate were it not for expletive profanity. We sort through millions of words for those that express our ultimate frustration, and none but the profane ones meet our needs. We don't speak so much, then, as gesture. We gesture with our lips and teeth and tongue and palate and velum in various combinations, and we push air past them, as hard as we can. We have a physical rather than verbal reaction, or, at least, our verbal reaction is more physical than lexical, though just as meaningful.

Although expletive *fuck* is bleached of lexical meaning, its etymology weirdly bears on its pragmatic meaning. As far as we can tell, *fuck* entered English sometime in the fifteenth century, and we have it in a text, though in code, roughly by 1475. The word was in print by 1508, in poems by William Dunbar. Richard Coates has discovered late fourteenth-century evidence of a Bristol place name, *Fockynggroue*, but the *OED* is skeptical. Before 1475, then, *fuck* may have had no history. Of course, there was a word of questionable repute for sexual intercourse—plenty of sex was had in medieval England, so there was bound to be a word for it, but that word was *swive*, not *fuck*. *Swive* struggled against *fuck* in the sixteenth century but eventually became obsolete, at least, in straightforward use. In the nineteenth century, it was archaic enough that it could serve as a euphemism for *fuck*, and Melissa Mohr claims that "it is undergoing something of an ironic revival today...as a jocular alternative to the f-word."

English got *fuck*ed in one of three ways. One of line of argument supposes that *fuck* developed from Latin. Eric Partridge suggests that it derives from the Latin verb *pungere* 'prick'; more recently, Jonathon Green favors *pugnare* 'strike'; but the derivation is not really plausible, which doesn't mean, by the way, that the Latin and English words are unrelated. The second line proposes a Proto-Indo-European

(PIE) ancestor—the *OED* accepts this possibility—perhaps the root **peuk-* 'prick', which eventually leads to Latin *pugnare*. In other words, *fuck* isn't *pugnare*'s grandchild, but it may be its distant cousin, both having descended from **peuk-*. Calvert Watkins, the late dean of American Indo-Europeanists, who contributed an appendix of PIE roots for the *American Heritage Dictionary of the English Language*, made the **peuk-/fuck* connection in the fifth edition (2011), after resisting it for decades. Anatoly Liberman represents the third line of argument, insisting that *fuck* and related words in other languages are purely Germanic in origin, unconnected to Romance or other Indo-European languages except when they borrow the Germanic words.

What's uncanny is that none of this linguistic lineage makes much difference to the original and early meanings of *fuck*, its closest relatives, or its distant cousins. They mean 'rub' or 'move back and forth' and 'flog, beat, strike,' whether they're Latin *pugnare*, German *ficken*, Dutch *fikken*, or German *fickfacken*, which Liberman defines as "run aimlessly back and forth; have a lot to do; scheme behind one's back, deceive, cheat; potter about; flog"; indeed, Liberman observes, "Noneuphemistic verbs denoting sexual intercourse, to the extent that they can be etymologized, usually mean 'thrust,' 'strike,' 'pierce,' 'prick,' rub.'" The point here is not that when I am at my wit's end and say *Fuck!* I mean 'beat' or 'strike,' but rather that striking and beating are what I'm doing with my mouth in order to exclaim it. The etymology describes the gesture I'm making, not its meaning.

Of course, *swive* is a gesture, too, but it's the wrong sort of gesture with which to confront the end of language. There is no exclamatory potential in *swive*, which is all sibilant and velvety *v* sounding. You cannot stand in the pouring rain, your open briefcase spilling classified documents into a puddle, suddenly shit on by a bird, and yell, "Swive!" with any satisfaction. By way of contrast, *fuck* is admirably expletive and well up to the task of expressing one's existential frustration. It beats against the barrier at the outer limits of language; it beats and beats, and crushes and smashes with the rage of something not fitting—with bruised and bloody hands, so to speak. Where expletive is all that works—the only means of expressing an overwhelming intensity of feeling—that rage is all the greater because one has found the end of language and can go no further. Profanity is no parochial gesture, then. It strikes a complaint against the human condition.

THE PARADOX OF EUPHEMISM

The title of Wat Hopkins's article discussed in the last section is "When Does F*** Not Mean F***?: *FCC v Fox Television Stations* and a Call for Protecting Emotive Speech." Those asterisks aren't fooling anybody, and there is no way for a reader who knows the word *fuck* not to interpret the euphemism as a profanity on the spot. Early in the article, Hopkins explains his recourse to *f-word* rather than *fuck* in a footnote: "The Author struggled with how to use the offending language in this Article, and ultimately decided to use the toned-down descriptor except in direct quotations or where the use of the full word contributes to a greater understanding of the issue or issues being discussed." Hopkins faces this dilemma because he is writing about profanity/obscenity in a legal context—he can't just ignore the words in question. Apparently, he assumes about his audience what Justice Brennan noticed in his colleagues on the Supreme Court, "a depressing inability to appreciate that in our land of cultural pluralism, there are many who think, act, and talk differently from the Members of this Court, and who do not share their fragile sensibilities." I suppose one can agree with Justice Brennan about people talking differently but still suffer from fragile sensibilities, and Hopkins registers this possibility by employing euphemisms in a discourse—a law journal's—that could survive profanity, even if those participating in it preferred more supposedly polite speech.

In other contexts, however, why use euphemisms at all? If the point is to avoid profanity, but the euphemism fills what speakers recognize as profanity space, profanity is still in the air. Why not speak in sentences without space for profanities or their substitutes? Just say things differently. Ruth Wanjryb, the title of whose book *CU Next Tuesday* (2004) is itself a very clever euphemism, observes of euphemisms that "they are all ways by which swearers manage to have their swearing cake and also eat it. Or break the taboo, but get away with it." She doesn't pursue this smart position, but it bears pursuing, which is what I propose to do here. We could say something bold about it, like, "There's no such thing as euphemism," but it would be more accurate instead to insist that euphemisms for profanities don't always work—at least, they don't work the way most people think they should, but are *both* euphemism *and* profanity.

TRUE EUPHEMISMS

Of course there are euphemisms. The question here is whether euphemism works well in response to profanity. If Aunt Helen dies, and you don't want to say *she's dead*, you can say instead that *she kicked the bucket*, or *passed away*, or *went to campground*, which are all euphemisms for 'is dead.' Even this short list suggests what Keith Allan and Kate Burridge prove exhaustively in *Euphemism & Dysphemism*, that euphemism is an intricate semantic web—you can have dysphemistic euphemisms, for instance, such as *kicked the bucket,* better than *died* or *dead* if you or your audience wish to deny the inevitable, but probably not the full-on euphemism Aunt Helen would like to hear about herself. Profanity is always and only dysphemism—or, as we just realized, maybe not. Dysphemistic euphemisms are a bit like tall short people and a reminder that adjectives like *short* and *dysphemistic* suffer from sorites paradox syndrome. *Profane* was diagnosed with the syndrome in Chapter 1, and determining what's euphemistic similarly depends on context. The most profane euphemism and the most euphemistic profanity may in fact be the same thing.

Some euphemisms for profane terms have been around a while—recorded, say, in the seventeenth century—and some are nineteenth-century innovations. Originally, the critical terms weren't *fuck* or *shit* or *prick*—though these weren't far behind—but names of the Christian God, *Jesus* and *Christ* and *Jesus Christ. Criminy* (1681) is an early euphemism for *Christ,* but synonyms closely related to it structurally, *cripes* (1820) and *crikey* (1832)—importantly, the first syllable of *criminy* shares the *i* of those words—are fairly recent additions to English vocabulary. *Gee* as a euphemism for *Jesus* must be old—it's so obvious!—but in fact it's newish, first recorded in 1851. Originally, these euphemisms may not have been very effective, because you could hear the swearer start to say *Christ!* get as far as *Chri-,* and then shift to sounds that supposedly made nonsense of the word.

To camouflage profane terms, euphemisms usually depend on what I call "distractors," and the relative success of one or another euphemism may depend on the strength of distraction. For instance, *cripes* is a less effective euphemism for *Christ* than either *crikey* or *criminy,* because it's a one syllable replacement for a one-syllable word—the extra syllables in *crikey* and *criminy* are mild distractors. *Cripes!* is a perfectly good exclamation, but it's not such a good euphemism, because it's easier to recognize *Christ!* beneath the camouflage. Similarly, *gee!* and *geez/jeez!* as shortened forms of *Jesus!* are less euphemistic than *jeezle peezle!* or forms that Lise Winer recorded in her *Dictionary of the English/Creole of Trinidad & Tobago* (2009): *jeezan ages! jeezan peas!*, and *jeezan rice!* or *Geez, Louise.* My own preferred form on this pattern, *geez-o-peez!* is unrecorded in any dictionary I've consulted, but I've used it regularly throughout my life, so I know it exists. *Peezle, -o-peez,* and *-an peas,* are all effective distractors—when you use them, you sound less like you're taking the Lord's name in vain. You could say **Jesus Pesus!* I suppose, but it wouldn't camouflage the profanity at all, because, far from being a distractor, *Pesus* reminds us of the oath *Jesus* and doubles down on the profanity.

Modern speakers of English have come up with all kinds of distractors. Not all of them work especially well. *Jesus!* you cry, and your stern Presbyterian grandmother, unexpectedly and unfortunately in hearing, stares you down. "Jesus what?" she asks. *Jesus wept!* is the best you can do, but the distractor doesn't camouflage *Jesus,* so you're likely to feel the hickory switch despite your best effort. Similarly, *bejesus* is not particular effective as a euphemism—again, that's not a criticism of it as a word, it's a favorite word of mine, but if profanity were a loaded weapon, it's not the camouflage you'd choose to wear. *Bejesus* started out as a euphemism for *by Jesus*—just a routine oath—according to *Green's Dictionary of Slang,* and it served as "a general intensifier, esp. with implications of assurance, arrogance," which I never knew, but which is perfectly consistent with the way I've always used the word, conventionally in the phrase *scared the bejesus out of me*—next time I'll be a bit less arrogant or assured.

Some distractors have proven very effective, and most people whose euphemisms incorporate them don't even realize they're euphemizing. *Gee whillikers* and *gee whillikins* are good examples, as are related forms like *gee whittaker* and *gee whittikins*. One moment you're blaspheming, but the next you seem to be talking about some guy named G. *Whittaker*; *-kin* is a cute diminutive suffix, familiar from *lambkin* and *munchkin*, and *whittikins* seems made of whiskers and kittens—*Aw, little kittikins!*—and the *Jesus* present at the alpha of these words isn't at the pragmatic omega. A form apparently restricted to New York City, *jeeswax*—probably from *jeez* + bee(s)*wax*— is likewise hard to identify with the hero of the Gospels. *Jiminy!* (1686) is an old euphemism for *Jesus*, but why risk any association of the former with the latter? By 1845, someone had added yet another distractor to *Jiminy!*, and people began to say *Jiminy Cricket!* instead, the strategy for which is a little dangerous—as with *Jeepers Creepers!*— because the phrase's initials are the same as *Jesus Christ*. In a sense, these are the very best sort of euphemism, because they pull closer to the original profanity even as they distract us from recognizing it. Obviously, when the phrase *Jiminy Cricket* became a name in Walt Disney's *Pinocchio* (1940), the personification—not to mention Disneyfication—fully camouflaged its blasphemous origins.

There's no reason to think that any of these euphemisms is easily come by. It takes some experiment to make over a euphemism with potential into one that withstands suspicion. *Jeepers Creepers!* was preceded by *Jeepers Cripus!*, first recorded in W. D. Edmonds's novel about love on the Erie Canal, *Rome Haul* (1929). Drawing on *Cripes!*, it was too close to *Christ* for comfort. Colin MacInness tried out *Jeepers-Deepers!* in the second novel of his London Trilogy, *Absolute Beginners* (1959), which might seem a strong euphemism just because—with the *d* in *Deepers*—it moves away from the ideal structure of an exclamatory expletive. For some reason, however, perhaps because *creep*'s meaning is so striking that it distracts us further—*Jeepers Creepers!* finally emerged in 1959. Quite a few other candidates for euphemism have been tested and retired in favor of more robust forms.

Most people who speak or hear *Gee whiz!* or *Golly!*—from *by Goll!* with *Goll* a phonetic prevarication on *God*—don't hear them as euphemisms, because they can't "see" the underlying profanity. Euphemisms like these effectively camouflage their expletives. We probably also assume that—as with so many words—a long time passed and what was obviously euphemistic back in the old days isn't anymore. Who knew that *derrick* was originally the surname of an executioner who invented a gallows with a long arm useful for hanging lots of criminals at once—no one on a twenty-first-century construction site. How would modern speakers of English know that *Golly* is a euphemistic substitute for *God*? Sure, they could look it up in a dictionary, but why would they think to look?

Another factor helps to detach these more or less successful euphemisms from their original blasphemy. Kids started to use them, and they became natural to youth-speak, and before long we began to associate them with wide-eyed Andy Hardy innocence—*Aw, gee whiz, Dad!*—rather than the pool halls in River City. The rise of the cool factor in youth culture and the ways in which youth mark cool has profoundly influenced language attitudes. Some curmudgeons still complain about slang, but most curmudgeons alive today grew up as culturally powerful teenagers, and slang doesn't seem so bad to them, even if they're no longer hip to what the kids are saying. Arguably, because youth, having got beyond their grandparents' *Gee whiz!* and *Golly!*—they're young, no mere reiteration—adopted profanity as a mark of coolness, profanity is less vulgar than it used to be—taboo but not taboo. We haven't forgotten that profanity is profanity, but we have forgotten, since it evades taboo, that certain euphemisms are—or perhaps we should say "were"—euphemisms.

If these *Jesus, Christ, Jesus Christ,* and *God* derived words still really are euphemisms, instead of just value-free interjections, then in a narrow sense they are nonetheless also profanity, as Allan and

Burridge noted in exactly the case of *Jeepers Creepers!* When it comes to profanity that takes God's names in vain, euphemism is no better than a fig leaf covering up our once and always fall from grace. God's not listening to what you say, he knows what's on your mind, and you can't distract him with an *-eezle* or by calling Christ an insect, and never mind the top hat and tails, because Jesus wasn't fancy like that. Wish upon a star if you like—dream on.

Of course, if people today use *gosh* and *golly* without knowing they once were euphemisms for blasphemies and without intending them to cover blasphemies currently, they may not invite the wrath of God, but neither, one suspects, will the high school girl who cries "Shit!" when everything falls out of her locker burn eternally in Hell. You might think we were using euphemisms, not so much to please God as to please our neighbors, that our motives aren't theological but social. This doesn't mean they aren't ethical, or that there's no reason to resist using profanity in some social settings, but it's also to say, once we're no longer insulting God in any of God's persons, the terms on which we swear and hedge swearing with euphemism are negotiable, and negotiate them we do, in each and every context.

EUPHEMISM AND POLITENESS

We are obsessed with politeness, not just because we want to be polite—very often we do, much to our surprise—but because we want to pursue our own ends by manipulating politeness rules. Penelope Brown and Stephen C. Levinson lay these rules out in a cross-cultural mosaic in their foundational book, *Politeness: Some Universals in Language* (1987). Brown and Levinson develop their elaborate theory from some basic concepts introduced by Erving

Goffman, who argued in "On Face-Work" (1955) that we have two faces, positive and negative, that we are always trying to save. We want our positive faces—the more or less consistent personality we perform in a social relationship—to be admired by others; our negative faces reflect our desires to preserve and protect our "space" and to achieve our social goals unimpeded by others. We register our social disapproval in what Brown and Levinson call face-threatening acts—FTAs. If I call you out as *Bitch!* or *Prick!* I'm probably not admiring you any more than if I tell you to *Fuck off!* If I'm the president of the Senate and I tell you, a senator, to *Go fuck yourself* in the hearing of others, I'm not only busy not admiring you, I'm undermining your leadership, challenging your negative as well as your positive face.

If Brown and Levinson are right, we can't escape politeness, because it's essential to language use. From another point of view, it's justified on ethical terms. Our current philosopher of manners, Karen Stohr, begins her book *On Manners* (2012) with a couple of plausible propositions: sure, manners are social conventions, but "[s]ocial conventions help us communicate and act upon shared moral aims," and "good manners go hand in hand with good moral character." We may disagree about the meanings of profane words, about their propriety and their effects once they're let loose in the world, but we might agree not to use them in many settings because doing so is good manners, and manners are an expression of moral aims. We all want to be moral, even if we also want the greatest possible freedom of expression. Euphemism is a politeness strategy, a way of respecting other's faces while promoting our own interests, not just saving but preferring our own faces while negotiating the social maze.

As with most philosophical inquiry, we need to distinguish among terms that, though often used interchangeably, are importantly different, in our case *manners, politeness,* and *etiquette.* Stohr helpfully quotes Judith Martin, who for a long time wrote a syndicated newspaper column as "Miss Manners," on this point:

> Miss Manners uses the word "manners" to refer to the principles underlying any system of etiquette, and "etiquette" to refer to the particular rules used to express these principles.... Because etiquette rules are fashioned to pertain to a particular time and social setting, they are subject to development and change. However, the principles of manners from which they derive their authority remain constant and universal. Even directly contradictory rules of etiquette prevailing in different societies at the same time or at different times in the same society, may derive their authority from the same principle of manners.

Brown and Levinson articulate all of those contradictory rules, but Martin captures the insight sufficiently without laboring the details. *Politeness* is the linguistic term for the philosopher's moralized *manners*, while *etiquette* is the mere and perhaps not very reliable expression of politeness or manners. Much more is at stake in manners and politeness than in etiquette, though when confronted with a dozen forks at a fancy dinner, etiquette may seem, for the moment, a life-and-death matter.

Sometimes those inclined to proscribe profanity are more concerned with etiquette than with manners. I don't feel it a breach in manners when a truly frustrated person says "Shit!" Indeed, I may recognize the frustration, sympathize with the person, and experience relief when I hear the profanity. The frustrated person and I share moral aims and I have to make some room for the expression of authentic feeling. If someone I don't respect comments negatively on my appearance, and I respond, "Fuck you, shit-for-brains," I've committed an FTA, but tit for tat—your positive face is no more important than mine. If I object to the frustrated person crying "Shit!" however, I am also committing an FTA, interfering with a negative face that just wants to go about the business of expressing frustration—to no one in particular—unimpeded.

Still, saying "Shit!" may violate a social convention and even if it doesn't, even if conventions are changing and different auditors gauge the authority of conventions differently, exclamatory profanity nonetheless rubs some "fragile sensibilities" the wrong way. What if your negative face merely wants peace and quiet, or to be spiritually undisturbed? Is someone else's frustration—when expletively expressed—an imposition on those who unexpectedly witness it? And should we avoid profanity in order to save others' faces rather than threaten them? These are all reasonable questions, especially if one is cautious about answering them absolutely, because the rules are complex and flexible. As Stohr points out, you ask people to pass the salt, please; you don't say, in a face-threatening way, "Pass the salt, you idiot." But what obviously applies in one social situation doesn't necessarily apply in another—pragmatics matter. For, as Stohr argues, "I can say, 'Pass the salt, you idiot' to my brother without necessarily being rude if I am doing so affectionately and my brother understands 'you idiot' to be a term of endearment rather than an insult." In some situations, *bitch* isn't face threatening—it's hard to imagine when *cunt* isn't—and *Fuck you* can be endearing, an expression of intimacy or solidarity, rather than a challenge, said to the right person, for the right reason, in the right tone.

Can't we all just get along? Surely, we can negotiate our way through our myriad, often competitive needs and desires. Surely, we can find room for strong expression but in less obtrusive forms of speech. Perhaps the very frustrated person could say—as some people do—"Sugar!" instead of "Shit!" Everyone sidesteps a steaming heap of scatology, and no one need take offense. Euphemism compromises strong expression but insists that speakers can say some version of what they want to say. You can avoid saying, "So, your grandmother's dead" by saying "So, your grandmother kicked the bucket," though a dysphemistic euphemism like that is likely to threaten a lot of faces, not least grandmother's posthumous one. But "So, your grandmother's gone to a better place" gets the death idea across while giving it a positive spin and threatening no face at all. *Sugar!* isn't *Shit!* in expletive force, but it's at least some sort of release—it expresses frustration as well, some would argue, as politeness allows.

Who can argue against being polite? We interpret politeness as private virtue in the public interest. In general, we follow the principle Edwin L. Battistella advances in his elegant book, *Bad Language* (2005): "Avoiding coarse language in public signals an understanding of the boundary between public and private discourse and a tacit acceptance of that boundary." But politeness can be put to complex and, if not malignant, certainly not benign social purposes—power takes advantage of our "tacit acceptance." The linguistic category politeness may be universal, but profanity isn't universally or historically framed as impolite. The question arises under certain conditions, as Tony McEnery argues in *Swearing in English: Bad Language, Purity, and Power from 1586 to the Present* (2006), and he lays them out as follows:

> [M]odern attitudes to bad language were established by the moral reform movements of the late seventeenth and early eighteenth centuries ... [and] were established to form a discourse of power for the growing middle classes in Britain[, and] ... the moral and political framework supported by a discourse of power can be threatened by the subversion of that discourse.

Thus, the motive for euphemism may be a matter of manners, but manners may be a means of social subordination, and language policy deriving from manners may end up serving the interests of the few rather than those of the mass of speakers.

McEnery derives his account from Pierre Bourdieu's *Language and Symbolic Power* (1991), which is especially interested in euphemism, because

> [d]iscourses are always to some extent *euphemisms* inspired by the concern to 'speak well,' to 'speak properly,' to produce the products that respond to the demands of a certain market; they are *compromise formations* resulting from a transaction between the expressive interest (what is to be said) and the censorship inherent in particular relations of linguistic production (whether it is the structure of linguistic interaction or the structure of a specialized field), a censorship which is imposed on a speaker or writer endowed with a certain social competence, that is, a more or less symbolic power over these relations of symbolic power.

In the end, whether it's a matter of deliberate language policy or just the sort of self-censorship we administer when we understand the limits and know we're going too far, language use conforms to parameters imposed by power. So, Bourdieu says,

> symbolic power does not reside in 'symbolic systems' but...is defined in and through a given relation between those who exercise power and those who submit to it.... What creates the power of words and slogans, a power capable of maintaining or subverting the social order, is the belief in the legitimacy of words and of those who utter them. And words alone cannot create this belief.

In other words, the "problem" isn't profanity or euphemism, but the interests outside and beyond them that govern value in social markets.

When we swear, we create and enact power, which is, indeed, related to extralinguistic power, and that power—the nonlinguistic kind—certainly shapes language use but it also simultaneously depends on it. The notion that the power of words and slogans either maintains or subverts the social order doesn't account for the complexities of profanity. When the vice president uses profanity to construct his relationship to a senior senator, is he maintaining or subverting the social order? Both, it seems to me, and would he have said what he said if saying it had been irrelevant to his extralinguistic power? Isn't saying it a proof of that power, but also a sign of weakness, in the sense that the power needs proof? In profanity, as well as in euphemism, linguistic and extralinguistic power interact, and the point of profanity might well be to draw our attention to interaction we overlook in commonplace discourse.

It's easier to see Charlo Greene's on-air expletive as subversive, as constructing power in response to that of the Man and, in order to do so, challenging politeness—what marijuana activists would see as bad manners in a good cause. But it's harder to see how a frustrated exclamatory expletive either maintains or subverts the social order, except insofar as it reiterates the loosening grip of taboo. Euphemism meant to control profanity in public discourse is also complicated. We may want to speak well or properly, as Bourdieu insists, and euphemism may help us to do that, but it also helps us— at least in some situations—subvert social order at the same time as we maintain it, or maybe we maintain social order while we subvert it. Politeness, after all, is often double-edged—ask any woman from the American South, bless her heart. Euphemism sometimes allows us to swear while being polite, or at least polite enough. As we considered in Chapter 1, the terms *profanity* and *obscenity* are flexible enough that we can sometimes negotiate relative politeness within them, without even resorting to euphemism.

EUPHEMISM AS PALIMPSEST

Allen Walker Read noticed that some mid-twentieth-century speakers of English—mostly Americans, if Read's evidence is representative—were hiding behind what he called "A Type of Ostentatious Taboo" (1964). Rather than announce a topic they shouldn't talk about, they would point to it cryptically, with *you know who* or *you know where* or *you know what*: "You know who did you know what to the guy and then dumped the body you know where." That's how you talk if you don't want to get whacked yourself. Read's examples—and as usual with Read, there are lots of them—are much less dramatic. Read calls these prevarications "ostentatious" because even though they're meant to deflect specific meanings, they draw attention to themselves. The best euphemisms—like *jeezle peezle* and *gee whillikers*—won't draw attention; instead, they distract us from the underlying profanity. People who take a second look at them realize that euphemisms for profanity are, in fact, odd words and out of place—seriously, *jeezle peezle*? Newly aware, these onlookers can just make out the profane figure underneath the camouflage.

We can also, more colloquially, define *ostentatious* as 'over the top,' and we can think of euphemisms for profanity as written over the profanity, so that the relationship between the euphemism and the profanity is like a palimpsest, parchment from which earlier writing has been scraped so that later writing can take its place. If you inspect the manuscript, though, whether with the eye or under ultra-violet light, you can still see the older text. You can see it because it's still there—faint, partially legible, perhaps, but present in spite of its apparent absence. Legibility varies from word to word and depends on the situation, too. In *Jesus H. Christ*, the profanity hasn't been scraped so much as embellished, and the profanity underlying *gee whillikers* is well and truly scraped away, though you can reconstruct it from vague lines and curves with the help of a good dictionary. In the Rankin-Bass Claymation version of *Rudolph the Red-Nosed Reindeer* (1964), Rudolph's father, Donner, can't believe his eyes when his son's nose lights up: "His beak is blinkin' like a blinkin' beacon." The literal sense of *blinking* covers the euphemism and the euphemism covers the profanity, alliteration and repetition distract us for a while, but the profanity is still there.

One modern euphemistic strategy has preferred forms like *F****—illustrated in the title to Hopkins's article—*c**t, b*—, *m*****f******, and the like. We tend to think of such forms as having replaced letters with asterisks or em dashes, but the forms are immediately recognizable as the profanities they've supposedly replaced, and it's thus more accurate to say that the asterisks are written over the letters that confirm profanity. I can't explain how my brain works through the problem—I'll have to leave that to the neurophysiologists, and I may eventually discover I'm wrong—but when I look at *b*— and see it for the covert profanity it is, I don't insert the supposedly missing letters, but rather peel away the euphemistic overlay, or maybe it's more precise to say that I see through it to the underlying word, which suggests that to all intents and purposes the profanity is there all along.

If this sort of euphemism is polite, it's because we pretend it's polite. If our shared moral aim is to respect one another, and if profanity is disrespectful and thus bad manners, it's hard to imagine how *c**t* is better than *cunt* unless we just agree that it is—without such prevarication, *c**t* is just as subversive of the social order. Indeed, it could be more subversive, because it's self-revealing: it's subversive because though it's a euphemism it's still a profanity; it's further subversive because its euphemism is a pretense—we're not just guilty of obscenity but of lying about or, at least, misrepresenting whether we're using it. Could it be that, though intended to be good manners, euphemism of profanity—at least, this kind of euphemism—is morally more corrupt than the profanity itself? Anyway, as Read saw it, it's distasteful: "I do not favor the use of the 'euphemistic dash'; it succeeds only in throwing a smutty atmosphere over a subject." Asterisks are just as bad. "The proper course is to print a word in full or not at all."

Or, is much euphemism morally acceptable because, since we can see through it, it's not really a lie? The failure of such euphemisms is too obvious, even—or perhaps especially—when they're clever. Asked the entertainment site TMZ, "Amy Smart vs. Ali Larter: Who'd You Rather?"—you know what—one commenter— I call him the Sofa King—wrote, "I would sofa king do both of them, they are both sofa king hot and sexy." Syllable stress is unexpectedly the distractor, but it confuses us only temporarily, because we can't figure out what sofas and kings have to—oh, I get it.

Let's examine some other ways in which euphemism fails because profanity is still written in it. For instance, some euphemisms for the F-word don't try very hard. The Irish came up with *feck*, the Australians with *fark*, and the future—as described in *Battlestar Gallactica*—*frak*. The FCC allowed *frak* to occur in network television, which suggests that it's not profanity, but the vestige of profanity is undeniable. Is it really possible that change of vowel makes *feck* more polite than *fuck*? Yes, it is, because we rely on such changes to generate any number of distinct words: *bat, cat, fat, mat, rat,* and *sat* are different words to which we conventionally ascribe different meanings and they're all exactly one sound apart; *bite, bit, bait, bet, bat, but, boot, boat,* and *bot* are all exactly one vowel apart, no different in that regard from *feck* and *fuck*.

In lexical terms—to the extent that lexical meaning is even relevant, as it probably isn't in cases like *What the feck!* and *What the fuck!*—*feck* and *fuck* mean the same thing. They differ, however, in their pragmatic meanings, because one is a euphemism and polite and the other a profanity and impolite, even though there's no rational basis for the assignment of one meaning to one or another form, even though the profanity is immanent in the euphemism, even as we allow it to be polite—when one says *feck* or hears it, one is immediately reminded of *fuck*. The same is true of *fark* and *frak*, *ferp* and *frap*, and *frick* and *frig*. The further the euphemistic form is from *fuck*, the more polite it can be, because we don't have to admit as readily that we know what we're doing, know what we "really" mean. The *r* is a distractor from *fark* to *frig*, but anything that begins with *f* and ends with a velar stop—*g* or *k*—is easily identified with the form we're trying to make polite, so there's a limit to the distraction, a limit to the politeness, a limit to how successful the euphemism can be. By contrast, *ferp* and *frap* are more likely to be truly polite because truly euphemistic because farther from the profanity they're meant to cover.

But even *ferp* and *frap* are suspect euphemisms, for a couple of reasons. Compare them with two euphemisms for *motherfucker*, *mofo* and *motherfather*. These are ostentatious euphemisms because they are brazen: with *motherfather*, you're almost there before the speaker pulls back from committing outright profanity, but the euphemism is humorous. Hank Moody's idiosyncratic *Muthafucka!* may be jubilant and socially productive, though your average *motherfucker* just seems mean, but it's not a joke. *Motherfather*, however, is a joke and prompts self-aware laughter—laughter because the form is so preposterous and self-aware because while laughing, the laugher thinks -*fucker* in spite of the attempt at euphemism. Drawing attention to a form as a joke is perhaps not the best way to ensure a euphemism's success. *Feck* is brazen, too, ostentatious insofar as it doesn't take euphemism very seriously. It dares you to question whether it's done enough to avoid *fuck*.

Read observed that "ostentatious taboo is usually accompanied by well-known paralinguistic features—smirking, the arched eyebrow, a slyness of manner." It's certainly true of *You-know-what*, but also true of *mofo* and *feck* and probably, early on, *frig* and *frick*. Because *fork* means 'eating utensil' most of the time, its use in *What the fork!* or *No forking way!* or *Fork off!* calls attention to it and reminds those within earshot of what's behind it. At the core, all of *fuck's* effing euphemisms are ostentatious because in context they are all recognizably euphemisms for profanities. Except for a few, like *fork*, they are nonsense except as euphemisms for profanities, so we understand when using them that profanities lurk underneath. In this way, euphemism manages simultaneously to cover and to expose profanity, then we must wonder about the relationship status of profanity and euphemism. Apparently, it's complicated.

Very often, when we try to pass off euphemism as innocuous— as the answer to profanity—we see it fail on those terms. Sometimes even ultimate camouflage proves transparent. For instance, *fucked* would seem to be pretty well concealed in *SNAFU* 'situation normal all fucked up', a euphemism borne of the U.S. military's love of acronyms. The army didn't invent *RSVP*, and all sorts of bureaucracy— United Parcel Service, my own university—relies on acronyms and initialisms. You'd think such burgeoning abbreviation would successfully euphemize the profanities they supposedly hide. But it's not always the case. Consider initialisms now commonplace in texting: *NFW* 'no fucking way' (first recorded 1974, military), *BFD* 'big fucking deal' (first recorded 1971), *OMFG* 'oh my fucking God'— doubly profane (first recorded first recorded 1997 in use on the Web), and especially *WTF* 'what the fuck' (first recorded 1985, also originating on the Web).

As with so many other euphemisms, abbreviations like these can cause as much trouble as they solve—which, of course, is their pragmatic point. If you want to hide a profanity, an acronym is likely to prove more successful than initialism. Most people have no idea that *scuba* 'self-contained underwater breathing apparatus' is an acronym, and the *fucked* in *snafu* may be sufficiently obscure. Speaking or writing initials as a word that isn't spoken as a series of initials works as a distractor. Nevertheless, some acronyms—like *MILF* 'mother I'd like to fuck,' for instance—beg us to find the profanity. Initialisms, too, call attention to themselves. We know that each letter stands for a word, and we translate the abbreviation, or maybe we articulate the full form mentally and translate it into the abbreviation. Regardless, once again, we're inevitably aware of the underlying form.

In cases like *WTF* and *NFW*, we're further brought to mind of the profanity within because they are exclamations. Exclamations draw our attention anyway, but we know that some exclamations are profane, and so the *F*s in question are suspect the moment we say or hear them. In other words, the pragmatic environments and grammatical uses of profanity work against the effectiveness of some euphemisms, as in the following examples, culled from Sheidlower's *The F-Word*:

FARK They did walk and they di[d] see in each other that words could not express how beautiful these dirty grotty streets in this farked up hostile world look looked to them. (*Hairball Goulash*, 1998)

FECK I went on clinging to the wall until old Fanning made feck-off gestures of great savagery. (H. Leonard, *Out After Dark*, 1980); "Fecker," said Hazel passionately. "That's all he is, a fecker. I can't stand the sight of him." (D. Purcell, *Falling for a Dancer*, 1993)

FORK "Go fork yourself," he said. Maggie smiled with confusion. (A. Neiderman, *Dark*, 1997)

FRAK You know this game's got frak-all to do with the real thing, right? (*Battlestar Galactica*, 2007)

FRAP   She and her boss didn't give a flyin' frap about space. (W. B. Scott et al., *Space Wars*, 2007)

FRICK   Well, I'll be fricked. (J. F. Powers, *Wheat that Springeth Green*, 1988); "Absofrickin'lutely!" (*21 Jump Street*, 1989)

FRIG   Better frig it before it frigs you. (W. Manchester, *City of Anger*, 1953); Tell the bastard to go frig himself. (W. J. Sheldon, *Troubling of a Star*, 1951)

All of these words are what linguists and lexicographers call "partial euphemisms," which means they have to be partial something-elses. I suggest that they are more obviously profanities than they are euphemisms, that they are more precisely "very partial and not especially credible euphemisms."

It's odd, we never think about it, but there aren't many occasions on which we tell someone *to go* _____ *himself*. We might say, of a five-year-old, *I think he should go dress himself*—five-year-olds can put on their own clothes, but they aren't always willing to do it, and so parents might comment on the problem in a *go* _____ way. A surprising number of people, if we're to believe the Web, advise others *to go shoot themselves*, which may be a literal injunction or alternatively a euphemism for *go fuck yourself*. However possible it is to use it for other things, however frequently we do so in other idiomatic ways, we nonetheless associate the construction with profanity. Similarly *a flying* _____ is almost always *a flying fuck* that we don't give, or some partial euphemism for it. How many ways can we be _____ *up*? *Choked up, pent up, shook up, fed up*—so when we hear something was *farked up*, we're unlikely to miss the profane option, especially given phonetic reminders of it. How many *-all* constructions are there besides *fuck-all*? *Bugger all* is less profane, but not quite unprofane. If we insist on using euphemisms in just the same way we use their corresponding profanities, we're likely to realize that one lurks behind the other.

In the entry for *frig*, Jesse Sheidlower's *The F-Word* (2009) includes quotations that illustrate *frig you, frig him, frig them, frig me*.
It's true that we can say things like *scold him, remind them, blame me*,
but profane alternatives to them will come to mind when _____ *me*
is exclaimed or uttered in tones of voice often used for swearing—
angry, frustrated, provocative, derisive, or dismissive tones of voice.
Also, while we can create unprofane infixings, the profane ones are
more frequent and more idiomatic: so *Battlestar Gallactica*'s "I
guaran-frakkin-tee you, I will put you down this time for good," the
infixing suggests profanity to the listener, and the message it frames
confirms it. One reason we recognize *WTF* so readily as profanity is
that the interrogative + *the* _____ construction is predictably profane or euphemistic: *What the fuck? Who the fuck cares? What the
blazes? What in hell? What in tarnation?* If you say *What the puppy?*
everyone knows what you really mean.

Oddly, too, we sometimes use euphemisms right alongside profanity. In *The F-Word*'s entry for *ferk*, Sheidlower includes the following from Ken Tout's *By Tank: D to VE Days* (2007): "Bloody SS.
Shit on you, rotten buggers. Shooting our colonel. Why don't you
ferk off back home and shoot bloody Hitler." Apparently, *bloody*,
shit, and *buggers* don't require euphemism, whereas *fuck* does, but
ferk is nonetheless profanity by association in a context like this one.
The context need not include outright profanity for context to signal
profanity. In "Better frig it before it frigs you," the repeated euphemism calls attention to itself and more or less demands that we take
it for what it is, a barely concealed profanity. When Robert Graves
writes in *Good-by to All That* (1929), "The Bandmaster, who was
squeamish, reported it as: 'Sir, he called me a double-effing c___,'"
the bandmaster may be fooling himself, and Graves fools only the
censors. Given all of these factors, no matter how hard we try, euphemisms do not reliably cover, avoid, or even greatly improve profanities,

yet because they allow us to perform various shades of politeness, we depend on them without realizing the very complex language attitudes they address and deliver.

Again, to be clear, I am arguing that although people usually think euphemisms work because they substitute for profanity, in fact many euphemisms are themselves partially profane, because they more or less cover up profanities—usually less—that are still inscribed in the situations of their use, and our minds' eyes see through them to the profanities, until, we have to admit, we just see through euphemism. That's not the same as saying that euphemism isn't meaningful. You can say *What the puppies?* in settings where *What the fuck?* would be rejected as profoundly impolite, while in other settings *What the ferk?* might get by with a sly nod of acceptance, since it helped to avert all out profanity. Still, what makes profanity and the relevant euphemisms pragmatically powerful and interesting is that the euphemisms are often both euphemisms *and* profanity, a fact not unknown in linguistic circles but too often overlooked when we calculate the logic of language attitudes.

PARODIES OF EUPHEMISM

Long ago, in an article in *New York Magazine* (1970), euphemism seemed to work as supposed: " 'Frickin' kids...those frickin' kids.' Frank never swears." Good for Frank. But things changed by the time a *Washington Post* (1998) article, in dictionary style, explained the *fuck* euphemism, *frap*: " 'Frap,' a way to curse without cursing." No one needed Wanjryb or any other linguist—not even the one writing this book—to tell them that euphemism was paradoxical. In the twenty-first century, euphemism parodies profanity and— because much euphemism is actually a hybrid of euphemism and profanity—euphemism increasingly also parodies euphemism. So, nurses can argue with doctors on the following terms in the beloved situation comedy, *Scrubs* (2009): "[Elliot]: 'You know what? Frick them!' [Carla]: 'Frick them? I'm one of them.' [Elliot]: 'But they're acting like a bunch of frick-heads. Sorry about all the F-bombs." Of course, *frick* isn't exactly an F-bomb, except that, inexactly, it is.

We parody profanity plenty today—remember Lily and *Modern Family*'s "Little Bo Bleep"—for it's a symptom of lost taboo that we can make such fun of something once so socially disapproved, and the cleverness involved in parody suggests that intellectual, social, and aesthetic status attach to profanity play. For instance, my father often said, *I don't give a shit,* but *I don't give a fuck* is a longstanding alternative, and recently lots of people have had lots of fun playing the claim in meme-ingful ways. "All the fucks I give are on this shelf" captions a photo of a guy gesturing toward empty shelves. Two people look at a map; one points and says, "Maybe the fuck I give went that way." A guy looking into the distance through binoculars sighs, "There goes the last fuck I'll ever give." Data of *Star Trek: The Next Generation* explains, "Giving a fuck is not part of my programming." Sean Connery smirks over the lines, "I'd give a fuck...but I already gave it to your mother last night." You can take some DIY advice about "How to: Create a fuck to give." In one of those *Leave-It-to-Beaver*ish line drawings, a secretary talking with her boss on the telephone places a document in a folder: "Yes sir. I will file it right under I don't give a fuck." Similarly, a woman blowing a bubble: "I'm sorry.... My give a fuck is broken but my go fuck yourself is functional." This sort of Web-based parody is infectious, but it's where parody fades into monotony.

Parodies of euphemism have been going for a long time, and it isn't worth belaboring the timeline. Shakespeare's plays are filled with the sort of double entendre useful in such parody, so we've been engaged in it more or less since we had any claim to be modern. Later, the almost anonymous Walter who wrote the pornographic picaresque titled *My Secret Life* (1902, but probably written in the 1880s) recognizes the real point of euphemism, which is to protect the women with whom he has all kinds of sex. Walter is free with his obscenity—"I played with my prick, which was in an inflammatory state, feeling it made me much randier, I called through the door how I wanted to fuck her, how my prick was bursting, how I would frig myself if she would not let me"—but he asterisks people and places—"Neither had ever tasted champagne I found, so ordered some, telling the woman to get it at **** a well-known place for food and wine [then]. Madame S***k*n**s fetched it and I gave her a glass." Readers are as unlikely to be fooled by reference to "L**c**t*r S****e" as they are by *frig*, but in a parody of official euphemism, Walter disagrees with the authorities and most of his neighbors about what constitutes real politeness, so he reverses the conventions.

But parody of euphemism has recently intensified—at least, in America—and, rather than hiding in pornographic closets, once again plays to the groundlings. A parody of profanity, "Little Bo Bleep," in its continual bleeping, is a parody of euphemism, as well. The recording artist and celebrity CeeLo Green is most famous now for a song called, in its unexpurgated version, "Fuck You." Another guy has stolen his girl, and CeeLo is hatin' with a "fuck you" to him and a "fuck her, too." CeeLo doesn't have as much money as the other guy, and he can't believe that's the reason she left him: "Ain't that some shit?" he asks, and we agree, it's just wrong. A song of universal interest, nevertheless, it's banned from radio, because it's got a couple of George Carlin's seven words in it, and those two are repeated often. The radio version, the version your kids can hear is "Forget You." Sheidlower records *forget* as a euphemism for *fuck* in *The F-Word*, but the censors were satisfied. The song was a big hit in both versions, but "Forget You" won the Grammy Award for Best Urban/Alternative Performance and was nominated for Record of the Year, which proves the value of euphemism.

Soon thereafter, the television series *Glee*—which was about a high school glee club that rips songs from the Top 40—covered "Forget You," and I hope they paid enough for CeeLo to flash some cash and get his girl back. The demographic for *Glee* isn't the same as the song's album, download, or radio demographics. *Glee* is aspirational television for junior high schoolers and those on the cusp of junior high. So, it seems a little inappropriate that the song euphemizes *shit* with *shhh*—"Ain't that some shhh." Except when it hushes people up, *shhh* is not an English word, which leads kids to ask, "Hmm, what does *shhh* mean? What does it stand for?" *Shit* comes to mind, and tweens know what it means. Once they've got *shit*, by the principle of proximity illustrated earlier, they realize *forget* is also a euphemism. They look it up in dad's copy of *The F-Word*, just to make sure. In the song, both *forget* and *shhh* make fun of the very notion of euphemism for *fuck* and *shit*.

Similarly, in the television series *Don't Trust the B____ in Apt. 23*, for an older audience, the title song begins, "I'm not perfect, I'm no snitch/But I can tell you she's a . . . " and then you hear the initial *b* and a buzzer, which sounds a bit like the *itch* sound. We remember Read's paralinguistic features, the "smirking, the arched eyebrow, a slyness of manner" that supposedly accompany ostentatious taboo, and these euphemisms are sly—the b and buzzer are ostentatious in the sense that they are conspicuously contrived—but we're smirking at what they say about euphemism before what they say about profanity, and what we're enjoying now that we didn't so much earlier in the history of humankind is the duality of euphemism, admitting in parody that euphemism isn't what it once was and probably can't be anymore.

Examples of euphemism undermined by euphemism abound in media. In *New Girl* (2013), the lights go out at a school dance that the heroine, Jessica Day, is head-chaperoning. In understandable frustration she's about to swear but attempts to stop herself, for the sake of her G-rated audience: "What now? Ahhh...Son of a... uhhhh...penis. Uh, that wasn't better. Sorry, everyone." But it was better—*penis* is not profanity, but it's a stretch to use it as a euphemism for *bitch*. In *The Unbreakable Kimmy Schmidt* (2014), Gretchen Chalker, one of the Mole Women, along with Kimmy, who had been held captive in a bunker by charismatic cult Reverend Richard Wayne Gary Wayne, is the only one who still follows him when he goes on trial for kidnapping and abusing them. She forgives him, noting that "The Reverend only has to answer to Gosh himself." She has picked the euphemism up from the Reverend himself, who arguing his case in court observes, "See, I'm a man of faith. I believe in Gosh and his son Jeepers." Most viewers, I'm sure, hadn't realized, that *gosh* and *jeepers* are historically linked to profanity, but they did after watching this episode, and euphemism is no longer a face-saving strategy but a joke.

What are the effects of parody on the very nature of euphemism, and, indeed, by reflection on profanity? Mikhail Bakhtin, a principal literary theorist of the twentieth century, took parody seriously as a stage of literary development. He argued that any novel incorporates many languages—really, many varieties of a language—and brings them into contact on idiosyncratic, that is, artistic terms. "The novel," he wrote, "is the expression of a Galilean perception of language, one that denies the absolutism of a single and unitary language—that is, refuses to acknowledge its own language as the sole verbal and sematic center of the ideological world." So, the novel represents "fundamental liberation of cultural-semantic and emotional intentions from the hegemony of a single and unitary language, and consequently the simultaneous loss of a feeling for language as myth, that is, as an absolute form of thought." In a less structured, less aesthetically composed way, profanity also challenges the notion of a unitary language and similarly liberates "emotional intentions" from control by censorship, whether official, social, or self-imposed. When profanity isn't really profanity, as in the case of much exclamation, but still is, and when euphemism is still profanity though it tips a cap to politeness, we have heteroglossia—Bakhtin's term for many-languaged language—in a word.

We constantly test discourse of any kind, whether that of the novel or everyday conversation. No matter the mode of expression, we are somewhere between mildly and wildly dissatisfied with its performance on the job. So, we write poetry, speak slang, and even invent languages, both to register that dissatisfaction and to find some way of saying fully what we mean. But the poetry fails, too, and so does the novel, and so does profanity, and so does euphemism. Parody is a test of language's adequacy: Does it meet our expressive needs, our expressive ambitions? Is it less than or different from what it appears to be? "As a rule," Bakhtin thought, "the testing of discourse is coupled with its being parodied—but the degree of parody, as well as the degree of dialogic resistance of the parodied discourse, may be highly varied." In the end, though, once parody questions the adequacy of a literary genre—when its audience expects the parody and the genre can no longer resist—it is overcome and changes or is replaced by another. Parody is the generic end game.

We must wonder about the effect of euphemism as a parody of profanity and euphemism as a self-parody. As taboo further weakens and profanity becomes less and less profane, as euphemism for profanity is less and less plausible, not raising an eyebrow even when it's ostentatious, what chance does either have? How can they still signify in a language? Euphemism per se isn't going anywhere. Our relatives still die, and we need ways to talk about that politely. "All our evidence," Brown and Levinson conclude, "indicates that euphemisms are a universal feature of language usage," and within a language as euphemisms "become conventionalized there is constant pressure to create new euphemisms for truly taboo subjects." But what if profanity and its subjects are no longer truly taboo? In that case, profanity and euphemism may be problems dissolving into the future.

REFERENCES

I quote Helen Macdonald from *H Is for Hawk* (New York: Grove Press, 2014), p. 141. After her goshawk, Mabel, had vexed her enough, MacDonald reflected, "Now I know why austringers have, for centuries, been famed for cursing" (p. 139). Erving Goffman's argument about interjection and cries appears in *Forms of Talk* (Philadelphia: University of Pennsylvania Press, 1981), pp. 93–95. The comment on *Jeepers Creepers* is the entry point into Keith Allan and Kate Burridge's *Euphemism & Dysphemism: Language Used as Shield and Weapon* (New York: Oxford University Press, 1991), p. vii. William D. Hopkins, Jamie L. Russell, and Jennifer A. Schaeffer are quoted from their article, "The Neural and Cognitive Correlates of Aimed Throwing in Chimpanzees: A Magnetic Resonance Image and Behavioural Study on a Unique Form of Social Tool Use," *Philosophical Transactions of the Royal Society B* 367 (2012): 37–47, at pp. 38, 39, and 44, in series. Rob Waugh writes about their research in "Monkeys Throwing Poo? It's Actually a Sign of Intelligence—Especially If They Score a Hit," *Daily Mail*, http://www.dailymail.co.uk/sciencetech/article-2068645/Monkeys-throwing-poo-Its-actually-sign-INTELLIGENCE.html. Michael C. Corballis's book, *From Hand to Mouth: The Origins of Language* (Princeton, NJ: Princeton University Press, 2002), is quoted from p. 77 and then from p. 80. David F. Armstrong, William C. Stokoe, and Sherman E. Wilcox propose, more aggressively than Hopkins, Russell, and Schaeffer, and Corballis that "The earliest linguistic units may have been either visible or vocal gestures, or, quite likely both" in *Gesture and the Nature of Language* (Cambridge, U.K.: Cambridge University Press, 1995), p. 19, and they argue that speech is gesture in the same book, pp. 8–11 and throughout. Naïve sound symbolism is engagingly represented by Roy Blount, Jr., in *Alphabet Juice* (New York: Farrar, Straus and Giroux, 2008) and the etymological role of sound symbolism is argued by Anatoly Liberman, *Word Origins* (New York: Oxford University Press, 2005), pp. 15–43. I quote Steven Pinker's *The Stuff of Thought* (New York: Penguin, 2007), from pp. 331, 366, and

366 again; he, too, entertains the power of sound in profanity on p. 339. My account of teaching "Maledicta" at Albright College forms part of "Teaching 'Bad' American English: Profanity and Other 'Bad' Words in the Liberal Arts Setting," *Journal of English Linguistics* 30 (2002): 353–365. Pinker's swappability comes up on pp. 362–363 of *The Stuff of Thought*, and profanity's zing on p. 357. I deal with infixing and interposing in English extensively in *Slang: The People's Poetry* (New York: Oxford University Press, 2009), pp. 120–144. On processing, see Marjorie Barker and T. Givón, "On the Pre-linguistic Origins of Language Processing Rates," in *The Evolution of Language Out of Pre-language*, edited by T. Givón and Bertram F. Malle (Amsterdam: John Benjamins, 2002), pp. 171–214. The processing of sound is "almost instantaneous" for physical reasons explained by A. J. Hudspeth in "The Energetic Ear," *Dædelus* 144 (2015): 49; "the central nervous system can calculate what word was spoken while also abstracting such nuances as accent and emotional inflection" (p. 47), but it takes a while to get from which word to which meaning. Gavin Francis explains how much in "The Mysterious World of the Deaf," *The New York Review of Books* (November 20, 2014), p. 46. *How I Met Your Mother* was created by Carter Bays and Craig Thomas and aired for nine seasons on CBS, mostly directed by Pamela Fryman; Neil Patrick Harris's performance as Barney Stinson is legen-wait for it-dary. You can count on V. S. Ramachandran, like Steven Pinker, for a reliable and readable account of complex subjects, like mirror neurons, here in *The Tell-Tale Brain: A Neuroscientist's Quest for What Makes Us Human* (New York: Norton, 2011), quoting p. 129 and 121. Is chimpanzee shit slinging meaningful in the way "Fuck you!" is meaningful? "Only humans, as far as we know," Ramachandran writes, "can use metaphor and analogy, although here we are in a gray area: the elusive boundary between thought and language. When an alpha male ape makes a genital display to intimidate a rival into submission, is this analogous to the metaphor "F—k you" that humans use to insult one another? I wonder" (p. 163). W. Wat Hopkins' "When Does F*** Not Mean F***?: FCC v. Fox Television Stations and a Call for Protecting Emotive Speech," appeared in the *Federal Communications Law Journal* 64 (2011), and is quoted from pp. 7, 18, 22, 7 again, 9, and 37. *The Wire* aired on HBO for five seasons from 2002 to 2008. "Old Cases" was directed by Clement Virgo and written by the show's creator, David Simon. Dominic West plays McNulty; Wendell Pierce plays Moreland. Drake Bennet comments on the show in "This Will Be on the Midterm. You Feel Me? Why So Many Colleges Are Teaching the Wire," in *Slate*, March 24, 2010: http://www.slate.com/articles/arts/ culturebox/2010/03/this_will_be_on_the_ midterm_you_feel_me.html. The dispassionate jargon is quoted from the first episode of *CSI: Miami* (September 23, 2002) on CBS, directed by Joe Chapelle and written by Steven Maeda, and spoken by Lieutenant Horatio Caine, played by David Caruso. Lenny Briscoe was a central character on NBC's *Law & Order* for twelve seasons (1992–2004), brought to life by the late Jerry Orbach. The comments on dissatisfaction with the language we're given is a quick summary of my position

in *Slang: The People's Poetry* and *From Elvish to Klingon: Exploring Invented Languages* (Oxford: Oxford University Press, 2011), and especially Suzanne Romaine's comment on the subject in the latter (p. 215). For William Dunbar's use of *fuck*, see *The Poems of William Dunbar*, edited by James Kinsley (Oxford: The Clarendon Press, 1979), p. 40. Richard Coates presents the evidence for "*Fockynggroue* in Bristol" in *Notes and Queries* (December 2007), pp. 373–376. I quote Melissa Mohr's *Holy Shit: A Brief History of Swearing* (New York: Oxford University Press, 2013), p. 97, on jocular *swive*. Eric Partridge's etymology is in *Origins: An Etymological Dictionary of Modern English*, 4th ed. (London: Routledge & Kegan Paul, 1966); Jonathon Green's is in the monumental *Green's Dictionary of Slang* (London: Chambers, 2010); Calvert Watkins's is in *The American Heritage Dictionary of the English Language*, 5th ed. (2011); and Anatoly Liberman's comprehensive treatment is given in *An Analytic Dictionary of English Etymology: An Introduction* (Minneapolis: University of Minnesota Press, 2008), pp. 78–86. Passing from expletive to euphemism, though relying on some of the same sources, W. Wat Hopkins's concern about representing "offending language" is registered on pp. 2–3 of his article, note 13; one of my heroes, Justice William C. Brennan, is quoted from p. 22. Ruth Wajnryb's pithy formulation of the euphemism problem is in *CU Next Tuesday* (London: Aurum Press, 2004), pp. 133–134. Allan and Burridge are cited above. Throughout the rest of the chapter, histories of words are borrowed from the indispensable *Green's Dictionary of Slang*, cited above; since dictionaries are arranged alphabetically, they're easily found there, so I don't provide page numbers. When I reproduce citations from this and other dictionaries, I do not provide separate bibliographic information for the cited works, though I do expand author names and titles so that anyone who wants to locate the original can do so more easily. Lise Winer's *Dictionary of the English/Creole of Trinidad & Tobago* was published by McGill-Queen's University Press in 2009. The fact of *jeeswax* comes to us courtesy of Volume 3 the *Dictionary of American Regional English*, edited by Frederic G. Cassidy and Joan Houston Hall (Cambridge, MA: Belknap Press of Harvard University Press, 1996). *Word Histories and Mysteries: Abracadabra to Zeus* (Boston: Houghton Mifflin, 2004) explains the history of *derrick*. When it comes to politeness theory, you can't do better than Penelope Brown and Stephen C. Levinson's *Politeness: Some Universals in Language* (Cambridge, U.K.: Cambridge University Press, 1987). Erving Goffman's "On Face-Work: An Analysis of Ritual Elements in Social Interaction," *Psychiatry: Journal for the Study of Interpersonal Processes* 18 (1955): 213–231, is the classic underlying Brown and Levinson's work. I quote Karen Stohr's *On Manners* (New York: Routledge, 2012) from pp. 4, 22—for the passage from Judith Martin—and 31. I quote Edwin L. Battistella's *Bad Language: Are Some Words Better Than Others?* (New York: Oxford University Press, 2005) from p. 83. I quote Tony McEnery's *Swearing in English: Bad Language, Purity and Power from 1586 to the Present* (Abingdon, U.K.: Routledge, 2006), from p. 3, and Pierre Bourdieu's *Language*

& Symbolic Power, edited and introduced by John B. Thompson, translated by
Gino Raymond and Matthew Adamson (Cambridge, MA: Harvard University
Press, 1991), pp. 78–79 and 170. Allen Walker Read's typically perceptive "A Type
of Ostentatious Taboo" was published in *Language* 40 (1964): 162–166, and is
helpfully reprinted in a collection of his most important essays, *Milestones in the
History of English in America*, Publication of the American Dialect Society 86,
edited by Richard W. Bailey (Durham, NC: Duke University Press), pp. 270–
276. The Rankin/Bass *Rudolph the Red-nosed Reindeer*, which first aired on CBS
on December 6, 1964, was directed by Larry Roemer and written by Romeo
Muller and Robert May; Donner was voiced by Paul Kligman. Johnny Lopez
wrote the article "Amy Smart vs. Ali Larter: Who'd You Rather?" for the celebrity gossip site *TMZ* (July 31, 2010). Our euphemist calls himself RJ Hunt.
I trade freely on Jesse Sheidlower's *The F-Word*, 3d ed. (New York: Oxford
University Press, 2009) for information on the several partial euphemisms.
Read is quoted from p. 271 of *Milestones*. UPS jargon is discussed briefly in my
Slang: The People's Poetry (2009), pp. 25–27. The preparodic quotations at the
outset of the parody section are also pulled from *The F-Word* s.v. *frick, frap*, and
frick, respectively. The memes are borrowed from the inspirational websites,
http://www.quickmeme.com and http://www.someecards.com. Walter's sex-
capades are the subject of the abridged (!) *My Secret Life: An Erotic Diary of
Victorian London*, edited by James Kincaid (New York: Penguin/Signet, 1996).
W***** is quoted from pp. 183–184 and 451. CeeLo Green included "Forget You"
on his album *The Lady Killer* (Elektra, 2010). *Glee* aired on the Fox Network
(2009–2015), and "Forget You" was featured in "The Substitute" (Season 2, episode 7), on November 16, 2010. Gwyneth Paltrow as Holly Holliday, Amber
Riley as Mercedes Jones, and Kevin McHale as Artie Abrams were the song's
principal singers. "Forget You" is included on *Glee: The Music, Volume 4*
(Twentieth Century Fox/Columbia, 2010). Many of us lament the untimely
demise of *Don't Trust the B____ in Apt. 23*, created by Nahnatchka Khan, which
had just two seasons (2012–2013) on ABC. The theme song was written by Katie
Hampton. Thankfully, *New Girl* has been going strong on Fox since its premiere
on September 20, 2011. The episode "Dance," directed by Trent O'Donnell and
written by Elizabeth Meriwether, Rebecca Addelman, Ryan Koh, and Camilla
Blackett, aired on April 29, 2014. Jessica Day is performed by the inimitable
Zooey Deschanel. *The Unbreakable Kimmy Schmidt* is a Netflix original created
by Robert Carlock and Tina Fey and starring Ellie Kemper as Kimmy Schmidt.
The dialogue quoted here is from "Kimmy Rides a Bike!" which aired on March
6, 2015. Lauren Adams plays Gretchen Chalker, while the Reverend Richard
Wayne Gary Wayne is played by John Hamm. Mikhail Bakhtin is quoted from
The Dialogic Imagination, edited by Michael Holquist and translated by Caryl
Emerson and Michael Holquist (Austin: University of Texas Press, 1981), pp.
366, 367, and 413, in series. Finally, Brown and Levinson are quoted from
Politeness, p. 216.

Chapter 4

Artful Profanity

Profane exclamations may sound atavistic, but much profanity has in fact been civilized. Profanity is not merely rough-and-tumble language of the streets, nor even merely verse graffiti on toilet walls, but also literary language, not just the language of pulp fiction, either, or fiction generally, but an atavistic echo in the ether of poetry, as well, perhaps because the profane poet gets away with mixing the low and the high and thus asserts a powerful poetic license. So, the Scots "makar" William Dunbar contributes one of the earliest known instances of *fuck*—very late fifteenth or very early sixteenth century—in a poem beginning:

> In secreit place this hinder nycht
> I hard a bern say till a bricht:
> My hunny, my houp, my hairt, my heill
> I haif bene lang your lufar leill
> And can of you get confort nane.

The *bern* or 'lover,' we are told further along in the poem, is *ourgane* 'overcome' with *the glaikkis* 'sexual desire' and, but for his *feiris* 'manners,' would have *fukkit* his *bricht* 'lady fair,' Quite a bit later, before 1673, John Wilmot, the libertine Earl of Rochester, in "A Ramble in St. James's Park," observes with tumescent glee that point in the ramble

Whence rows of mandrakes tall did rise,
Whose lewd tops fucked the very skies.

This is all pornographic stuff, and profanity serves it well, but it is also, paradoxically, great poetry, satire by two of the most stylistically sophisticated poets who ever wrote in English.

Profanity in "A Ramble in St. James's Park" and "In secreit place this hinder nycht" is subversive, but not in the commonplace way, as naughty language that flouts decency or authority. Rochester wrote vigorous poems on public subjects, like "To Her Sacred Majesty the Queen Mother," as well as elegant love poems, without a touch of profanity. But satire is another thing, and he wrote of Charles II, with whom relations were often strained by Rochester's bad behavior,

And Love, he loves, for he loves fucking much.
Nor are his high Desires above his Strength,
His scepter and his Prick are of a Length,
And she may sway the one, who plays with th'other.

Charles was,

'Tis sure the swaucyest that ere did swive
The proudest peremtoriest Prick alive.
Though Safety, Law Religion, Life lay on't,
'Twould breake through all to make its way to Cunt.

None of this was untrue of Charles, though perhaps better left unsaid. Or, at least, it would have been better had Rochester not accidentally presented this poem to the king rather than another the king had requested. A letter of the period tells us that "Lord Rochester fled from Court," for neither the first nor the last time.

"A Ramble in St. James's Park" mocks Edmund Waller's "A Poem on St. James's Park" (1661), a dreamy pastoral poem. Rochester was not a fan of pastoral. In order to prick and deflate the dream, he replaces Waller's lines, "Bold sons of earth that thrust their arms so high/As if once more they would invade the sky," with lines about mandrake roots—supposedly sprung from ground where semen had spilled—resembling a line of penises swaying in the breeze, fucking the sky, because there is absolutely nothing pastoral about that. Dunbar's poem is similarly a send up of courtly love: his *bern* is a priest, the *bricht* a kitchen wench, and when they *fukkit*, Dunbar says with great poetic authority, "Go fuck yourself" to the tradition of *amour courtois*. Like Rochester, Dunbar wrote plenty of clean poetry, and his "The Golden Targe"—*targe* means 'light shield'—a dream allegory, represents the golden style of early Scots poetry. But in "The Flyting of Dunbar and Kennedy"—a flyting is a poetry battle—he announces to the court that his adversary Kennedy is *beschittin* 'covered in shit' and—my favorite Dunbar word—*cuntbittin* 'sexually diseased or impotent.' Dunbar was a university-educated priest from a good family, but he was famous and valued, among other things, for public obscenity.

The profanity in evidence here is not accidental or habitual, the kind that people supposedly use because, as my grandmother used to say, they don't know any better. For poets, profanity is specific to the purpose. Dunbar and Rochester knew what they were doing. They chose *fuck* or *cunt* or *shit* or *prick* to occupy that particular place in that particular line of that particular poem because doing so accomplished a specific aesthetic object or effect. Profanity isn't necessary, we're told. You can always find a polite way of saying it, we're told. Perhaps expletive isn't a necessary component of language in the sense that we couldn't have language without it. But literary profanity *is* necessary, precisely on the terms that authors use it. If it's there, the author proposes, it's necessary, or I wouldn't have put it there.

Not all authors of all times have felt free to use profanity in their work. As Melissa Mohr explains in *Holy Shit* (2013), the Renaissance—perhaps more accurately in the history of English, the Early Modern period—marks "The Rise of Obscenity," and it wasn't until later, in the late eighteenth century, that we reached "The Age of Euphemism." Dunbar, a medieval poet, and Rochester, writing before euphemism held sway, perhaps felt no inhibition. Of course, some writers did use profanity in the Age of Euphemism, and, as we have seen, euphemism can itself be obliquely profane. Authors of the twentieth and twenty-first centuries have rediscovered profanity's expressive power, and it's written indelibly throughout modern literature. In Claire Messud's recent novel, *The Woman Upstairs* (2013), Nora Eldredge, the narrator, begins with profanity:

> How angry am I? You don't want to know. Nobody wants to know about *that*. I'm a good girl, I'm a nice girl, I'm a straight-A, strait-laced, good daughter, good career girl, and I never stole anybody's boyfriend and I never ran out on a girlfriend, and I put up with my parents' shit and my brother's shit, and I'm not a girl anyhow, I'm over forty fucking years old, and I'm good at my job and I'm great with kids and I held my mother's hand when she died.... It was supposed to say "Great Artist on my tombstone, but if I died right now it would say "such a good teacher/daughter/friend" instead; and what I really want to shout, and want in big letters on that grave, too, is FUCK YOU ALL.

I take it that this isn't a good time to question Nora's recourse to profanity or, by extension, Claire Messud's, either—it's the language they need to say what they have to say.

In this chapter I consider the roles profanity plays in three quite different literary settings: the television series, *The Sopranos*; James Kelman's Booker Prize–winning novel, *How Late It Was, How Late*; and songs written and performed by Nellie McKay. I chose these three from an unknown number of works in all literary modes and genres that include profanity, hoping that, given their differences, they will illustrate the role of profanity as expressive, essential language. I also hope to demonstrate that taking profanity as a point of interpretive departure can be especially productive, at least with some texts. But on the principle that any interpretation should account for the language of the text it addresses, explaining the role of profanity in any given text is necessary to understanding it fully.

PHILOSOPHICAL PROFANITY

In the fall of 1990, David Lynch's weird and wonderful television series, *Twin Peaks*, was the subject of every dinner party. What was it about? What was it trying to achieve? People I knew couldn't stop talking about it. I'm still not sure what it was all about, but I know what it achieved. It initiated—clumsily, for it only lasted thirty episodes—a new television genre, the dramatic series with a long story arc. Without *Twin Peaks*, there wouldn't have been *Buffy the Vampire Slayer*, *Six Feet Under*, *The Wire*, *The X-Files*, or any number of other such series, and that, in my opinion, would have been a damned shame.

One of the most important of these long-form shows, the one that proved cable networks were here to stay, is HBO's *The Sopranos* (1999–2007). You would think that, a decade on from *Twin Peaks*, the genre would have made some progress, that *The Sopranos* would be thematically coherent—it was bound to be more coherent than

Twin Peaks. But it isn't easy to say what *The Sopranos* is about. Is it about how you just can't keep a good sociopath down? Is it about addiction? Is it about therapy? Is it about how sociopaths appropriate therapeutic methods and perspectives to manage crime syndicates? Is it about men hating the men they love or about women hating the men they love, or men loving the women they hate? Is it about Jersey? About the decline of America in the late twentieth century? About family? About Cosa Nostra, what Tony Soprano—the series' central protagonist—calls "this thing of ours"? Of course, it's about all of these themes and more. A thematically narrow series wouldn't be interesting. Fundamentally, however, it's about anger.

The anger is marked by killing and beating and mayhem, often in combination, but it's also marked by profanity. In *The Sopranos,* people get beat up—sometimes killed—in a hail of profanity. Franco Ricci explains that in *The Sopranos,* "Fury and action will triumph over words and images, reality over fantasy, left-brain linearity over right-brain holism, the reality of the mob world over the symbolism of art." And while this is true, it is only half true. For, as we know, fury can burn in words, and words can act as an accelerant in fury; expletive is action; and while the reality of the mob triumphs over art *within* the show's fiction, ironically, the artful use of profanity proves that symbolism ultimately overwhelms "reality."

There is a lot of violence in *The Sopranos* and a lot of profanity, too. If you watched the series regularly, you knew this and probably also noted the connection between these two modes of expressing anger. I made the connection, too, yet I had no idea how much profanity occurs in the show until I counted it all up, every *fuck, asshole, shit,* and *cocksucker.* I also counted any derivative of *fuck* (like *fucker*), *shit* (like *bullshit*), *cocksucker* (like *cocksucking*), as well as just plain *cock, prick, dick, cunt, hell, bitch* and *son of a bitch,* and also real profanities, like *goddamn, hell, Jesus,* and *Jesus Christ.* I counted *finook*

'gay male', from Italian *finocchio* 'fennel'—recall Rochester's mandrake roots—because homosexuality is profane from the mobster's
point of view, something the show amply illustrates in the story
of gay *capo* Vito Spatafore, a family man and great earner, who is
brought down first by self-loathing and finally by his wife's cousin,
Phil Leotardo, who watches while two of his soldiers beat Vito to
death for being who he is. Obviously, given the preceding chapter,
I also counted obscene gestures, though not the nightstick dead Vito
took up the ass.

Some of these items may sound more like slang than profanity,
but as I argued in Chapter 1, the line between the two—if there's any
line to draw—depends on context. In *The Sopranos*, all of the items
in question are uttered, whether you think they're slang or profanity,
with exclamatory force. (This is not the same, though, as saying that
items are used exclusively in expletive ways.) On an exclamation
scale from 1 to 100, no profane utterance rated lower than a 35, and
most of them, frankly, exceeded 100, though I admit to making this
scale up just to register my intuitions. Casual profanity from the
mouths of babes and their mothers scored lower, as when, in the pilot,
Tony's son, A. J., complains on his thirteenth birthday, "So what, no
fuckin' ziti now?" Without ziti, it's not a birthday. A. J. asserts his
coming of age in front of his parents and Father Phil, who react, but
mildly, in that indulgent way you do when you know you can't really
control a child anymore. The kid grows up, he swears—whaddya
gonna do?

Alternatively, bad men left to their own devices—especially
shooting, beating, or threatening other bad men—broke the scale,
over and over again. The winning episode, hands down, is "The Pine
Barrens," in which Christopher Moltisanti and Paulie "Walnuts"
Gualtieri think they've killed a member of the Russian mob while
they try to collect from him. They wrap the putative corpse up in a

rug, throw him into the trunk of their car, and take him to New Jersey's Pine Barrens to dispose of him. When they open the trunk, they discover he's alive, chase him around the Barrens, shoot at him— in the end, he may or may not escape.

Profanity is part of the violence when Christopher and Paulie fight the Russian (who, they discover later, was in the Russian special forces) and the register of their humiliation and frustration when they chase after the Russian and then are stranded in the Barrens overnight—stranded in winter without appropriate clothing or food beyond fast-food packets of ketchup and relish. Add to this storyline a drag out fight between Tony and his depressive girlfriend, Gloria Trillo, in which steak as well as profanity is hurled around the room, and the profanity rate soars. As television viewer and profanity aficionado, I was both delighted and appalled, which may indeed be the aesthetic point. The moral point, and I think there is one, is more complex and has nothing to do with delight.

What one might call *The Sopranos*' "profanity rate" is jaw-droppingly high. Basically, each episode of the show runs 53 minutes. So, let's set a reassuring threshold—you may not agree that all of what I counted counts as profanity. *Fuck* and forms built on it always constitute the bulk of the profanity in any episode, and the questionable cases occur only once or twice. *Cunt* and *cocksucker* are reserved to amplify the force of profanity in certain contexts, as against the rate. Thus, 60 seems a good threshold—in how many episodes, in other words, do instances of profanity amply exceed the number of minutes aired? The answer is remarkable: in 69 (81%) of 85 episodes, the profanity rate was more than one item per minute, on average. As many as 19 episodes (22%) had rates of 100 or more; that is, more episodes had rates over 100 than had rates below 60 (19%). Over the 85 episodes, rates ranged from 36 to 177—that's right, from 60% of the threshold to 295%. Counting all of it up, there are 7037 profane instances in 85 episodes, at a rate of 82.788 per episode, or 138% of the per episode threshold. That's a lot of profanity. Within the series, it's spontaneous; looked at from outside, it's not there by accident.

It's reasonable to ask what motivates the exceptions, the unusually high rates but especially the low ones. In Episode 1.5 (36 profanities), Tony takes his daughter Meadow to Maine on a college tour; his wife, Carmela stays behind to dally with Father Phil, her priest. Father Phil has already established himself as a profanity milquetoast. In the pilot episode, he says things like "Geez, Louise" and "Darn, these laser disks are incredible." In Episode 1.5, he manages "Yipes!" One of Tony's "problems" is that he loves his children and wants to set the best example a mob boss dad can. In fact, all mobsters apparently want normal relations with the families of other made men. This is always amusing to watch: cold-blooded killers like Silvio Dante and Paulie stop by for dinner as Uncle Sil and Uncle Paulie. And it's in this spirit of euphemism—not just word euphemism but life euphemism—that Tony, a World War II buff, can say to Meadow, "Potsdamned if I know." Anyway, everyone knows there's less swearing in Maine than in New Jersey.

Episode 3.1 (51 profanities) has the FBI planting a bugged lamp in the Sopranos' basement because Tony holds conferences with colleagues there. Carmela is at tennis lessons, everyone drives here and there, the maid and her husband meet in the park for lunch, the FBI waits undercover in vans—the series is about anger, but the episode is not. The pilot episode (44 profanities) is a soft landing for the audience, suggestive but leaving plenty of room for us to learn more in future episodes, to learn gradually how angry the citizens of Sopranoland really are. The final episode ends cryptically: maybe it just ends, or maybe we imagine the family or part of it has gone into witness protection, or maybe Tony gets capped in front of his family in their favorite diner—they love the onion rings. But up until that terminal point, the episode keeps suggesting a happy resolution to all that's gone before, an escape from responsibility. With 44 profanities, it comes full circle, by my idiosyncratic count.

Viewers who paid attention to the pacing of episodes remember that along with all of the sound—conversations in the Soprano kitchen, often loud spats among the family; planning sessions at the Bada Bing, with pulsating music and pole-dancers in the background; movies and television on the big screen, never at a low volume; the creepy singing fish, Paulie's perpetual chatter, talk therapy session after session, and the soundtrack—there is a lot of silence. Tony fetches the morning paper in his robe. Tony smokes a cigar while watching ducks swim in his pool. For a while, no one talks in a hospital room. Tony and Dr. Melfi analyze whatever, but then there's a pause, during which you can hear hearts beating, maybe your own, before they continue. When we leave Melfi's office, there will just as likely be silence as we enter a new scene. The final episode ends utterly, in silence. In and around the silence and the ambient noise of living come the arguments between Christopher and Adriana, between Tony and Carmela, and they're violent, and there's plenty of profanity.

But most of the profanity is saved for major eruptions, with five wiseguys simultaneously swearing while kicking the shit out of someone who crossed them. In other words, the profanity can be measured against the 53-minute duration of an episode, but it is even more expletive—meta-expletive—when stuffed into short segments of the most profane episodes. Soprano profanity is not distributed evenly throughout an episode, and the more superfluous profane items there are—I mean, really, 177 such items in one episode—the more absurd and frightening and meta the explosion is when profanity spews like rapid-fire from a roomful of semi-automatic mouths.

In these cases, whatever purpose profanity serves within an episode, its larger purpose is to comment on anger and its expression in words and deeds.

In his *On Anger*, the Roman philosopher Lucius Annaeus Seneca (4 BCE–65 CE) explained of that malicious motive, "No pestilence has been more costly for the human race. Butchery and poisoning, suits and countersuits, cities destroyed, entire nations wiped out... dwellings put to the torch.... Consider the cities of great renown whose foundation stones can hardly be made out: anger cast these cities down. Consider the wastelands, deserted, without an inhabitant for many miles: anger emptied them." *The Sopranos* includes some butchery, less poisoning, suits and countersuits, so to speak, within the mob economy. But what's true for the mob is to some different extent also true of America. Mobsters are extreme characters, yet their characters are still, to some different extent, our characters.

For Seneca, the effects of anger aren't merely various at a variety of scales—they are all interconnected, and you can't have a mafia butchering and countersuing without civil and national decay entailed. Thus, *The Sopranos* is certainly about the decline of America, because anger fuels the decline. So, it's also about New Jersey, or a certain aspect of Jersey, not quite mythological enough. When I read about Seneca's wastelands, I think of all the deals cut and the gangsters capped in those empty tracts next to bridges. The correspondence is not exact, but such scenes serve as momentary moral emblems of the unarticulated message of the whole.

At the root of anger, according to Aristotle, lies incontinence, or *akrasia*—especially in the context of *The Sopranos*, unmanly lack of self-control. No one wants to do evil things, so the philosophy goes, and the philosophy itself, the stoicism of Seneca, for instance, can be understood as a kind of therapy—this is the formidable argument of Martha Nussbaum in *The Therapy of Desire*. Anger is not merely emotional or internal. As Nussbaum explains, "all major ancient analyses of [anger] understand the passion to be, or to involve, not only the reactive emotion that we most often think of when we think of anger, but also a component of active aggression." Seneca anticipates something like modern therapy as the practice most likely to save us from the destruction that follows in anger's wake: "The paradigm of philosophical interaction is the quiet conversation of friends who have an intimate knowledge of one another's character and situation. Conversation, writes Seneca, is 'more useful' than writing, even intimate letter writing, 'because it creeps bit by bit into the soul.'" Of course, your therapist isn't supposed to be your friend or to have certain types of intimate knowledge about you, but that's exactly the boundary over which therapy between Tony and Dr. Jennifer Melfi continually trespasses.

So, Tony goes to therapy, but he doesn't go to fortify his will against incontinence or to overcome anger. In fact in several episodes, we see him angry—even violent—in therapy. Sometimes the violence is manifest, but sometimes it's registered symbolically, as when Tony says to Dr. Melfi, "I dreamed I fucked your brains out, right on that desk, and you loved it," and Melfi responds, "Well, you threw that at me like a rock" (Episode 2.13). Sometimes the violence is that of expletive: Melfi explains that she could never have a personal relationship with Tony because she "couldn't bear witness to violence," upon which Tony shouts, "Fuck you, you fucking cunt" (Episode 5.1). The therapy was never going to take, as Tony himself suggests time and again. So, Melfi: "But who said that, after getting out of the dirt and the poverty, do we have to stop looking for pain and truth"; answered by Soprano: "Pain and truth? Come on, I'm a fat fucking crook from New Jersey" (Episode 4.11). Tony goes to therapy to flirt with an inaccessible woman and deal with his anxiety. Anger he can use in his business, but anxiety gets in his way.

Anger, Aristotle noticed, is hard to manage: "Anyone can get angry—that is easy," he writes in the *Nicomachean Ethics*, "but to do this to the right person, to the right extent, at the right time, with the right motive, and in the right way, *that* is not for everyone, nor is it easy." This is what hooks us: both anger and the problem of resisting it, resisting *akrasia*, are fundamental human issues. Anger is ignited by a slight, according to Aristotle, and though the slight is painful, avenging it is a pleasure. Phil Leotardo is an icon of this relationship between slight and revenge. A ruthless *capo* in New York's Lupertazzi crime family, but dedicated to the old ways, Phil is more easily slighted than most, which is saying something. In Season Four, Tony's cousin, Tony Blundetto, kills Phil's brother. Phil wants to kill Blundetto back, and he wants the satisfaction of doing it personally, with torture. Tony kills his own cousin, to spare Blundetto the torture, of course, and also to avoid all out warfare between the New York and New Jersey families, but that doesn't work: Phil's persistent sense of injury—he is never unslighted—is one factor in the wars that follow.

The tragic story of anger in *The Sopranos* belongs to John "Johnny Sack" Sacrimoni, underboss and then boss of the Lupertazzi family. Unlike most Mafiosi in *The Sopranos* (Bobby Baccalieri is another rare exception), Johnny Sack is faithful to his wife, Ginny, even though she wears a very plus size. Ralph Cifaretto insults Ginny by joking about her weight, and thus he also slights Johnny Sack, who puts a contract out on Ralph when Carmine Lupertazzi refuses to sanction an execution—on the not-entirely-unreasonable principle that made men shouldn't be clipped for their bad jokes—but he cancels the contract at the last minute. I see Carmine's point, but my sympathies are with Johnny. What sort of pleasure can he take in a tax on Ralph's earnings? How does that address an insult to honor? The surplus of anger, slights coming at you from all directions, can eat you up. Johnny Sack dies horribly of cancer. So, Seneca reminds us, "As the saying goes, 'No sooner do we turn and look around than death is at our elbow.'"

Slighting others is an inevitable outcome of the mob's atavistic economy. It's a form of mutualism, or "cooperation resting on simultaneous benefits to all parties involved," as the primate expert Frans de Waal puts it. If you've watched *The Sopranos* or any film about the Mafia, you are familiar with "the meet," where business is divvied up among the families or among the capos within a family. *The Sopranos* is replete with squabbling about whether one or another of them got a fair share, whether New York ought to get more out of the Esplanade, or what Paulie Gualtieri, the senior soldier in Tony's army, ought to get out of any business in which he had a hand. Seneca could be addressing the Mafia directly when he says, "You don't keep true accounts: you put a high value on what you've given, a low value on what you've received." It's a recipe for slights that drive them to anger and if not immediately to violence at least to profanity. Then, probably, violence *and* profanity.

This confusion of motives and the recalibration of them to an Aristotelian middle way required philosophy in the ancient world, and, Aristotle argued in the *Rhetoric*, the orator incites anger or calm by persuading those listening into an imbalance of those motives. Today, *The Sopranos* proposes, just living in America throws them out of balance. Philosophy is no longer enough—when we're confused, we demand therapy. Yet therapy is no panacea, and some therapists aren't ready for the anger slouching in their armchairs. "I guess I'm out of touch with the climate of rage in American society, the casual violence," says Dr. Melfi early in the series (Episode 1.4). She nailed the diagnosis in four episodes. The long rest of the series demonstrates the limits of diagnosis.

Clearly, Seneca has seen some angry people: "As madmen exhibit specific symptoms—a bold and threatening expression, a knitted brow, a fierce set of the features, a quickened step, restless hands, a changed complexion, frequent, very forceful sighing—so do angry people show the same symptoms." And we've seen them, too, characters of *The Sopranos*: the first three symptoms have Tony as he appears in every publicity shot. We see the rage in Tony's father, Johnny, but also in his son, A. J., when he starts to beat kids up later in the show, thus proposing a heritage of anger. But most of the mobsters show that face—Ralph, Paulie, Silvio, Christopher, even the mild-mannered Bobby Baccalieri. Watch the episodes again, and you'll see that some of them, Tony especially, do in fact have restless hands.

Therapy won't work for this crew. "Your mind," says Seneca to the angry man, "which weaves a growing web of crime, is beyond healing; already you need no motives...to set you off, but wrongdoing itself is a sufficiently strong motive for doing wrong. You have drunk deep of wickedness and so steeped your guts in it that it cannot be expelled save with those very guts." This aptly describes real criminals, of course, but that's because criminals, at least mobsters, are angry for the reasons described above. Aristotle too saw that, at least in some cases, the angry man enjoys *akrasia*, will not relinquish it, and it spells his doom: "But to the incontinent man may be applied the proverb 'when water chokes, what is one to wash it down with?'"

What's required, before one chokes on rage, is self-control, control to counter incontinence. No one on *The Sopranos*, certainly none of the mobsters, ever manages to exercise the requisite self-control, nor does any of them want to—they enjoy pissing on one another, in spite of the risks it entails. Beyond *akrasia*, there is self-indulgence, incontinence in the extreme, and there is so much of it in *The Sopranos*. Carmela has furs and jewelry and a Mercedes. Tony has women and booze and a big fuckin' Escalade, and he eats capicola by the fistful.

And this is the problem with the twenty-first-century mob. Tony, *capo regime* of the Soprano crew in the DiMeo crime family, lives in a fancy house, while his mother lives in the house he was brought up in, the one bought by his father, Giovanni Francis "Johnny Boy" Soprano, formerly the *capo regime* of the Soprano crew in the DiMeo crime family. Sometimes, it's good to keep your head down.

Seneca argued for self-control and against self-indulgence, with anger a form of the latter. He registers the objection an angry person might make to his stoicism: "Are you telling me that a good man doesn't become angry if he sees his father being murdered, his mother being raped? No, he will not become angry, but he'll be their champion and defender. Why are you afraid that a proper sense of devotion won't goad him sufficiently, even without anger?" Anger is superfluous and destructive, and this is why, in the Stoic program, it must be understood and then erased from one's character—anger, for Seneca, is not innate. Tony makes gestures toward Stoicism, which, like most Americans, he waters down. Seneca's answer to self-indulgence is what we now call "apathy," but we've watered that down, too. Seneca's word was *apatheia*, literally "without passion"— you can only be happy when apathetic, because you are then free of the push and pull of various passions and their imbalance.

Even Tony's diluted Stoicism entails a certain restraint, of course, but it's restraint in expressing what's dysfunctional, not therapy designed to cure dysfunction, as he makes clear to Dr. Melfi:

> Let me tell you something. Nowadays, everybody's gotta go to shrinks, and counselors, and go on *Sally Jessy Raphael* and talk about their problems. Whatever happened to Gary Cooper? The strong, silent type. That was an American. He wasn't in touch with his feelings. He just did what he had to do. See, what they didn't know was once they got Gary Cooper in touch with his

feelings that they wouldn't be able to shut him up! And then it's dysfunction this, and dysfunction that, and dysfunction *vafancul*!

What starts out as a criticism of modern America ends with profanity, the climbing wave of anger finally overcoming Tony's argument. Importantly, Gary Cooper—or at least the characters he played, strong and silent as they were—did not use profanity. "He just did what he had to do" isn't quite the same as "He did *only* what he had to do to be a good person." Gary Cooper may have been a Stoic, but, in spite of his aspirational diatribe, Tony is not.

Those who argue that profanity must express anger—a claim we've already questioned stringently, one we'll continue to question in the pages remaining—want to eradicate it from language, but that would be dangerous. Anger figures regularly in human behavior, which is why it so interests Aristotle and Seneca and any number of younger philosophers. If therapy—philosophical or psychiatric— will rid us of anger, then, by all means, but as long as there's anger around us we are better off hearing it. Though at times Tony and his crew seem like lambs, and at others wolves in sheep's clothing, when they are profane, they are wolves in wolves clothing. But let's not throw little Profanity out with the raging bathwater. Solving the problem of anger does not entail the end of profanity, which, as this book has tried to explain, is good for a lot of things besides expressing anger—though express anger it certainly does, when called forth to do so.

Just as the end of anger doesn't spell the end of profanity, so the end of profanity would not much threaten anger. Anger would lose a mode of expression, but what the enemies of profanity miss is that that many modes of expressing anger are considerably worse than words. Profanity, after all, exposes anger. Anger can hide in mere emotion, but profanity brings it out into aggression, if only verbal

IN PRAISE OF PROFANITY

aggression. Anger doesn't disappear when profanity disappears, and *The Sopranos* proves that in Tony's mother, Livia. She's not strong and silent like Gary Cooper—she is, in fact, a chronic complainer and devoted narcissist, so she perceives slights in nearly every inter-action—but she is surprisingly resilient and, cunningly, more of a Stoic than her son. The carping is often a distraction, a misdirection; if you watch Livia's eyes or her restless hands, you find the anger.

Livia is an interesting choice of name for Tony's mother. Livia Drusilla was married to the Roman Emperor Augustus, after Scribonia, with whom he'd had his daughter, Julia. He had no children with Livia, who is the very type of the stepmother. But Augustus was succeeded by his stepson, Tiberius, Livia's son from her first mar-riage to Tiberius Claudius Nero, and her line gave Rome Caligula, Claudius, Nero, all of them poster boys for conspiracy and violent resolutions. Seneca was Nero's tutor and advisor but later became a republican, so Nero ordered him to commit suicide, and we must hope that apathy served Seneca well at the end. Anyway, there was venom in Livia's blood. Tacitus surmised that Livia and Tiberius had murdered Augustus's grandson and presumptive heir, Postumus Agrippa, "the one from fear, the other from a stepmother's enmity." That was Livia all over as far as Tacitus was concerned, "terrible to the State as a mother, terrible to the house of the Cæsars as a step-mother." There is no pestilence more costly than anger, none more difficult to avert when hidden away in the stepmother's bosom.

David Chase, who conceived *The Sopranos*, claimed, "Livia was modeled *somewhat* on my own mother—an acerbic and fearful woman. Though Livia is the name of Tiberius' scheming mother in *I, Claudius*, it was also the name of one of my maternal aunts." You can guess what Jennifer Melfi would do with this information. Chase, soaked in 1970s TV, can't dodge his character's association with Livia Drusilla. Anyway, why bring it up if it wasn't at least subconsciously

relevant to naming Tony's mother? *I, Claudius*, based on Robert
Graves's novel of the same name, is a proto-example of the very sort
of long-arc television series Chase would make, though it has a very
(early) BBC rather than an HBO feel to it. Chase is his own mother's
son, and Tony Soprano is no stepson to Johnny Soprano. Nevertheless, as Seneca warns, "Anger makes a mother a stepmother," and
thus the Livias converge.

For Livia Soprano is selfish, manipulative, and mean-spirited.
She persuades Junior Soprano, both Tony's uncle and his rival, to
put out a contract on her own son—it sounds like ancient Rome,
though Rome isn't Sicily isn't Jersey. Tony inconveniently survives
the shooting, proving why ancient Livia preferred poison to con-
frontational violence. Marginalized in the mob world by her gender,
degraded by her cheating, lying husband, disappointed in her children, to whom, according to her repeated account, she gave everything on a silver platter, she is one angry stepmother. Visiting her
in her retirement home, Junior guesses, "Boy, Anthony must have
really gotten under your collar. Admit it. You're looking to crack his
calione for putting you in here." Livia responds with a characteristic
hand wave and furtive eyes, "I don't know what you're talking about."
She is the angriest Soprano, but she hides her anger, and she never
utters a profane word.

Well, almost never. She says of the activities director in the
nursing home, "She's a real pain in the ass." Later in the series, she
says to her grandson, A. J., "I know your father forbids your coming
down here," that is, to her retirement home—she perceives a slight.
A. J. denies it: "He doesn't. Honest. He just doesn't want us to talk
about you in the house." So, she had the wrong slight but, probing,
discovered another. "Well," she replies, "you can go shit in his hat."
But then she catches herself and reminds A. J., "I shouldn't use that
kind of talk. Don't let me ever catch you talking that way." When she

focuses attention away from herself and onto A. J., her anger, just momentarily expressed in profanity, recedes once again in to her dark interior. The rest of the time, as the cursing goes on all around her, she says to anyone who will listen—none of them does—"I don't like that talk" or "I am the only person in this family who doesn't curse—so do me the favor."

How does a literary work explore the problem of anger and its manifestations? It might be too much to say that profanity is required in such an exploration, yet it seems so well suited to it, especially because literary works depend on language. Even a television series, built partly on musical and visual materials, is still basically verbal art, and profanity is the most viscerally angry language available to us. When an episode is full of it, we're reminded of how destructive anger can be, how it casts civilization down and razes all opportunities—nothing lives when struck by that pestilence. When an episode is quiet, when anger burns hotter unspoken, we fear its hidden malignancies.

POLITICAL PROFANITY

In a chapter celebrating the literary value of profanity, mentioning James Kelman's Booker Prize–winning novel *How Late It Was, How Late* (1994) is obvious verging on cliché. The novel is about a Glaswegian down-and-outer named Sammy, who lives on disability insurance after an earlier life of petty crime, goes on a drinking binge, fights with police, lands in jail, wakes up blind, and has to negotiate a hostile—especially bureaucratic—world even less able than he was before. The story is told in a narrative voice that rarely speaks in pure third person. As Tom Shone put it in *The New Yorker*, not far into the novel "you begin to see what you've let yourself in for: a narrative voice that manages to try on first, second, and third person for size and yet feels as spacious as a straightjacket." Much of the novel unfolds in Sammy's interior monologue, in which he refers to himself in third person, and, of course, there's dialogue, as well.

Here is a typical passage of Sammy thinking and narrating simultaneously, as he is wont to do:

> Naw, but he was gasping for a smoke he really was he was fucking gasping: he smiled and tried to stop it but couldnay; stupit: hell with it but he kept going, his feet kicking into the steps; but that was alright man it was okay, just the stick banging away and the jolt when the bus started but he was fine and fucking great man and nay cunt could see him; nay cunt could fucking see him! Know what I'm talking about, the glasses and that, the shades, the auld shades, the bold yin, yer man. And then he was up there: there he was—holding on for dear life, the auld pole and that.

Apparently, there are some four thousand instances of *fuck* and its derivatives dispersed through the novel, and that's just to account for the f-word. The c-word gets a lot of play, as well, and other more or less profane items appear with less frequency, such as the *hell with it* of the passage quoted here.

At some moments, as the events and commentary wash through his mind, Sammy is "the bold yin," but the profanity doesn't surge into his narrative because he's bold. Rather, profanity expresses deep frustration at shit that happens and the System that sometimes causes it but rarely mitigates it. Alongside the frustration is plenty of existential anxiety. More than once, in more than one way, Sammy wonders, "What was gony happen to him but that was the real question. That was the one he wasnay asking. No seriously. But it was like the basic thing of it was there in his head, it just couldnay materialize;

maybe it was him stopping it." I've known people who couldn't materialize the basic thing of it, and in all humanity, where everyone is
the hero of his own story, this sort of story is a tragedy, for in this
sort of story events in the world and the self, such as it is, never align.

The value of feeling as though caught in a narrative straitjacket,
for Sammy and readers, is that the crisis of agency is underscored. Is
"what was gony happen to him" better conceived as "what will he do
about it," if anything? Sammy has plans in mind:

> He could vamoose but if he wanted to. Who was gony stop him?
> He could go back to the flats and pack his stuff and just saddle up
> and move em out. A blind man hits London. He would get off at
> Victoria. It was aye a great feeling that when ye left the bus. All
> the Glasgow accents disappear. As soon as ye step down onto the
> ground; everybody merges into the scenery, no one looking at
> one another. And then ye're anonymous. That was the fucking
> crack man know what I'm talking about getting anonymous, that
> was what it was all about, getting fucking anonymous; nay cunt
> giving ye hassle.

For much of the rest of the world, the fucking crack is having a
family, getting ahead, and in our strange, not particularly attractive,
celebrity even if only for a moment culture, having a media presence, being on Facebook, the opposite of anonymity. But Sammy
needs a rest. He needs to take himself out of the way of all of the
cunts. I'm not sure London is the best place to hide from them, but
when he gets into the taxi at the end of the novel, I wish him luck—
and I'm sure I'm not alone.

Kelman had long been a champion of the Glaswegian underclass
when *How Late It Was, How Late* was published. That novel was "the
latest installment," according to Shone, "in a career spent waging

war against the higher registers of the English language; his past fiction...has delighted in seizing English by the lapels, dunking it into the gutter, and shaking it into vulgar idiomatic life." Everyone paying attention to contemporary fiction knew what he stood for when the Booker Prize was in danger of being won by him. Appropriately, in my view, narrative structure and the motivating forces of linguistic register and language attitudes are never far apart in Kelman's work. But one of the judges of the 1994 competition, Julia Neuberger, nevertheless announced that the novel was a "disgrace" and "deeply inaccessible for a lot of people."

How many people a prize-winning novel—even a Booker Prize–winning novel—has to reach is unclear, but it's very clear how unreadable it was to a certain stripe of the English establishment. Charles Bowen, newly CEO of Booker in 1994, admitted that Kelman's novel "was the only one on the shortlist I couldn't get through." And 1994 wasn't the only year in which judges and others found Kelman's work impenetrable. When *The Busconductor Hines* (1984) was considered for the prize, Richard Cobb, a "professor of history at Oxford and a former Booker judge, memorably rejected" it "because it was 'written entirely in Glaswegian....I found him very heavy-going and only read two chapters....It was in dialect, like Burns's poems.'" Which is to say, I suppose, that Burns, had he written fiction, would not have been awarded the Booker Prize, though, surely, that stands as criticism of the prize, not the poet. Glibly marginalizing the vernacular, however, is ill-judged. After all, lots of people speak one or another variety of it, and few enough people speak a standard variety of English.

Profanity, of course, is not primarily a matter of dialect. It's shared among the rich and the poor, the rural and the urban, the black and the white. But how it's applied in context—the contexts in which it's acceptable, its frequency—can figure in a dialect. And it's also possible to misunderstand profanity as dialectal because people hear it differently when representatives of different classes or other social groups speak it. Occasional profanity from a supposedly genteel person is only the exception that proves the rule of gentility—at least, that's how it sounds to people similarly genteel. To some—certainly not all—of those genteel listeners, profanity from a down-and-outer like Sammy is uncouth as it wouldn't be from couther mouths. For those listeners, it merely confirms not only his marginality, but also the rightness of that marginality. Profanity, then, serves as an instrument of our assumptions. Neuberger castigated *How Late It Was, How Late* as a "disgrace" because "it was deeply inaccessible for a lot of people" who couldn't understand what might justify Sammy's language. Neither she nor they spent much time looking for a justification, though it's not all that difficult to find one.

Kelman responded to vilification of his novel after he'd won the Booker, pointing especially to ways in which he politicized narrative by removing an intermediate layer of irony: "I saw the distinction between dialogue and narrative as a summation of the political system," he wrote. "It was simply another method of exclusion, of marginalising and disenfranchising different people, cultures, and communities. I was uncomfortable with 'working-class' authors who allowed the 'voice' of higher authority to control narrative, the place where the psychological drama occurred." Narrative intervention in its very form questions the legitimacy of that drama—one can think of it as a "nonstandard drama," and Kelman refuses to let Establishment ideologies—especially those of standard English—"correct" what's naturally nonstandard.

Tom Leonard, a poet who often writes in Glaswegian dialect, and in many ways Kelman's fellow traveler, agrees with Kelman on this technical point. Leonard writes in a stunning essay, "Reclaiming the Local," that in conventional narrative, "The personae are trapped within the closed value-system that denigrates their use of language, while the writer-narrator communicates with the reader over their heads." Leonard's essay was written some years before publication of *How Late It Was, How Late,* but Leonard and Kelman had already been in league, and narrative in *How Late It Was* appears to enact the critical principle Leonard had advanced. Certainly, the response to *How Late It Was* proves the wisdom of Leonard's principle and Kelman's subsequent narrative innovation.

For, as Kelman observes, "You cannot write a short story without language. That seems an odd statement. Yet received wisdom in society has demanded it. Yes, they say, go and write a story, whatever story you want, but do not use whatever language is necessary. Go and write any story at all, providing of course you stay within the bounds.... What it amounts to is... [w]rite a story wherein people are talking, but not talking the language they talk." So, fiction must react to the received wisdom, which demands that it give voice to dialect and, yes, if a character's speech is speech of a "type" of person, whether regionally or socially identified, and that speech includes plenty of profanity, the profanity must be presented as essential to the character's voice—denying the dialect or the profanity is to deny the legitimacy of that voice. No one, not even a Booker Prize judge, has a right to do that to another person.

Judges are supposed to act impersonally or impartially—in the case of the Booker Prize, judges should be looking out for literature, not exercising their own biases, but as soon as you read that, you'll think, "It can't be done," and Leonard, probably Kelman, too, would agree with you. "The trouble with asking humans to enact the impersonal," Leonard points out, "is that they usually do so by objectifying the humans around them. The humans around them won't behave like objects, so the 'impersonal' diagnostician has to construct mechanistic models of those humans that turn them into the objects they have refused to become. The models of depersonalisation are inevitably linguistic, and thus at the heart of politics is language, at the heart of language is politics." Some of the judges responded far from impersonally to *How Late It Was*, but in the attempt at impartiality rejected both Sammy and his creator—neither of whom likes to be treated as objects and won't voluntarily behave like them—on superficially linguistic grounds, though the rejection is in fact moral and political. Shone talks about Kelman's advocacy for the "vulgar idiomatic life," but who's to say what's vulgar and what's not?

Kelman is determined in *How Late It Was, How Late* to let Sammy speak without a narrative filter pretending to an objectivity or impartiality that can't be maintained, to let Sammy speak as himself without typifying anything, without reifying his style of speech, for as Leonard notes:

> It's in the reification of linguistic codes and their possession by dominant and powerful classes wherein lies real danger.... That reification will always contain as part of its mechanics the device to maintain the illusion that social conflict does not exist, or that such conflict as exists can be meaningfully recreated, and resolved, within its own perimeter. Self-expression outside that code becomes simply a mechanism of self-elimination. The dominant refuse to recognize that all language is an instrument of consciousness: instead, it is held as a symptom. Others don't 'have' a language—they 'are' it. In dismissing the language, one dismisses the existence of its users—or rather,

along with Neuberger, Bowen, Cobb, and many more, "one chooses to believe that they have dismissed themselves." If no one listens to Sammy, well, that's Sammy's fault for being so disordered, so profane, so self-involved, and then—as Sammy puts it of himself in the novel—"Okay; so that was him fuckt."

How Late It Was, How Late is in effect a sort of test about how well you can accommodate Sammy's difference from yourself, whoever you are, and recognize his humanity, in spite of the fact that all of the profanity and the outlook in which it participates may make you uncomfortable. So, says Kelman, "Good literature is nothing when it is not being dangerous in some way or another and those in positions of power will always be suspicious of anything that might affect their security. True literary art makes some folk uncomfortable. It can scare them. One method to cope with being scared is not to look, to turn away and then kid on whatever it is does not exist." And, in fact, many readers of *How Late It Was*—probably a lot of its nonreaders, too—did turn away from it in discomfort, all the while blaming the suffering Sammy and his creator for readerly disaffection.

But it's really a problem of listening, which is Kelman's point. I had a friend who used to put it this way: "People talk the way they talk for a reason, and if you can tease out what the reasons are, you have contributed to scholarship. There's no point to being irritated or making fun of them." Instead, he suggested, "Shut up and listen." Don't speak from on high as though you understand those to whom you're not listening. You can't understand if you don't listen; you can't listen if you turn away. Can you look someone like Sammy in the eye? Can you imagine why he curses as much as he does? It's a matter of sympathy. Adam Smith wrote, "As we have no immediate experience of what other men feel, we can form no idea of the manner in which they are affected, but by conceiving what we ourselves should feel in the like situation." Earlier, we considered how the mirroring of experience leads to pleasure in someone else's profanity. It's interesting that we feel a frisson of intimacy with someone who drops an F-bomb over spilt milk, but we can't muster sympathy for someone in Sammy's condition, just because he utters too many F-bombs. As Neuberger admitted, "I did not care in the end what this drunken Glaswegian thought." You can't imagine Pat Conroy thinking or saying this about the kids he taught on Yamacraw Island, about whom he cared more the more he listened to them.

We may not take pleasure in Sammy's profanity, but we can respect it, indeed, we must do so, if we are following Smith in *The Theory of Moral Sentiments* (1759), the ethical theory that underlies capitalism as described in *The Wealth of Nations* (1776).[1] Smith wrote the *Theory* while occupying the Chair of Moral Philosophy at the University of Glasgow, and I don't think that's quite a coincidence—he had been a student at the university, too, and over decades had seen misfortune enough in the city streets to provoke his theory of sympathy. In the *Theory*, Robert Crawford writes eloquently, "he championed the kinds of social cohesion and mutual sympathetic awareness that counterbalanced the alienating effects of an increasingly industrial society." Sammy is nothing if not alienated, and all of the turning heads resist awareness and reject cohesion with his kind, preferring to objectify the kind and reify its language. Remember Tony McEnery's words: "Broadly speaking, the discourse of power excludes bad language, the discourse of the disempowered includes it."

There is a wide range of morally responsible reactions to Sammy, and there's no reason to suppose that Smith would have approved of Sammy's character or his language, but approval isn't really the point. "How selfish soever man may be supposed," Smith argued,

---

[1] I'm fairly sure Kelman would reject my turn toward Smith here, but I'm doing so because many readers, as supposed capitalists, should take it seriously. I am at the distinct disadvantage in this chapter of admiring all the authors therein—Kelman, Leonard, Smith, Jane Gardam, Edward St. Aubyn, and even, on occasion, Kingsley Amis—though they might not manage a civil conversation among themselves. But the conversation they would have, civil or not, is important, and it's what I'm constructing here, admittedly without permission from the principals.

"there are evidently some principles in his nature, which interest him in the fortune of others, and render their happiness necessary to him, though he derives nothing from it except the pleasure of seeing it. Of this kind is pity or compassion, the emotion which we feel for the misery of others, when we either see it, or are made to conceive it in a very lively manner." In the incessant profanity of *How Late It Was*, Kelman hopes to "make" us conceive Sammy's misery in a lively manner, that is to say in a fictionally concentrated manner. It's hard to see how Neuberger and others missed this point, not to mention sidestepped derelict Sammy—perhaps their reaction to the novel refutes Smith's assumption, or perhaps their mirror neurons misfired during the award season.

I mean, "We sympathize even with the dead," as Smith puts it, so it seems as though we ought to be able to sympathize with Sammy. But Smith's sympathy is always registered from a distance, and it's ephemeral: "the emotions of the spectator will still be very apt to fall short of the violence of what is felt by the sufferer. Mankind, though naturally sympathetic, never conceive, for what has befallen another, the degree of passion which naturally animates the person principally concerned. That imaginary change of situation, upon which their sympathy is founded, is but momentary." In *How Late It Was*, Kelman sustains that moment, and Sammy's profanity is the force driving our impressions. It's clear from some reactions, however, especially Neuberger's, that it doesn't always have even an ephemeral effect. Or, instead, the effect is far from ephemeral, but entirely negative, and the opposite of what Kelman intends and Smith proposes.

Neuberger, who is senior rabbi of the West London Synagogue, became a Dame of the British Empire and is now Baroness Neuberger, a life peer. Once a Liberal Democrat member of parliament and party whip, she is now, given her religious role, independent as a legislator. She has been prominently involved in healthcare issues, for instance, as head of the King's Fund, a think tank. She taught at Leo Baeck College in London for twenty years and was Chancellor of the University of Ulster. Her husband, Albert Neuberger, is a professor at University of Warwick; her brother-in-law Michael Neuberger was a professor and Fellow of the Royal Society, who won the GlaxoSmithKline Prize—GlaxoSmithKline partners with the King's Fund to examine better ways to deliver healthcare in the United Kingdom; another brother-in-law, James Neuberger, is Professor of Medicine at the University of Birmingham; and a third, David Neuberger, is also a life peer, Baron Neuberger of Abbotsbury, and is President of the Supreme Court of the United Kingdom.

No doubt Baroness Neuberger has done good works, but all in the Establishment frame, such that only momentary sympathy is required, and good can be accomplished even when one's head is turned. I do not exempt myself from the criticism. On a committee, as a legislator, through alms the synagogue or church distributes, you can do some good even on the basis of types, constructed and considered impersonally, even while reifying the social characteristics—including speech—of the very underclass you are determined to help. The repetitive, self-absorbed, profane complaint of the dispossessed will not interrupt your own self-absorbed self-talk: you won't have to listen to individuals other than yourself. I often wonder, when reading *How Late It Was*, whether Kelman intends to prove that we're not listening and not given to listening to people of the wrong class just as much as he intends to represent Sammy faithfully and engender sympathy for him: look on your fellow human, Sammy Samuels, gentle reader, and feel sympathy, but I know you won't, and this book will prove it. Were this Kelman's motive, the book would still be a great one, and profanity, which sets us up to react like Neuberger, just as essential to the fictional project at hand. Of course, there is no Baron Sammy Samuels, nor ever will be.

If one lacks Kelman's political commitment, profanity can take a much different fictional guise. Jane Gardam's wonderful story, "The Great, Grand, Soap-Water Kick," is about an aging tramp named Horsa, who breaks into a house for his periodic and effectively ritual bath. Sammy, too, longs for a bath: "He did need a fucking wash. A bath, a real yin, a lie down and a steep. Ye couldnay do much damage there; surely to fuck." There are similarities between Gardam's technique and Kelman's—we are mostly inside Horsa's head, in which the monologue sounds a bit Joycean: "So finds this house, oh very-nice. Verygoodclassperson. Green grass of Mugstown well cut, metal-edges. Keep grass not feeling too fullofself. Keep place. Gravel paths of mustard yellow. Windows white nets, swags like innertent. Front door smart boxsweets. Good chain for pullbell." In the end, Horsa not only has his glorious bath but finds both clothes and food to take away from the house he's invaded. We like him; we're glad it worked out. This is Neuberger's kind of tramp, one suspects—in and out, no contact with the middle classes or life peers, happy with his lot, no complaints, worthy of our sympathy.

Gardam plays it all for comedy, and this probably doesn't sit well with Kelman. Though I'm not here to comment on his sense of humor, I imagine Kelman would see Gardam's approach as patronizing, though the degree of agency preserved in Horsa's antics is worth considering. He's not condemned narratively for breaking and entering and bathing, even though he more or less destroys the house. He's a down-and-outer who finds it easier than Sammy to look out for himself and even to be joyful, but from a certain perspective, again, aligning with Kelman's, that may seem like so much comfortable mythologizing, a euphemism for the desperation men and women like Horsa and Sammy feel—they rarely go on a cleansing spree.

The status of Horsa's speech is unclear. It certainly doesn't make sense to those who get in its way. To a woman who drops by the invaded house to pick up "some old clothes for charity," Horsa says—this is what he hears in his own mind—"Nothing about me, ma'am, nothing about me." But if I'm reading correctly, the parenthetical statement that follows—"(Wurbly-burbly-gloshy-woshy-WAH)"— is what the woman hears, and she reacts thus, again from Horsa's interior perspective: "'Eeeeeeeeeek!' screams good woman, 'Helphelp. Mad man.' Nobody notices. Goodbye friend." The parenthetical seems to transcribe babble, but I'm not so sure that's what it represents. Horsa sheltered in a barn because "Rain turn snow. Horsa shacks up barn. Farmer looks. 'Get out there, you or I'll getmegun. So pushoff. Pram sticks every ten yards icymud. Sits down splat. 'Great goodfornowt,' yells farmer. 'Firing hay bloody fags.' 'No fags,' says Horsa. 'Don't smoke, farmer,' but comes out bad: "burble-wurble-yah-blah-splot.' Tramp, see. Loner. No practice mouth, tongue, vocal cordage of sarcophagus. 'Bad words, filth,' yells farmer." But, considered dispassionately, *burble-wurble-yah-blah-splot* is not filth, so one suspects it stands for something else.

A writer may not wish to avoid profanity entirely or represent it obliquely in the way Gardam does. Nevertheless, writers of a certain class disapprove of Kelmanesque cascades of *fuck*s and *cunt*s. Kingsley Amis writes about deploying profanity judiciously in his usage guide, *The King's English* (1997), and, without naming it, he has *How Late It Was, How Late* in mind:

On the whole, the thinning-out of spoken ribaldry is a loss. An entire way of being funny, and entire range of humorous effects, has been impoverished, except probably on the lower deck of our society. At first sight, the case with the printed four-letter word is different, though here I detect a similarly unwelcome drift towards serious aesthetic purpose. A bit of that can be seen in one of the last and least of the big fuck-novels, the winner of the 1994 Booker Prize. The doggedness with which its author keeps on trotting out the great word and its various derivatives already has something old-fashioned about it.

I like the transparency of this waspish comment, the carefree way in which it asserts a middle upper middle class superiority, the sort of superiority you need to feel if you write a book about how you think others should write their English. In that doggedness, Kelman is too earnest for Amis, trotting words out isn't art, and putative overuse of *fuck* belongs to the vulgar people on the lower deck, and you can tell where they stand even when they pretend to "serious aesthetic purpose."

"Naturally, someone in my position has had to devise some rough rules governing the use of such words," Amis writes, and we suppose he means someone in his position as a writer, though there's also a residual sense that he's in the position of arbiter. "My own set of rules," he continues, "I now put in writing for the first time. In what follows, *they* and *them* stand for what were once obscenities. 1. Use them sparingly and, as classicists used to say, for special effect only." And this principle certainly seems to guide the practice of poets like Dunbar and Rochester, or Philip Larkin—"They fuck you up, your mum and dad"—whom Amis probably had in mind as a prime example of profanity decorum, given their friendship and close correspondence. But Amis misses a crucial point, as people who know the answer before considering the evidence often do— not all special effects are achieved by sparing use of profanity and abundant use is essential to the special effect Kelman has in mind for *How Late It Was, How Late.*

Class makes a great deal of difference in the poetic license for literary profanity. Edward St. Aubyn, an upper-upper-middle-class writer on the cusp of the lower upper classes doesn't hesitate to use profanity in his tetralogy of Patrick Melrose novels, but he does so with the restraint Amis recommends. So, at a crucial moment in *Bad News* (1992), the second novel in the series, "Patrick shot bolt upright and banged his head on the leg of the chair. 'Shit, wank, fuck, blast,' he said in his own voice at last." Well, good for him, to find his own quite profane voice at last. Somehow, this transformative moment invites approval in *Bad News*, perhaps precisely because it marks a transformation rather than business as usual, the consistency of Sammy Samuels, for instance. Sammy speaks in his own voice throughout a Booker Prize–winning novel—it's just that few listen to it.

There's an interesting but unsavory political twist to all of this: the privileged can use profanity because they know how to use it, and they carry a poetic license to do so. Leftist Glaswegian activists like Kelman shouldn't misuse bad language, because they only spoil it for the other authors. To many readers, it's much more acceptable for a completely irresponsible, drugged out almost aristocrat to swear than it is for a Glasgow down-and-outer who is caught in profanity as long as he's caught in the pain of living. "Wait," you say, Patrick is, after all, in New York arranging the funeral of the father who abused him sexually throughout his childhood—you can see why he might need some cocaine or heroin to help take the edge off of that experience. Perhaps. But I admit I'm certainly no less aware of Sammy's plight, that of the excluded, marginalized, disenfranchised, objectified, depersonalized Glaswegian.

According to the Sapir-Whorf hypothesis, differences among natural languages reflect and perhaps impose different conceptions of the world. As the linguist Edward Sapir, who put the Sapir in Sapir-Whorf, explained, "The 'real world' is to a large extent unconsciously built up on the language habits of the group. No two languages are ever sufficiently similar to be considered as representing the same social reality. The worlds in which different societies live are distinct worlds, not merely the same world with different labels attached." *How Late It Was, How Late* plays with the notion that the "real world" is unconsciously built up on the language habits of the individual, Sammy, who sees things as he expresses them. Is Sammy's social reality limited by his language, or do our social realities exclude Sammy because they are limited by our linguistic capacities, by our capacity to hear what's contained in the language of another? Is there an ethnographic aspect to our experience of Kelman's novel? If we observe carefully what we don't understand easily, will the sympathy we can't help but feel for Sammy, at least ephemerally, lead to better knowledge of the overlap between our social realities?

Profanity proves essential to Kelman's approach to these matters, not just about Sammy in particular, but how we know about others, how we consider them from an ethical perspective, how we challenge ourselves to apprehend and evaluate and accept social and moral difference without losing sight of the individual who poses the challenge. For middle-class people—not for those organizing charity from on high—this is the moral and emotional crisis of the soup kitchen, the homeless shelter, the free clinic. It isn't enough for a character in a novel to embody the Sammies around us; the character has to speak experience we won't like to hear about in his or her own voice, which is bound to be an intensely vernacular voice, a voice that bothers us, that turns experience inside out, almost in the way that fantasy shifts the epistemological ground on which we prop our knowledge of the world. The religious detractors of profanity will point to Ephesians 4:29: "Let no corrupt communication proceed from your mouth, but that which is good to the use of edifying, that it may minister grace unto the hearers." But what if profanity, even when corrupt, is at least also edifying? In *How Late It Was, How Late*, profanity is the grit on which the pearl of moral understanding forms. The novel isn't a disgrace, but an opportunity.

PROFANITY PERFORMED

In very early February 2013, the girls of Queen of Peace High School in North Arlington, New Jersey, were cajoled into pledging not to curse for a month. More precisely, some succumbed but some refused, because the boys of Queen of Peace were neither expected to pledge nor to resist the supposedly inherent masculine impulse to swear. Girls are sugar and spice—not too much spice, not girl power, certainly not Roman Catholic roller derby grrrl power—and boys curse. According to *The Record* of Bergen County, Brother Larry Lavallee, the school's principal, insisted that "the girls have the foulest language.... 'It's unattractive when girls have potty mouths,' noted Nicholas Recarte, 16. A pitcher on the school's baseball team, Nicholas said he can't help shouting obscenities from the mound after mishaps. He said he didn't expect that to change." WTF, Nicholas, unattractive to whom, and why must girls follow your rules but not your example?

Plenty of research shows that contemporary girls and young women swear plenty, but not more than boys and men of the same age. Surely, though, many of us find it unattractive when boys have potty mouths, too; at least, we need a better explanation of why what's cool for guys is crass for girls. Both Brother Larry and Nicholas reflect fairly common attitudes about profanity and gender, attitudes rooted deeply in our mythologies about gender and character and propriety and morality. If you believe that Eve's forked tongue caused the Fall of Man and gave Adam a reason to curse, you may be suspicious of whatever comes out of women's mouths ever after and accept, encourage, and even benefit from a double standard about profanity. Of course, there are other ways of interpreting the Genesis story.

Notably, in the story of the Fall, only God curses—he curses the serpent. And, when expelling Adam and Eve from Eden, he doesn't tell Eve to go forth and multiply and Adam to curse as much as he likes. Of course, God can curse all He likes—I could choose another pronoun, but men tend to curse more than women—and, looking around Creation, He has had plenty of reason to do so, self-satisfaction recorded in Genesis notwithstanding. Made in His image, suffering from our self-imposed Fall, we have plenty of reason to curse, too. Men are ashamed of having fallen, so spend all of eternity claiming a closer relationship with God. Women, however, reflect God's nature as well as men so should be able to swear equally with them. We should avoid using profanity to harm others, but it's not such a bad way of expressing our existential frustrations.

In fact, we should encourage girls to swear, because pitchers on private Catholic school baseball teams grow up to run things, and when they're in the locker room or the board room, when they're on the golf course or a training course, they swear freely. Not swearing is part of the politeness structure that restricts girls and women but part of the power structure that enables boys and men. So how does a woman achieve power if she can't be one of the boys? In *Verbal Hygiene* (1995), Deborah Cameron describes the trap laid for women by notions of "correct" language. One might suggest to the ambitious woman that she "talk like a man," Cameron notes, but that "carries the risk of trapping women in the familiar double-bind. Insufficiently 'feminine' women may be labeled deviant, and powerful women are almost by definition threatening. On the other hand, a display of femininity can be used as a justification for not taking women seriously. The problem for ambitious women...is how to resolve this real contradiction."

Women should swear more, and they might as well start swearing while they are girls, right alongside the boys. Cameron shows how some solutions to the paradox she poses suppress women, for instance, assertiveness training, a regimen that helps the little lady figure out how to function in masculine work settings. But, honestly, there's nothing more naturally assertive than *Fuck you* or *Go fuck yourself*, or, in answer to a male colleague's uninspired suggestion, *Fuckin'-A, Pinkerton, fuckin'-A*. When you talk like this, people know where you stand. Two famous news anchors, Katty Kay and Claire Shipman, wrote recently about the confidence gap between men and women and how it affects women's success. They, too, identify correctness as a false idol; they wonder whether "being good" doesn't get in women's way, because "while being a 'good girl' may pay off in the classroom, it doesn't prepare [women] very well for the real world," and "Soon they learn that they are most valuable, and most in favor, when they do things the right way: neatly and quietly."

Well, fuck that. I have a daughter, Amelia, and she's a stinker, but at three or so her language isn't salty—not yet. I don't want her to use profanity just for the sake of using it, but I don't want her to be neat and quiet, and I want the entire repertoire of language— including profanity—at her beck and call. Especially, I don't want boys' interests to overwhelm hers because their profanity drowns out her polite speech. I don't want her to suffer expectations like "be straight-A, strait-laced," as Nora Eldredge puts it in Claire Messud's *The Woman Upstairs*, as though being that girl will make all the difference. Nora explains of herself, "I thought I could get to greatness, to my greatness, by plugging on, cleaning up each mess as it came, the way you're taught to eat your greens before you have dessert. But it turns out that's a rule for girls and sissies." Nora's is not an idiosyncratic response to the double standard: "Don't all women feel the same?" Nora asks. Yes, and so a girl possessed of herself will swear a blue streak—not a pink one—every now and then.

How do women solve the "real contradiction" Cameron and others identify in women's linguistic behavior? One way is to own the deviance Cameron mentions and thus challenge conventional assumptions about feminine language—just flout the supposed rules. Mary Prankster was a flouter, but *Mary Prankster* was the pseudonym for someone else, so the flouting was part of a self-conscious performance of deviance. Like a lot of deviants, Mary started out in Baltimore, then moved to New York, and occasionally played at The Brass Lantern, in Reading, Pennsylvania, where I heard her perform. In the song "Breakfast" (1998), she is "really stoned" and thinks her Mom has dosed her orange juice with acid "again." She's having a confusing conversation with the Aunt Jemima syrup bottle. "Fuck fuck fuck fuck fuck fuck fuck," she sings, "You're not my problem—I'm my problem." What does Aunt Jemima think of all the f-word? She tells Mary "How she hates being a stupid fucking racial stereotype," and suddenly race and gender join in performing profanity. "Fuck yeah," the song ends. And there you have it, the beginning of the "Fuck yeah" attitude behind that deviant Internet organ, Tumblr.

In "Tits and Whiskey" (1998), Mary cries "Fuck me, fuck me, fuck me, fuck me/I am Ernie's rubber ducky"—deviant. And deviant is what she's going for: "So fuck the rhythm and let's break out the tits and whiskey/'cause that shows that we're anarchists." "Mercyfuck" (1998) plays on the variety of *fuck* forms and meanings. Sometimes, *fuck* is patently sexual: "I wish I could fuck all my sorrows away / And fuck till the dawn of the next fucking day." But on that *fucking*, which is a pun, the song pivots from the sexual to the expletive: "Fuck the chorus and verse, fuck the pain getting worse" and she identifies herself as the "worst fuck up in all history." With this level of expletive, you kind of have to go all the way, and perhaps there's no return: "I'm fucked if I do and I'm fucked if I say / I'm fucked if I don't, so I'm fucked anyway." Still, she doesn't "need your mercyfuck sympathy," you stupid fuck. You can't reject her because she isn't conventionally feminine, because she isn't conventionally feminine—the profanity and a lot more tells you that—and has already rejected you. End of contradiction. Fuck yeah.

Or, one can try to solve the "real contradiction" in some form of rebellion rather than straight up deviance. Such rebellion addresses power, attempts its redistribution. Liz Phair is a rebel, or at least she started her performing career as one. Timothy White calls her early songs "affectionately uncouth"—so, challenging but not necessarily as threatening as Cameron supposes—and notes that in her first album, *Exile in Guyville* (1993), she "is ingenious at restoring sex and other ceremonies of self-revelation to an ordinary, freshly affecting scale," in which, one might argue, profanity promotes vernacular confrontation with such fundamentally human issues. Or, perhaps, and unexpectedly, profanity isn't vernacular but ceremonial language; or, further, in the mystery of performing such ceremonies, both vernacular and ceremonial.

Early Liz Phair just says it like it is. In "Fuck and Run," from *Exile*, she declares what a lot of young women, hedging commitment, are prone to think, but more important, she declares it in the way they at least occasionally think it: "I want a boyfriend / I want all that stupid old shit." In "Supernova," from the subsequent album, *Whip-smart* (1994), she deadpans, "You fuck like a volcano." And, while we're talking about profanity in the sexual register, "Chopsticks" from *Whip-smart* explains of one gentleman caller, "He said he liked to do it backwards / I said that's just fine with me. / That way we can fuck and watch TV." Slackers are busy, too, being slackers, so they fit the sex in where they can. In the grey of morning, the singer drops him at his house and then drives home, " 'Cause," she admits, "secretly, I'm timid." That's a change from the persona of *Exile*'s "Flower": "I want to fuck you like a dog," she offers, "I'll fuck you and your minions, too"—whether in series or one big clusterfuck isn't clear— and, to conclude, "I'll fuck you 'til your dick is blue." The setting of

"Flower" isn't clear, but could it be spring? "I only ask because I'm a real cunt in spring." Despite appearances, Phair's early songs aren't always densely profane, but the list represents well how they perform profanity.

Meghan O'Rourke would later characterize early Phair as speaking to "a collective village of young Americans whose defining idiom was ironic detachment." Strategically performative casual use of profanity—or perhaps performatively strategic casual use—promotes that idiom. And it was no accident that "her signature style of singing... made a mockery out of all that was feminine about singing." But by *Whitechocolatespaceegg* (1998), Phair had stopped performing the rebel, and there's not much profanity in that album or in the eponymous *Liz Phair* (2003), which prompted O'Rourke's caustic review: "She has committed an embarrassing form of career suicide," disappointingly subject to "the desire to infantilize herself." I remember as if it were yesterday how vehemently many of my Liz Phair listening friends agreed.

In *Liz Phair*, the songs are often sexual, even intensively so, but the ironic detachment has gone missing. You might consider "H.W.C." the signature song. It's got a bit of profanity —"All you do is fuck me every day and night"—but it's mainly about the restorative properties of the lover's hot white cum. That's right, "H.W.C." is a euphemism, and the song celebrates the power of a younger man to make an older woman younger again, an ancient and very suspect trope of Western literature. The promotional photograph accompanying the album, the one in the jewel case, shows Phair in something like sexual pleasure with an upright guitar between her legs. This is an old trope, too. The "O" of the lute, over which the male player would strum in paintings and poems of the Renaissance, represented the "nothing" of the woman's sexual part. The woman who gives into that image, Ariel Levy argues in her *Female Chauvinist Pigs*, has joined a raunch culture that works against her interests, not to mention those of all women.

The photo in question isn't a naked selfie, and "H.W.C." isn't profanity, perhaps not even as a euphemism, because you really need to be in the know before the initials make any sense. BTW, I'll bet the girls of Queen of Peace High School could get away with using *HWC* among themselves for quite a while, LOL. I mean, OMG, parents and teachers are totally clueless about initialisms in teen discourse, and so—unlike *fuck* and *bitch*—*HWC* isn't a detention word. O'Rourke wasn't sure what motivated Phair's detachment from ironic detachment and rebellion, "unless it's that Ms. Phair, perennially willful, wants to buck expectations and write home about it." In other words, having rebelled, and still rebellious, she had to rebel against her own rebellion. This all suggests that rebellion is mundane and comes in stages—stages you grow out of, stages you grow into, but temporary in both directions—and it's not a fully persuasive answer to Cameron's "real contradiction."

Nellie McKay's solution may not be fully persuasive, either, but it's compelling. McKay is a Manhattan-based cabaret singer, a twenty-first-century chanteuse. She has built a career on singing dirty while sounding nice. She has an album titled *Normal as Blueberry Pie: A Tribute to Doris Day* (2009), and she has a lot of Doris Day in her—I don't doubt the tribute is sincere—but she isn't close to normal, and the portmanteau of these sensibilities is what makes her a great artist. On her breakthrough album, *Get Away from Me* (2004), the title an arch revision of Norah Jones's warm and earnest *Come Away with Me* (2002), McKay has a song titled "I Want to Get Married," which runs through all the picket fence, starched-aproned, "leave it to beaver-ish" marriage fantasies feminists hate. Such a "display of femininity can be used as a justification for not taking women seriously," but that would miss the point of McKay's performance.

Terry Gross—like just about everyone else who heard it—thought "I Want to Get Married" must be a satire, but when she proposed this to McKay on *Fresh Air*, McKay was unwilling to confirm her suspicion. "You can criticize something you strive for, you can avoid something you dream about," McKay explained. This ambivalence is fundamental to her blended performance as a writer, singer, and instrumentalist. I can't afford to include a sampler of her songs in this book, so you'll just have to find out what I mean by her sound on your own dime. But I can explain a bit about her lyrics here, how they take us by surprise, as all great art will, how they resist settling for picket-fence language just to feel secure. As Gene Bertoncini characterizes her songs, they are a "purposefully zany and disarmingly melodic assault on modern times and timeless ills." You have to take McKay seriously because in that assault she throws you off balance.

Often, then, barbed lyrics are sung to dreamy tunes on perky instruments. On *Fresh Air*, for instance, McKay sang a version of "Mother of Pearl," the lead song on *Obligatory Villagers* (2007), to ukulele accompaniment. The song begins, "Feminists don't have a sense of humor." It's like the Cretan Liar Paradox! And one suspects it really is partly disingenuous: the song ends by throwing vegetarians in with the feminists, but on the back cover of an earlier album, *Pretty Little Head* (2005), McKay sports a sweatshirt with "VEGAN" printed across the front. She looks straight into the camera with a smile that could be taken as forced or facetious, even though it's also bright and friendly—it's like a slang smile, a pretty slang smile. So, is she a vegan or a carnivore making a joke about vegans? She's also "a proud member of PETA," according to the cover copy of *Get Away from Me*. Is she a vegan but not a feminist? Are we to suppose that because feminists and vegetarians are similar that she's also a feminist? If feminists don't have a sense of humor, what about the ukulele, what about that smile?

Like Livia Soprano, McKay is often most cutting when she isn't using "that language." In "Ding Dong"—the sound of a doorbell, not the snack cake—from *Get Away from Me*, the singer announces that her cat has died. Lonely, she looks for company, as anyone would:

> Do you have a little time?
> Would you like to ease my mind,
> Talk for hours and never stop,
> Chop your head off,
> Be a lighter person, brighter person, nicer?
> But you've heard it all before.

There's got to be a less violent way to become a nicer person. And stanza by stanza the singer—by whom I mean the performed character, not Nellie McKay—is visited by anonymous men—a man in white, one in red, another in black—who don't satisfy her loneliness and who seem to get the same advice about head-chopping and such. I would say, "It's just a cat," but then I remember that Tony Soprano, in a fury, kills Ralph Ciffaretto, his best earner, over a horse, and I don't want Nellie McKay coming after me with that ukulele.

Many elements combine in the song's unique affect. The music is bouncy and the diction is light, playful, almost silly: "God, I loved her, oh so much / Miss her little kitty touch." But it's also a romp of alcoholic depression: "My cat died, and I quickly poured myself some gin.... I'm smarter than you think. / Do I sound like an old bore? / Oh man, it's just the drink." That's the point, I think, when she heads to the closet and pulls out the axe or whatever, for the chopping that leaves everyone feeling lighter and brighter. The song's ambivalence is intoxicating. At her best, McKay sounds a bit like a slurry of gin martini and vanilla ice cream—it's wrong, but you've never tasted anything like it before, and, maybe because the ice cream is sweet and cold, it takes the juniper off the gin, though you can still taste it, just a little.

But in all of that Nellie McKay, where's the profanity? It's in the lethargic "Really," from *Get Away from Me*, in which the singer isn't mad enough or sad enough or tough enough do deal with the injustice around her. "I feel sympathy, empathy / It's just that I'm super busy right now.... I'm such a shit.... It's just that I'm a yuppie fuck." And though she is, she can also imagine herself a victim, one of the downtrodden. "Sometimes I feel like I shouldn't apologize so much"—a very Sammy Samuels thing to say—and then "I'm bein' attacked / tit for tat / you fuckin' bureaucrats / you can just apologize back," which—in spite of the F-bomb—is a yuppier way of saying what Sammy so often says. It's just that, given her performance as a latter-day Doris Day, it's surprising to find her reminding us of Sammy Samuels at all. Are we unexpectedly experiencing sympathy through profanity?

Profanity isn't frequent in McKay's songs, so when it occurs, it slaps the face of conventional language and living, which, however, she mocks subtly and with much technical cleverness when she's not swearing, too. In "Identity Theft," from *Obligatory Villagers*, McKay's persona rages against the education establishment. She's "runnin' from the thought police" and she doesn't want to assimilate into hypocrisy, so she decries the diploma, the "passport," on which you "get that stamp," all of which, she claims, is "funny like a nazi camp." At first, this last seems just tasteless hyperbole, but, as we'll see below, tastelessness has its self-effacing place in this kind of social critique—the singer has a point, but when she stretches the rubber band too far, it snaps back at her. Again, McKay intends to have it both ways, to propose what the singer proposes through the singer, and then to turn on her in a further layer of critique.

"Ignorance is a right," McKay's persona cries,

not a privilege
I've finished done and had it
And while you fucks are at it,
As far as I'm concerned
Pluto's still a planet.

I think I'm one of the fucks she has in mind. And the persona in this song certainly bears some relation to McKay, who studied jazz voice at the Manhattan School of Music but left without getting her passport stamped. She wanted to go her own way; it didn't do her any harm; I for one, take great pleasure in all she does. So I can live with the assessment she delivers in the *Fresh Air* interview: "You know, institutions of higher learning themselves are always suspect," even if I don't agree that education is identity theft.

I notice that in the liner notes for "Identity Theft," *fucks* is *f***s*, but the euphemism doesn't make this fuck feel any better. The lines, "Because I'm tired of being nice / Fuck you once and fuck you twice," which I wish I could say to real people now and then, have got a couple of *f**ks* in them, too. Since the profanity in question is well articulated on the recording, it's not clear what's gained by emending the liner notes, except, possibly, to make a point about profanity and politeness—you may not be willing for print to preserve what you're nonetheless willing to say. In a rousing sort of Irish pub style, "Livin," from the same album and the same set of liner notes, announces that "Oh, livin's a bunch o' s**t / S***tin's a part of livin." How odd that the first *t* is asterisked but not the following *t* and *i*—it could be an error, just a thoughtless lapse, or it could be a preference, but it could also be a joke about euphemism, from a singer-songwriter well aware that she's at play on the borders of propriety.

Atavism winks from behind the cabaret sophistication of McKay's work. McKay's art lies in the seamlessness of her music, lyrics, and performance: you can't locate an "authentic" or "sincere" idea among them. They might all be authentic and sincere; they might all be sly and facetious; or they might paradoxically—the positive spin on ambivalence—be all of them at once. Profanity plays an important role in McKay's performance because it is apparently disruptive, yet somehow appropriate and plausible, perhaps what Judith Butler has called a "subversive confusion." It is the incorporation of the anger and violence that lurks within, not behind, civilization, and that complex relationship is hard to express artistically without recourse to profanity or some other similarly effective gesture, not merely symbolic, but physical in the way of expletive, a slinging of the self into resistance.

Obviously, too, this sort of performance resists the notion that women are held to a standard of correctness in speech that doesn't apply to men. McKay chooses to do so in a particularly clever, a particularly effective way, not in a barrage of profanity, but with just enough profanity to assert authority over language without the profanity itself distracting from that authority. Profanity in *The Sopranos* is anger unleashed in language—it isn't disciplined, though the undisciplined use of it reflects an artistic motive. And, without second-guessing Kelman's motive or narrative strategies, it's nonetheless true that Sammy's profanity does distract some listeners from getting the point, though the point may be that they're not getting it, that they're not listening to the dispossessed. McKay uses profanity when she wants to, and, as Amis suggests, she amplifies it by minimizing it, though that works, not because she's upper upper middle class and using her profanity license—which *is* stamped— but because the rest of her performance—including her smile—is deceptively sunny.

McKay's performance is, in the way of art, unique, but it's not without parallel. Sarah Silverman is a notorious American comedian.

She's had a series on Comedy Central but is best known for her stand-up act. She's not a potty mouth per se, but her comedy certainly includes raunchy elements. (She is capable of the raunchiest possible comedy, as demonstrated in her version of the classic vaudeville joke, "The Aristocrats.") Mostly, it's wickedly politically incorrect. It depends on a sort of clueless persona, who doesn't understand why African Americans or Asian Americans or Jews—she is herself Jewish—are the way they supposedly are. Thus, Silverman pokes fun at Americans who don't get racial or religious or sexual politics as well as feminists and vegans who can't take a joke. Like McKay, she handily has it both ways. Silverman's stereotypes are broad, and yet they can be very funny, coming from the mouth of someone apparently so naïve.

Incongruity is Silverman's stock in trade. In her film, *Jesus is Magic* (2005), she has a character in a psychedelic pink above-the-knee dress, white platform knee boots, shoulder-length bob, and (mostly) sweet, cheery smile stride through various scenes in a jaunty way, playing her acoustic guitar and singing a song titled "I Love You More." She seems like a free-wheeling American hipster troubadour, until the lyrics hit: "I love you more than Jews love money.... I love you more than black people don't tip." It's completely outrageous crap coming out of pink-and-white cute. As *Variety* put it, it's "explosively funny and perversely adorable," and wrong—very, very wrong. What bothers the character most is Jewish people driving German cars: "What the cock is that shit?" she asks, in the one profane line of the song. The profane line is less offensive than any other line in the song, so, I suppose, score one for profanity.

Silverman's comedy, however, is just that—the skit "I Love You More" is an extended joke, and though one can't separate Silverman from her art easily, it's clear from her *Fresh Air* interview—in which her voice diverges widely from that of a character like the singer of

"I Love You More"—that she's not engaged in the same level of performance as McKay. McKay's performance isn't comedy, even if it includes comedic notes. It's a finer performance, not in the sense "better," but in the sense "fine-grained" or "finely inscribed," and it is far less easy from her public statements to tell where her performance begins and ends, if in fact it does either. In "I Love You More," the line "What the cock is that shit?" is a punchline, ultimately followed by this coda: "Cha cha cha!" It's the only way Silverman can get the character out of the song. McKay's profanity can't be separated in the same way from the rest of what she says, which makes a different statement about the status of profanity and therefore a different statement about women using it.

Obviously, there are alternative takes on profanity and its uses in both comedy and song. A stand-up comedian must forge a relationship with her audience. Silverman does this in a very odd way, by being sweetly objectionable from the beginning of her act, and occasionally allowing herself a sly look that announces her ironic awareness of her absurd character—in photographs, her lip often curls. Lots of people don't like Silverman's comedy, partly because her stage persona is not likable, and also because it's familiar only in its ventriloquism of stereotypes. Profanity isn't part of this address. Iliza Shlesinger, on the other hand, deftly uses profanity for various purposes in her stand-up act. Shlesinger is hot. In the publicity shot for her Comedy Central special *War Paint* (2013), she's naked and her blonde tresses cover her breasts. She wields lipstick in her right hand, and her lips curl in a knowing, smirky way, like Silverman's. She trades on some of the same incongruities as McKay and Silverman, but she's neither innocent nor pretending to be so.

Shlesinger swears throughout *War Paint*. She's not trying to shock or offend or even to perform a McKay-like paradox. Her swearing always sounds completely natural—it's hanging-out talk—and her closing material includes what some might consider obscenities, like *beej* 'blow job' and *handie* 'handjob,' but they're playful obscenities. She tosses off a casual "They teach us this shit in high school"— though probably not at Queen of Peace—mimics a certain type of young woman saying, "Sarah, you're being a bitch," drops a *fucktard*, and flips the bird. These instances are scattered over some twenty minutes, neither a cascade of profanity—think of how much profanity *The Sopranos* sometimes crams into twenty minutes—nor constant reiteration of it, as in some male stand-up. Shlesinger explains that she's invented the word *snootch* for 'vagina' because she greatly objects to *pussy*, which, she points out, is "not a word that women hear independent of men." That could be a feminist observation, one that perversely vindicates Jonathon Green's insistence that all slang and profanity is masculine language, that is, until a woman on the warpath, like Shlesinger, makes it new. But she offers another, very revealing evaluation of the p-word: "It's not a lady word."

How unexpectedly polite from a comedienne who slings shit with all requisite assurance, the assurance of a lady rebelling against captivity in masculine discourse! Recourse to politeness—"It's not a lady word"—might seem a retreat into femininity, but I think instead it's another paradoxical look at feminine performance. In this performance, profanity is normative rather than disruptive and politeness is disruptive rather than normative, in spite of the stereotypes Shlesinger literally embodies, as well as those she performs. Unlike McKay, however, she performs those stereotypes of feminine identity within quotation marks, often as another voice, a voice which, in *War Paint*, on occasion moves from feminine speech to a sheep's bleat. *Snootch* isn't entered in *Green's Dictionary of Slang*, and Shlesinger has thus done what she isn't supposed to do as a woman—not only does she invent slang, she invents it to resist men putting their slang where it isn't wanted.

Shlesinger's profanity performs solidarity with her audience. Shlesinger starts with a diatribe against the airlines, which is a good way to build solidarity, too—everyone hates the airlines. If you insist, Shlesinger says, that your cousin Sheila works for an airline and she's a fine person, Shlesinger's having none of it: "Fuck your cousin, Sheila...your cousin Sheila's a goddamn bitch." Airline employees are not the major problem, though—it's the zone boarding system and the accumulation of special categories of customer to which (supposedly) Shlesinger does not belong. "If you don't fly that airline often enough, you are S.O.L." she concludes, and then she goes on to demonstrate how well everyone but those seated in Zone 4 are treated. Those privileged to board for Zone 2 include "anyone who likes comic books—you're a fuckin' nerd...if you're old, hurry the fuck up...no, ma'am, you may not bring Coors Lite up in this, bitch," says the airline worker Shlesinger performs. You can board for Zone 3 "if you have a copperhead snake as a pet instead of a normal goddamn pet, like a dog or a cat. You're like, "Fuck it! I'm goin' to get me a snake, yeah, fuck you, Dad. I'm not goin' to law school...you may get in the plane, and Boarding Zone 4, you can go fuck yourself."

And so Shlesinger demonstrates how the putative airline employee, from a position of questionable authority, gets to pull a Dick Cheney. After this initial bid for solidarity, there's less profanity—it's already done its job. Shlesinger's rhetorical use of profanity is distinct from McKay's stylish profanity. Of course, one can't really talk about one performance being more performative than others; one can't even talk about one performance being more invested in style than another, because style figures in all performance. But perhaps we can talk about performance that's more stylish than others, and McKay's performance deserves this distinction, because it's a performance we can't see through. Oddly, profanity is an instrument of finesse.

In *Gender Trouble* (1999), Judith Butler agrees that in gender identity—in femininity—"coherence is desired, wished for, idealized," but, she goes on to argue, that's too bad, because it isn't coherent at all. We make gender an interior matter, a psychological "fact," Butler continues, because "the displacement of a political and discursive origin of gender identity onto a psychological 'core' precludes an analysis of the political constitution of the gendered subject and its fabricated notions about the ineffable interiority of its sex or of its true identity." It's safer for men, at least, if we avoid the politics of gender and the discourses of song and stand-up, among other arts that engage them on women's behalf. Although "parody by itself is not subversive," Butler endorses parodic performances of gender because "the loss of the sense of 'the normal'... can be its own occasion for laughter," and the laughter is political and subverts assumptions about gender. We lose the sense of "the normal" in McKay's songs, only partly but significantly in her effing ineffable performance of profanity.

PENULTIMATE PROFANITY

The store of profanity in literature is not limitless but it is extensive, and this chapter is necessarily only a sample of how authors can use profanity to accomplish big things and how reading profanity as essential to the texts in question—rather than as a sort of aesthetic lapse—enriches our reading of the texts and the cultures they examine and evaluate, whether medieval Scotland or twenty-first-century America. And in American literature today, there is so much profanity to consider that were we to grasp and grapple with it as in the contexts presented here, we would come to a new understanding of ourselves. Profanity as a key to cultural and perhaps even personal understanding—you probably didn't see that coming any more than I did when I first started writing this book.

Think of all that stand-up comedy, all that television, all those songs in which profanity figures to one or another degree. The uses to which it's put diverge widely and meaningfully: exclamatory *fuck* in Episode 4 of the first season of *The Wire*; the salty language of the Wild West in *Deadwood*; Hank Moody's jubilant *motherfucker*; euphemism in *New Girl* and *Don't Trust the B—in Apartment 23*; the Mandarin profanity of the future Wild West out in space, in Joss Whedon's *Firefly* and *Serenity*, which is cleverly both profanity and euphemism at the same time—and that's just some of the television. What about movies? What about drama? What about poetry? What about song?

I have profanity in songs on my mind a lot recently because of Garfunkel and Oates. These are stage, YouTube, and television personae of second-string songsters, not Paul Simon and Daryl Hall, but Art Garfunkel and John Oates. The songwriters/singers/actors behind the personae are Kate Micucci and Riki Lindhome. Although there are sentimental exceptions, their songs are usually raunchy and funny and meant to be offensive: "Pregnant Women Are Smug"— *bitch, effin son of a gun*; "Save the Rich"—*fuck* (v); "Fuck You," in which *fuck* is literal; "This Party Took a Turn for the Douche"— *motherfucker, fuckwad*; and "The Loophole," which proposes that anal sex is OK with God and includes the line, "Fuck me in the ass because I love Jesus." Songs like these mash up raunch and social critique, but they also play on gender assumptions we've already discussed. Micucci and Lindhome are wacky girls next door, with big eyes, earnest expressions, close harmonies, and even a ukulele. The profanity takes you by surprise. Well, the first time.

Nellie McKay has a ukulele, too, and an earnest demeanor, and a charming voice, but the McKay Project and the Garfunkel and

Oates Project are as different from each other as they are similar. Iliza Shlesinger uses *fucktard* in *War Paint,* while Garfunkel and Oates prefer *fuckwad* in "This Party Took a Turn for the Douche." The two profanities are similar in form—*fuck* + suffix—and meaning, but they are similar with a difference. As Sheidlower defines them in *The F-Word* (2009), *fucktard* means "despicably stupid person," which works really well from the domineering perspective of Shlesinger's airline worker, but *fuckwad* means "stupid or contemptible person, asshole" is a nearer synonym for *douchebag.* Even in the small domains of comedy and musical performance, performance of profanity is implicated in many subtle differences of approach, meaning, motives, voices, audiences, and irony.

You begin to wonder whether profuse profanity isn't characteristic of a cultural moment, the moment of "ephemeral" media, though what looks like it could be gone tomorrow—YouTube, tumblr, IFC comedies like the short-lived *Garfunkel and Oates*—is actually more or less permanently accessible. And no one really thinks of television as ephemeral, either, though the shows mentioned throughout this book belong more or less to the same moment. Or maybe profanity tends to appear more in performance than in books, where something like Amis's rule about restraint operates even if it isn't really justified. Messud's *The Woman Upstairs* begins with an explosion of profanity, but the fiction isn't built on bad words any more than Nellie McKay's songs are. Still, the profanity is important to all such texts, part of what and how they mean or opportunities for meaning.

Yet we don't want to believe it. In school, we read Chaucer and Shakespeare—undeniably great authors—and some of us revere them, but they are so given to obscenity that dictionaries are devoted to their bawdy language: Thomas W. Ross compiled *Chaucer's Bawdy* (1972)—246 pages of it—and Eric Partridge produced

Shakespeare's Bawdy (1947)—originally 225 pages but much revised and now a Routledge Classic at 294 pages. Melville, Hemingway, Updike, authors you also might read in school—male authors, of course—were given to profanity, too. Schools have solved the problem. They don't assign the profanity-laden works, and they edit profanity out of the ones too important not to assign. What they refuse to do is respect the authors and present the works in all of their meaning. They refuse to take on profanity as a subject, even though the authors thought it aesthetically essential to the works in question, even though doing so would enhance understanding of the text and language as well as the myriad social aspects and effects of both.

For when we read rather than avoid profanity in literature, we engage matters with significance beyond the text, because of the profanity. "When we talk about the relationship of a liberal education to citizenship," Martha Nussbaum writes in *Cultivating Humanity* (1997),

> we are asking a question with a long history in the Western philosophical tradition. We are drawing on Socrates' concept of 'the examined life,' on Aristotle's notion of reflective citizenship, and above all on Greek and Roman Stoic notions of an education that is 'liberal' in that it liberates the mind from the bondage of habit and custom, producing people who can function with sensitivity and alertness as citizens of the whole world. This is what Seneca means by the cultivation of humanity.

While we are entertained by the texts that trade on it, profanity in those texts also urges us towards an ethical consideration of anger, or an admission of common humanity with the likes of Sammy Samuels, or surprise that our grip on gender politics is not quite as sure as we thought. Literary profanity is significant aesthetically and socially.

But we are taught to see profanity in an author like Chaucer as mistakes we can overlook given his or her literary stature. The problem, we assume, is with Chaucer's language. Chaucer, however, identified us as the problem long ago. Like Absolon, the lovelorn parish clerk in "The Miller's Tale," we are squeamish about farting and we don't like the smell of the word much better than the offending act. In the *Canterbury Tales*, Chaucer the Author allows Chaucer the Narrator to retell the Miller's crude tale in spite of the profanity. The Narrator agrees with polite readers that the tale is grossly impolite. The Miller tells a bawdy tale—a *fabliau*—that turns the conventions of chivalry and courtly love upside down and inside out. His anti-hero, Nicholas, is a scurrilous clerk, nearly a priest, like Dunbar's *bern*, and the married woman he loves, Alisoun, is not too far above Dunbar's *bricht*—who, we discover later in Dunbar's poem, is a kitchen wench, and no lady—in the social scheme of things. When Nicholas declares his interest to Alisoun, he catches her by her *queynte* 'sexual part,' probably no better as an amorous tactic then than now, but it is fiction, after all. He takes this approach because he is vulgar in the most modern sense of the word, and Chaucer the Author, who is not squeamish, captures the vulgarity in *queynte*, which, you may be surprised to learn, derives from *quaint*, not *cunt*, though it is a euphemism for the obviously profane word. Thus, it's hard to know just how profane *queynte* is, but one thing's for sure—it's not a lady word.

REFERENCES

William Dunbar's poem, "In Secreit Place," appears in *The Poems of William Dunbar*, edited by James Kinsley (Oxford: Clarendon Press, 1979), pp. 40–42. "The Golden Targe" and "The Flyting of Dunbar and Kennedy" appear on pp. 29–38 and 76–95, respectively. Rochester's "A Ramble in St. James's Parke" appears in *The Poems of John Wilmot, Earl of Rochester*, edited by Keith Walker (Oxford:

Blackwell, 1985), pp. 64–68, and the satire on Charles II mentioned later in the chapter is on pp. 74–75; "To Her Sacred Majesty the Queen Mother," as a point of stylistic contrast, can be found on pp. 4–5. On Rochester's big mistake, see Walker's note p. 270; on "The Ramble" as a response to Waller, see Walker's notes on p. 263. The distinction between the Rise of Obscenity and the Age of Euphemism is drawn in the very structure of Melissa Mohr's *Holy Shit: A Brief History of Swearing* (New York: Oxford University Press, 2013). Claire Messud's *The Woman Upstairs* (New York: Knopf, 2013) gets off to a great start with the quoted passage. *Twin Peaks*, created by Mark Frost and David Lynch, lasted for just two seasons and just over a year on ABC but changed television history. *The Sopranos* changed television history, too, and profanity figured in its impact. The series, created by David Chase, aired on HBO from 1999 to 2007. The show's chief profaners are Tony Soprano, played by the late James Gandolfini; Silvio Dante, played by Steven Van Zandt; Paulie Gualtieri, played by Tony Sirico; Corrado "Junior" Soprano, played by Dominic Chianese; Christopher Moltisanti, played by Michael Imperioli; Salvatore "Big Pussy" Bonpensiero, played by Vincent Pastore; Janice Soprano, played by Aida Turturro; Adriana La Cerva, played by Drea de Matteo; Bobby "Baccala" Baccalieri, played by Steven R. Schirripa; Tony Blundetto, played by Steve Buscemi; and Ralph Cifaretto, played by Joe Pantoliano. A. J. Soprano is played by Robert Iler. Interestingly, though they are capable of profanity, the sleeker New York City mobsters swear less than their New Jersey counterparts, but we see them in fewer unguarded moments. Women characters, except perhaps for Adriana, swear a lot less than men, something to keep in mind given the premise of the section of this chapter titled "Profanity Performed." It is impossible to list every director and every writer of every episode of the series, let alone the actors who swear, since that would require a complete account of every episode. I provide that sort of information for the episodes from which I quote. Franco Ricci's *The Sopranos: Born Under a Bad Sign* (Toronto: University of Toronto Press, 2014) is quoted from p. 28. The pilot episode, which aired on June 10, 1999, was directed and written by David Chase. The magnificent "Pine Barrens" was directed by Steve Buscemi, written by Chase, Terence Winter, and Tim Van Patten, and aired on May 6, 2001. Gloria Trillo, a lady who can do lots of things, including swear, was played by Annabella Sciorra. Episode 1.5 (7 February 1999) is aptly titled "College"; it was directed by Allen Coulter and written by Chase and James Manos, Jr. Then, Episode 3.1, "Mr. Ruggiero's Neighborhood" (March 4, 2001), was directed by Coulter and written by Chase. There is a perceptive essay on "Silence in *The Sopranos*," by Steven Peacock, a chapter of *The Essential Sopranos Reader*, edited by David Lavery, Douglas L. Howard, and Paul Levinson (Lexington: University Press of Kentucky), pp. 277–285. Throughout, Seneca is quoted from Lucius Annaeus Seneca, *Anger, Mercy, Revenge*, translated by Robert A. Kaster and Martha C. Nussbaum (Chicago: University of Chicago Press, 2010). Kaster translated *De Ire/On Anger*, pp. 3–129, introduction and notes included. The first passage quoted here can be found on p. 15. Aristotle considers *akrasia* 'incontinence' in *Nicomachean Ethics*, Book VII: Chapters 1–10; see especially Chapter 3, which begins on p. 1039 of *The Basic Works of Aristotle*, edited by Richard McKeon (New York: Random House, 1941), which I bought during my first term at the University of Michigan, according to my end-paper inscription, and have used, in spite of its inadequacies, ever since. Martha Nussbaum's *The Therapy of Desire: Theory and Practice in Hellenistic Ethics* (Princeton, NJ: Princeton University Press, 1994) is quoted from pp. 243 and 337. Lorraine Bracco plays Dr. Jennifer Melfi, not usually a swearer, in "Funhouse," which aired on February 9, 2000, was directed by John Patterson, and was written by Chase and Todd A. Kessler; "Two Tonys," which aired on March 7, 2004, directed by Van Patten and written by Chase and Winter; and "Calling All Cars," which aired on November 24, 2002, directed by Van Patten and written by Chase, Robin Green, Mitchell Burgess, David Flebotte, and Winter; as well as many other memorable episodes, of course. Aristotle is quoted on the problem of anger from *Nicomachean Ethics* Book II: Chapter 8, p. 963 in McKeon's edition. On the slight, see Aristotle's *Rhetoric*, Book II: Chapters 2–3, pp. 1382–1386 in McKeon's edition. On death at Johnny Sack's elbow, see Seneca, p. 96, the very last words of the essay. Frans de Waal interrupts on mutualism, from *Primates and Philosophers: How Morality Evolved*, edited by Stephen Macedo and Josiah Ober (Princeton, NJ: Princeton University Press, 2006), p. 13. Seneca returns to the conversation, from p. 88. For Aristotle on the orator inciting anger, see *Rhetoric* Book II: Chapter 2, again. Melfi arrives at her diagnosis in "Meadowlands" (January 31, 1999), directed by John Patterson and written by Chase and Jason Cahill. For Seneca on fierce features, see p. 14; for the web of crime, see p. 27. Water chokes the angry person in the *Nicomachean Ethics*, Book VII: Chapter 2, p. 1039 in McKeon's edition. Seneca anticipates his detractors on p. 24. Tony Soprano's elegy for the strong silent type is spoken in the pilot episode, described above. I quote Tacitus from my cracked Modern Library edition of his *Complete Works*, translated by Alfred John Church and William Jackson Brodribb, and edited by Moses Hadas (New York: Random House, 1942), pp. 7 and 11; reconsidering the Latin, the translation is perhaps less fair to Livia than it should be, though it's a little late now to worry about her reputation. Chase is quoted on the name from *The Sopranos: Selected Scripts from Three Seasons* (New York: Warner Books, 2002), p. viii. *I, Claudius* was a BBC serialization of Robert Graves's novel of the same title, aired in the United Kingdom in 1976 and in the United States the following year. Livia Drusilla was memorably portrayed by Siân Phillips. Seneca on anger as stepmother: p. 16. Livia Soprano doesn't know what Junior is talking about in "I Dream of Jeannie Cusamano," which aired on April 4, 1999, directed by Patterson, written by Chase. Livia was portrayed unforgettably by Nancy Marchand. Livia and A. J. converse in "D-Girl," which aired on February 27,

2000, directed by Coulter, written by Chase and Kessler. The section on "Political Profanity" quotes James Kelman's novel *How Late It Was, How Late* (New York: Norton, 1995), though the book was originally published in the United Kingdom in 1994. Tom Shone's article about the novel, "Punch Drunk," appeared in *The New Yorker* (January 9, 1995), pp. 80–81. I quote it first from p. 81. *How Late It Was, How Late* is quoted from pp. 83, 114, and 255 in series. Then Shone, again, from p. 80 of his article. On Julia Neuberger's pronouncements, see William Russell, "Bickering Judges Give Booker to Kelman," *The (Glasgow) Herald* (October 12, 1994), p. 1. Sassenach papers also reported the verdict, including the *Evening Standard* (October 12, 1994) and *The Sunday Times* (October 23, 1994). Bowen and Cobb were quoted in P.H. S., "Closed Book," *The (London) Times* (October 13, 1994). All of these newspaper accounts were retrieved through Lexis Nexis Academic. Kelman responds to his critics in the title essay of *"And the Judges Said..."* (London: Secker & Warburg, 2002), pp. 37–55, and is quoted from p. 40. As Cairns Craig explains in a classic article, "Resisting Arrest: James Kelman," in *The Scottish Novel Since the Seventies*, edited by Gavin Wallace and Randall Stevenson (Edinburgh: Edinburgh University Press, 1993), pp. 99–114, "Kelman has had an enormous impact on the nature of writing in Scotland in three crucial areas: the representation of working-class life, the treatment of 'voice' and the construction of narrative" (p. 99), and he goes on to explain what Kelman would later claim about voice and narrative and class in the wake of *How Late It Was, How Late*. And here's an important point, I think—Craig's article was published a year before Kelman won the Booker Prize. Leonard is quoted from *Reports from the Present: Selected Works 1982–94* (London: Jonathan Cape, 1995). We're told that "Reclaiming the Local" (pp. 33–43) was written before 1990 (p. 2), and it's quoted first from p. 40. Kelman is next quoted from "Elitism and English Literature," also in *"And the Judges Said..."* (pp. 57–74), from pp. 64–65. Leonard follows, from pp. 35–36 and 41. Sammy's pith is reported from *How Late It Was, How Late*, p. 111, and Kelman's on dangerous literature from *"And the Judges Said..."* on p. 68. My friend had his say in "'Shut Up and Listen': An Interview with Richard W. Bailey," *Journal of English Linguistics* 37 (2009): 356–374. Adam Smith is quoted from *The Theory of Moral Sentiments*, edited by D. D. Raphael and A. L. Macfie (Oxford: Oxford University Press, 1976), p. 9. Robert Crawford epitomizes Smith in *On Glasgow and Edinburgh* (Cambridge, MA: Belknap Press of Harvard University Press, 2013), p. 269. McEnery returns from Chapter 1, quoted from *Swearing in English: Bad Language, Purity and Power from 1586 to the Present* (London: Routledge, 2006), p. 12. Smith, quoted further, from pp. 12, 9, and 21. "The Great, Grand, Soap Water Kick" is included in *The Stories of Jane Gardam* (New York: Europa, 2014), pp. 57–64. Sammy wants his bath on p. 117 of *How Late It Was, How Late*. Horsa and his interlocutors are quoted from Gardam's story, pp. 58–59, 64, and 58 again. All of the Kingsley Amis is taken from *The King's English: A Guide to*

Modern Usage (New York: St. Martin's Press, 1998), p. 75; the book was published originally in London, in 1997, by HarperCollins. Larkin's memorable and much-remembered line opens "This Be the Verse," in his *Collected Poems*, edited by Anthony Thwaite (London: The Marvell Press, 1988; New York: Farrar, Straus and Giroux, 1989), p. 180. Patrick Melrose finds his voice in Edward St. Aubyn's *Bad News* (London: Picador, 2012), p. 122; the novel was originally published by William Heinemann in 1992. St. Aubyn's *Mother's Milk* was shortlisted for the Man Booker Prize in 2006 but didn't win. His satire of the prize, *Lost for Words* (New York: Farrar, Straus and Giroux, 2014), unfortunately though I'm sure unintentionally, diminishes Kelman's accomplishment, because there is a Scottish novel with lots of profanity contending for the prize. Ian Parker, in a profile of St. Aubyn titled "Inheritance," in *The New Yorker* (June 2, 2014), pp. 43–55, draws this comparison on p. 51/c: "At a moment when the emerging British fashion was for spikily vernacular Scottish and Irish writers—Roddy Doyle, James Kelman, Irvine Welsh—the response to St. Aubyn's elegant prose was muted, reason, perhaps for St. Aubyn's antagonism toward vernacular in *Lost for Words*." The profanity in *Lost for Words* is distributed throughout, with restraint. Edward Sapir's classic article, "The Status of Linguistics as a Science," *Language* 5 (1929): 207–214, is quoted from p. 209. We learn of the girls of North Arlington from Lesley Brody, "Girls at North Arlington High School Swear Not to Swear as Part of Lesson in Civility," *The Record* (February 2, 2013) at http://www.northjersey.com/news/education/girls-at-north-arlington-school-swear-not-to-swear-as-part-of-lesson-in-civility-1.541770. Maureen C. McHugh and Jennifer Hambaugh summarize current research on whether men swear more than women, and on balance, research suggests that they do, though with some qualification, in ""She Said, He Said: Gender, Language, and Power," *Handbook of Gender Research in Psychology: Volume 1: Gender Research in General and Experimental Psychology*, edited by Joan C. Chrisler and Donald R. McCreary (Berlin: Springer, 2010), pp. 391–393; McEnery goes into the matter in detail in *Swearing in English*, pp. 34–43. I quote Deborah Cameron from *Verbal Hygiene* (London: Routledge, 1995), p. 184; McHugh and Hambaugh also discuss assertiveness training, pp. 382–383. Katty Kay and Claire Shipman are quoted from "Closing the Confidence Gap," *The Atlantic* (May 2014), p. 64. Messud is quoted from p. 15. The Mary Prankster songs mentioned here are collected on *Blue Skies Forever* (Baltimore: Palace Coup Records, 2002). Liz Phair's songs are from the albums *Exile in Guyville* (New York: Matador Records, 1993), *Whip-smart* (New York: Matador Records, 1994), *Whitechocolatespaceegg* (New York: Matador Records, 1998), and *Liz Phair* (New York: Capital Records, 2003). Meghan O'Rourke is quoted from her review, "Liz Phair's Exile in Avril-ville," *New York Times* (June 22, 2003), which I have accessed online: http://www.nytimes.com/2003/06/22/arts/music-liz-phair-s-exile-in-avril-ville.html?pagewanted=all. You should read

Ariel Levy's *Female Chauvinist Pigs: Women and the Rise of Raunch Culture* (New York: Free Press, 2005); in fact, you should just read things by Ariel Levy. I discuss Raunch as a slang aesthetic in *Slang: The People's Poetry* (Oxford: Oxford University Press, 2009), pp. 144–150. Nellie McKay's inspired albums include those cited here: *Normal as Blueberry Pie: A Tribute to Doris Day* (New York: Verve, 2009), *Get Away from Me* (New York: Sony, 2003), *Obligatory Villagers* (Santa Monica, CA: Hungry Mouse Records, 2007), and *Pretty Little Head* (New York: Sony, 2005). Norah Jones became a target of McKay's satire with *Come Away with Me* (New York: Blue Note Records, 2002). Terry Gross interviewed McKay on WHYY and NPR's *Fresh Air* on November 21, 2007, and you can listen to it at the end of this URL: http://www.npr.org/templates/story/ story.php? storyId=16503513. Gene Bertoncini, who knows something about cool music, comments on McKay's songs in "In with the New, Kicking Out the Jams," *New York Times* (December 28, 2007) at http://www.nytimes .com/2007/12/28/arts/28eve.html?_r=0. Sarah Silverman wrote *Jesus Is Magic*, Liam Lynch directed it, and they collaborated on the music. It was produced by Showtime and released November 11, 2005. I took the *Variety* quote from my DVD cover; the DVD also includes Silverman's "Aristocrats" performance. She spoke with Terry Gross on *Fresh Air* on November 9, 2005. Iliza Shlesinger's *War Paint*, directed by Jay Chapman, was released on Netflix on September 1, 2013, where you can still watch it, as I did. Judith Butler's *Gender Trouble: Feminism and the Subversion of Identity* (London: Routledge, 2011) is quoted from pp. 173, 174, and 176 in series. For *The Wire*, see Chapter 3; for Hank Moody see Chapter 2; for *New Girl* and *Don't Trust the B—in Apt. 23*, see Chapter 3. Garfunkel and Oates, played by Riki Lindhome and Kate Micucci, starred in *Garfunkel and Oates*, a short-lived television series on IFC—it premiered on August 7, 2014, and was finished by the end of September—created by Riki Lindhome and Kate Micucci and directed by Fred Savage. Some of the songs discussed here figured in the series, but all of them are easily available on YouTube. Jesse Sheidlower's *The F-Word*, 3d ed. (New York: Oxford University Press, 2009) is the go-to book when you need to split hairs between *fucktard* and *fuckwad* and just about any *fucking* thing. If you're really into the history of bad words, Thomas W. Ross's *Chaucer's Bawdy* (New York: E. P. Dutton, 1972) and Eric Partridge's *Shakespeare's Bawdy* (London: Routledge & Kegan Paul, 1947; 4th ed.— London: Routledge, 2001) are handy if not infallible guides. I take up the educational point in "Teaching 'Bad' American English: Profanity and Other 'Bad' Words in the Liberal Arts Setting," *Journal of English Linguistics* 30 (2002): 353–365. Martha Nussbaum is quoted from *Cultivating Humanity: A Classical Defense for Reform in Liberal Education* (Cambridge, MA: Harvard University Press, 1997), p. 8.

Coda

Ultimate Profanity

On May 27, 2015, I attended a conference banquet in Pembroke College, the University of Oxford. This setting is important, because I am about to tell a story of after-dinner conversation about profanity, and one doesn't often hear *Pembroke College* and *clusterfuck* in the same sentence.

The conference in question was called OX-LEX 4 among the cognoscenti, but Fourth Symposium on English Historical Lexis and Lexicography explains a bit more about what went on there. I heard many excellent papers and will mention some here, just to give a taste of the intellectual fare: John Considine (University of Alberta) answered his own question in *"Medulla, Promptorium, Catholicon Anglicum, Ortus*: How and Why Were They Made?"; Kusujiro Miyoshi (Soka Women's College, Tokyo) outlined "John Pickering's Reference to Dictionaries in his *Vocabulary* (1816)" and heralded it as "America's First Philological Exploration of Lexicography"; Allen Reddick (University of Zurich), explained the roles of "Contingency and Accident in the Construction of Johnson's *Dictionary.*" I'm not poking fun or marveling at exotic learning—I take such scholarship seriously. My own paper was titled "Trench's Richardson: Reading the Origins of the *Oxford English Dictionary.*" I fit right in. I enjoyed myself. And my point is that OX-LEX 4 was a professional conference populated by first-rate scholars, a site of culture at its highest and most rarefied. Except for me and my friend Jonathon Green, author of the monumental *Green's Dictionary of Slang* and *The Vulgar Tongue: Green's History of Slang*, none of the conferees was especially devoted—as a scholar, anyway—to low language.

Jonathon was sitting across from me and we talked during dinner, but by the time coffee was coming around, he was flirting with colleagues who would stop at his chair. Jonathon is a great flirt. He would flirt with a toad on a lily pad. He did when he was younger, legend has it, after he licked the toad. Thus ignored, I turned to companions on my left, both of them first-rate historical linguists, but also good at conversation—the two don't necessarily go hand in hand. We talked about many things, but eventually they asked me what I was working on, and I explained that I was writing this very book, the book you are reading, a book in praise of profanity.

One of them—significantly, a younger woman—asked, "What is your favorite profane word?" I didn't have a ready answer, but she did. "Clusterfuck," she said. She may have come up with *clusterfuck* on the fly but subsequently proved she had chosen it thoughtfully, before that evening. You might say she's a first-class historical linguist with a mild profanity obsession. Our third party, an older man, pitched in, and we enjoyed one another's company and our deviant topic—*clusterfuck*. In other words, we were building ad hoc group solidarity by using profanity. You might object: Doesn't our solidarity depend more on talking about profanity than on using it? You have a point—though *clusterfuck* and other profanity dropped continually from our oh-so academic mouths. Arguably, however, talk about talk—as the linguists put it—is part of the language system, the solidarity we felt no less solid though at one remove from profanity in its everyday expletive splendor.

We are lexicographers, after all, and we first considered the meaning and etymology of *clusterfuck*. Both of my companions thought the word means 'minor disaster, screw up, esp. involving many agents,' so one might say, "We tried to provide healthcare to millions of the uninsured, but then bureaucracy got in the way, and it was just one big clusterfuck." They agreed the word likely originated in military use, like *snafu* 'situation normal all fucked up'; there are plenty of military clusterfucks and plenty of aggravated military personnel to swear about them. I wasn't so sure. Could it be sexual, instead, a word for group sex? The military etymology and meaning made sense intuitively, but intuition isn't always the best lexicographical guide. I haven't memorized all of the big slang dictionaries, but I've been through them often enough to recall glimmers of data, and on hearing *clusterfuck*, group sex came to mind.

In fact, both explanations are true, though sex comes first. In the *Historical Dictionary of American Slang*, Jonathan Lighter—who is especially good on military slang—records *clusterfuck* 'bungled situation' first in 1969, quoting from Byron Holley's *Vietnam 1968–1969: A Battalion Surgeon's Journal*: "These are the screw-ups that the American public rarely hears about. They happen enough over here that we have a term for them—'cluster-fuck'!" But Lighter records *clusterfuck* 'orgy' somewhat earlier, in 1966. It isn't until 1969, though, in Gilbert D. Bartell's *Group Sex: A Scientist's Eyewitness Report on the American Way of Swinging*, that the meaning is crystal clear: "One advantage of open versus closed swinging, according to most of our informants, is the possibility of 'three-on-one' or 'gang bang' (sometimes called 'cluster fuck' activity)." Jonathon Green, in *Green's Dictionary of Slang*, starts the sexual sense in 1968—Lighter's earliest quotation is opaque—and includes the senses 'chaos' and 'group of ineffective people' with later dates and without anchoring them in earlier military use. Splitting hairs, it seems as though the military sense derived from the sexual sense, but frankly, it's too close to call.

There we were, stuck on the cut and caret of a single word among the heaps of lexical treasure stored up in compendious dictionaries of slang—we agreed that it's a gem. And though it's just one word, it represents the problem of defining profanity raised at the outset of this book. One strain of profanity is the oath/curse variety, the "goddamn you all to hell" variety you might expect from military personnel confronted with yet another massive cock-up. Another strain is sexually oriented, and if obscenity is what you expect of profanity, then the orgy origin of *clusterfuck* is plausible, if not preferable, to other etymologies of the word. The distinction matters: when you think of the lexical field Gem, do you see a ruby or a diamond? When you think of the lexical field Profanity, do you see the voluptuous ruby of sex *fuck*, or the unforgiving diamond of curse *fuck*? Mental associations—a word belonging to one group rather than another in the mind—matter in meaning and lead us to understand profanity in everyday usage as one kind of language rather than another.

Our fascination with *clusterfuck* didn't end with its semantics, however. We concluded that it's just about a perfect word structurally; it's perfect just in the aesthetics of its form. For instance, *clusterfuck* has both a vowel rhyme and a consonant rhyme internally: /k/ begins and ends the word, and the central vowel known as "wedge"—the stressed version of schwa—is the nucleus of /klʌs/ and /fʌk/, so there is a nice symmetry to the word, with the unstressed syllable /təɹ/ the fulcrum on which to balance the rhymes. Besides /k/, *clusterfuck* has four or five other consonant sounds, depending on which variety of English one speaks—my dialect of American English is r-ful, whereas my companions speak relatively r-less dialects of

British English. Regardless, there is a mouthful of sounds in *cluster-fuck*, set out in graceful proportions, and variety is counterpoised against balance in the construction of the word.

This sort of elegance cannot be taken for granted. Mark Peters, who writes about all kinds of outlandish language, fairly recently wrote about "Clusterboinks and clusterfornications: The children of clusterfuck," for the profanity blog *Strong Language*. These children of *clusterfuck* are not imaginary; Peters has found evidence of their use, even if they are used rarely. *Clusterbunch, cluster coitus, cluster-crap, clusterfrak, clustermolestation, cluster-naughty word, cluster nookie*, and *clustersmurf*—this list proves just how far apples can fall from a tree. The apples are all euphemisms, though I can't imagine why I'd rather endure clustermolestation than a clusterfuck. *Clusterbunch* gives us more consonant sounds than *clusterfuck*, it's true, but *cluster coitus* and *clustercrap* give us fewer. These words lack both the descriptive and expletive forces of *clusterfuck*. If we're talking about group sex, cluster nookie seems inexperienced, and if we're referring to a colossal cock-up, nookie has nothing to do with it. *Cluster coitus* is rhythmically balanced, though each part ends with an unstressed syllable, as do *clustermolestation* and *cluster nookie*—in a clusterfuck, you want a happy ending.

Some will argue that *clusterfuck* can't be elegant because it's about bad things, like fucking things up or just fucking. I'm not sure I can condemn orgies, and I don't think *clusterfuck* is a worse word for orgy than *orgy*. Indeed, though clusterfuckers may think *clusterfuck* is a bold word that flouts convention, I think the word has just enough whimsy to cover my discomfort with the idea. Thus, the paradox of elegant word form and the various, patterned sounds it represents, on one hand, and the supposedly vulgar meanings attached to the word, on the other, simply proves its excellence, in my view. It is arresting, an object of criticism like a painting on a wall—much more attractive and challenging than the portraits of long-dead masters and fellows hanging in the Hall at Pembroke College. *Clusterfuck* is not base lexical rock but, like the Hope Diamond or the Moussaieff Red, a work of art.

But enough of profanity, of its aesthetics, anyway. We left the Hall for a drink in the college bar with a score of our colleagues, after which we emerged into an unusually warm, clear March evening and gradually separated. From Pembroke, we could see stars in the heavens, and *clusterfuck*, it seemed, had a place in the scheme of things. We could see shadows against the stone walls and hear our soles scrape along the paving. Some went their own ways, but Jonathon and I, and some others, followed Considine to the Hi-Lo, a famous Jamaican eating house, his favorite undergraduate haunt— apparently the Rt. Hon. David Cameron's, too. It was no cluster- fuck—I was still wearing my bow tie—but we had a fucking amazing time, anyway.

REFERENCES

Two volumes of J. L. Lighter's three-volume *Historical Dictionary of American Slang* (New York: Random House, 1994 and 1997) have appeared so far, A–G and H–O. *Clusterfuck* quotations derive from this dictionary. Mark Peters's characteristically insightful and entertaining article, "Clusterboinks and Clusterfornications: The Children of Clusterfuck," appeared in *Strong Language: A Sweary Blog about Swearing*, on May 23, 2015, and can be found at https://stronglang.wordpress.com/?s=Clusterboinks+and+clusterfornications.

INDEX